RAVING REFERRALS

For Real Estate Agents

THE PROVEN STEP-BY-STEP SYSTEM TO
BUILD A PROFITABLE REAL ESTATE BUSINESS

BRANDON BARNUM

and

VERL WORKMAN

EXPERTISE PUBLISHING

@2025 All rights reserved. Brandon Barnum and Verl Workman
Raving Referrals For Real Estate Agents: The Proven Step-By-Step System To Build A Profitable Real Estate Business

Published by: Expertise Publishing
ExpertisePublishing.com

Paperback ISBN: 979-8-9907448-3-7
Hardcover ISBN: 979-8-9907448-4-4
eBook ISBN: 979-8-9907448-5-1
Library of Congress Control Number: 2025902380

Disclaimer: No part of the publication may be reproduced, distributed or transmitted in any form or by any means, including photocopying, recording, or other electronic or mechanical methods without the prior written permission of the publisher and authors of this book, except in the case of brief quotations embodied in reviews.

Note: I want to take a moment to address a critical aspect that underpins our professional integrity and legal compliance – the Real Estate Settlement Procedures Act (RESPA). RESPA, enacted in 1974, is a key federal law that has a significant impact on our industry. Understanding and adhering to RESPA rules is not just a matter of legal compliance; it's a testament to our commitment to ethical practices and our clients' best interests.

Publisher: Expertise Publishing – ExpertisePublishing.com
Editors: Ella Barnum & Harry Katcher
Interior Design: Noelle Peterson

Connect with Brandon Barnum
Email: brandon@ravingreferrals.com
Web: www.RavingReferrals.com
LinkedIn: www.linkedin.com/in/brandonbarnum
To book Brandon as a Speaker: www.BrandonBarnum.com

Connect with Verl Workman
Email: speaking@workmansuccess.com
To Book Verl as a Speaker: www.VerlWorkman.com
For Real Estate Coaching: www.WorkmanSuccess.com

Endorsements

"Whether you're a new Realtor or you've been in the industry for over 30 years, this book is a must read. You can read a couple chapters at a time and put those methods to work or read the whole book in one weekend like I did. Either way, by reading this book, you are GUARANTEED to gain a take away to try in your business today. I purchased this book for every one of my team members too."

Brooke Sines
RE/MAX Executive Carolinas
RE/MAX of Grand Rapids

"If you want more income, influence, and impact, this new Raving Referrals book teaches you what you need to succeed."

Mark Victor Hansen
World's #1 Best-Selling Non-Fiction Author
Chicken Soup For The Soul

"50% to 80%+ of most Realtors' business comes from referrals. This IS a referral-based business. People like to work with people they know and trust. It's been that way since the dinosaurs!"

Rob Leggat
EXIT Realty Premier

"You need this book! Decades of referral business experience and actionable information distilled into this indispensable guide."

Janet Choynowski
CEO Immobel Group

RAVING REFERRALS FOR REAL ESTATE AGENTS

"Raving Referrals provides the best strategies and tactics for learning how to ASK for and GET those referrals. Understanding your referral score, adopting the 7 laws of raving referrals and measuring referral lifetime client value are a few of the key concepts you'll learn in this idea-packed book. There is nothing more valuable to your career, business and team survival than getting great referrals. Start reading Raving Referrals today and be sure to purchase enough copies for your entire team!"

Dave Savage
CEO of Mortgage Coach

"Buy this book now. You'll attract more referrals, win more business, and take it to the BANK!"

Cheri Tree
CEO of Codebreaker Technologies

"What drives our businesses more than any other item? Referrals! This book is detailed and comprehensive in showing its readers exactly how to get those highly coveted referrals. Brandon and Todd are the best at giving the reader all of the necessary tools to remain at the top of the industry!"

Lance Billingsley
Navi Title

"When you incorporate the valuable information in this book, you'll find that you'll win more sales, do it in less time, and build a strong base of lifetime customers who will act as sources of raving referrals."

Dr. Tony Alessandra
Author of Room Full of Referrals &
The Platinum Rule for Sales Mastery

"Raving Referrals holds the secrets and strategies to gain your most ideal prospects from existing clients and business partners. Jump to the front of the line with referrals that easily convert with the know, like and trust factor!"

Debbie Allen
Bestselling Author of The Highly Paid Expert

"This book is a game changer for real estate agents who are looking to supercharge their referral game! The simple idea of leading with value and letting revenue follow is masterfully presented in these pages. "

Tony Dixon
Advanced Tax Group

PREFACE

"If you're tired of endlessly searching for new clients and want to grow a thriving real estate business rooted in genuine relationships and referrals, Raving Referrals for Real Estate Agents is a must-read. This book provides the tools and strategies to attract a steady stream of high-quality clients who come to you through trust and connection. It's a game-changer for agents looking to expand their business the right way!"

John G Stevens
Weekly Real Estate News

"Raving Referrals for Real Estate is a GAME changing way of building community and growing your business, authentically and from a place of service."

Sara Guildi
Director of Coaching, Workman Success Systems

"If referrals are at the heart of your growth strategy, put this book at the top of your stack"

Charles Furlough
Pillar to Post Home Inspections

"'Raving Referrals for Real Estate Agents' is a great book for agents looking to build a thriving, referral-driven business. Verl Workman delivers practical, proven strategies to turn clients into lifelong advocates. His insights on trust, value, and service make this a must-read for anyone serious about long-term success in real estate."

David Horsager, bestselling author and CEO
Trust Edge Leadership Institute

"Referrals are not only the best form of marketing (by far), they are also the least expense (they're usually free). If you want to experience the magic of growing your business through referrals, this is the only guide you need."

Sam Richter
SBR Worldwide, LLC
IntelNgin | Business and Sales Intel Engine program

"All too often, agents waste time looking for shortcuts. Instead, learn from those who have done what you want to do; it's right here!"

Chris Heller
President OJO Labs

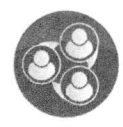

Dedications

Brandon's Dedication

I dedicate my life to glorifying God every day in every way. We are all blessed to live in a world with unlimited possibilities, and God, our creator, wants to co-create with you. I invite you to turn to Him and ASK for everything you want in life. Spend time in gratitude and prayer ASKing God to guide your life journey. As you invite God in and shine His light through your life, you will experience miracles and magic that lead to a life well-lived.

While my life is dedicated to God, this book is dedicated to my wife, Marlo, without whom none of my success would be possible. Marlo, you have stood by my side, supporting my dreams and aspirations for over 30 years. I have watched you grow, mature, and evolve into an incredible person. I am proud to call you my wife for life.

Verl's Dedication

I dedicate this book to the incredible members of my family who have been instrumental in my journey and invaluable to the success of Workman Success Systems. First and foremost, to my wife, Coleen, from the first time I saw her when she was 12 and I was 15, I knew she was special. Getting married and having her unwavering support and love have been the foundation of everything I do. Coleen, your belief in me and our shared vision has been my guiding light. You are the compass that guides me and our entire family to always want to do better. Thank you for being my partner in life and in business.

To my daughter, Brianne, who inspires me every day with her creativity, resilience, and passion. Watching you grow into the amazing person and leader you are has been one of my greatest joys. I am most proud of you as a dedicated mother and wife. Your example that one can really have it all is a true inspiration. Your determination and spirit remind me of the importance of pursuing one's dreams with vigor and heart.

To Nate, my oldest son whose fearless approach to sales, leadership, and marketing drive Workman Success. Your constant positive attitude and sincere desire to do the right thing for this business is inspiring and I am proud of you.

And finally, to Ryan, father of four beautiful girls, who has the kindest heart, thank you for pouring your heart into our clients through invitations to come into coaching. It's amazing to me that people want to stay connected to you after they have been through the sales process with you! You are a perfect example of building relationships that generate referrals. I can't wait to see what is next for you as you continue to grow.

Acknowledgments

FROM BRANDON: While there are so many people to thank for bringing this book to be, the most significant acknowledgment goes out to my friend and mentor, Mark Victor Hansen. Since meeting Mark on May 18, 2004, he has constantly elevated and expanded my thinking of what's possible. Over the past 20 years, Mark has taught me that anything I desire and ask for can be achieved. While he's over halfway to his goal of selling a billion books, the impact Mark has made on the world through Chicken Soup for the Soul, The One Minute Millionaire, and his other best-selling books, and he is well on his way to "make the world work for 100 percent of humanity."

In my life, family always comes first. I've been blessed to not only have an amazing wife to share the last 30 years with, but also three amazing kids that has given my life meaning and fulfillment. Sebastian, you are a brilliant man who has taught me so much and helped dramatically expand my view of the world. Thanks for teaching me what it takes to be a dad and accepting me for living in Wonkaland. You are doing so much to make my dreams come true, and for that, I am grateful more than you know. Jackson, you are a natural leader and I look forward to seeing everywhere your journey takes you. Regardless of the destination, I know you and everyone around you will enjoy the ride. Ella, you are so intelligent, talented, driven, and creative. You've grown so much these past few years and the best is yet to come. Your mom and I will be cheering you all on as you explore this adventure called life.

Of course, family would not be complete without the wise ones who taught us what we know. Mom, thanks for your unconditional love, endless optimism, and for holding your vision for the future you want for the world. I so admire your relentless belief in the best for all humanity and look forward to celebrating the great transition with you in the near future. Gayle and Don, you are amazing parents who have given so much love and support to your girls. You exemplify love in action, and I hope you know that the ripple effect of your caring and support is beyond measure.

This book came to be thanks to the passionate support of Emmie & Wil Saavedra whom I am beyond grateful to have as both business partners as well as friends. We have so much impact and empowerment to create, and I am thrilled we are doing it together.

A special thanks to Noelle and Robert Peterson for helping refine and improve this Raving Referrals book, curriculum, and course. You both go above and beyond serving everyone you can.

I'm also grateful for the support and partnership of the HOA.com team who are always in the lab testing and perfecting the referral partner process and co-marketing campaigns.

Thanks for bringing this book to life and helping the HOA.com referral network connect with homeowners through the power of hyper-local social farming. Together, we are revolutionizing and reinventing the HOA industry and truly creating Unity Through Community.

FROM VERL: I am grateful for the love and support I've received from everyone who has contributed to this book or allowed me to tell their story.

To Cleve Gaddis, a true leader and innovator in the real estate industry. Cleve, your commitment to excellence and your ability to inspire those around you have been a source of motivation for me. There are very few people in this world who have made such a lasting impact on everyone they touch. Thank you for your partnership and for being a beacon of integrity and success. We are better because we push each other to be better and I appreciate that more than you know.

I want to express my deepest gratitude to Jim Knowlton, whose mentorship and friendship have been invaluable. Jim, your wisdom and guidance have shaped my approach to leadership and business. From the very beginning you leaned in and helped us build our coaching program through practical experience, hard work, and learning as you go. Your example to not only me, but to all of our coaches, continues to be invaluable. I cherish our friendship. Your ability to see potential and nurture it has left a lasting impact on me and countless others.

ACKNOWLEDGMENTS

Sara Guldi, the Senior Director of Coaching at Workman Success Systems, continues to drive - and inspire - excellence and hold us all to a higher standard. Sara's commitment and selfless giving to our community is an example of what a leader should be. Sara leads our Directors of Coaching, Paul Sessum and MIchael Harmon, who, together, pour into our coaches and clients in a way that makes me humble to be part of their lives. I appreciate them, respect them, and honor their many contributions.

I feel it appropriate to recognize Mr. Mike Parker. When I met Mike he was one of the top agents in the country. He was a Howard Britton Star Power Star, and one of the best referral givers and receivers I've ever encountered. When I asked Mike what made his business so great, he said, "Every day I go through my list of 50 people that I call my top 50 list and I have a personal touch with every single one of them each month." Over the years, Workman Success coaches and clients have perfected the Top 50 system with a high level of execution on a basic fundamental system, creating the highest converted leads of all time. And we have Mike to thank and for that I will be forever grateful.

I would be remiss if I did not acknowledge Ms. Terri Murphy. As a Top 100 REALTOR® in the world for almost 15 years, Terri built her entire business on referrals and repeat business. When the Top 50 System was created Terri added the monthly touches and specific action items based on a lifetime of experience. Terri is a Master Coach with Workman Success, a sought-after speaker, and author, but more importantly, she is the best connector of humans I have ever met.

I am humbled by the sincere desire and hard work shown by the following Workman Success Systems Coaches and clients as they endeavor every day to help their clients achieve their dreams. I am also sincerely grateful for their contributions and willingness to share their stories which bring Workman's systems to life:

Christy Buck, Workman Master Coach, team leader, and Broker/Owner with Infinity Real Estate Group, in Pearland, Texas.

Mike Coke, Workman Master Coach and Broker/Owner of Terra Firma Realty, in DeForest, Wisconsin.

Anthony Dixon, Founder and Asset Protection and Tax Specialist at Advanced Tax Group (ATG).

Alvaro Erize, CEO of CINC - a leading provider of lead generation and CRM solutions.

Charles Furlough, President and CEO of Pillar To Post Home Inspections.

Cleve Gaddis, Workman Master Coach, team leader, business consultant, radio show host, renowned speaker, and Broker/Owner of Modern Traditions Realty Group, in Atlanta, Georgia.

Brent Gray, Workman Success Systems' Chief Operating Officer.

Denise Klein, Workman Senior Coach, top producer, speaker/trainer, agent, and team leader.

Rob Leggat, Workman Senior Coach, sales trainer, team leader, and Broker/Owner with EXIT Realty Premier of Massapequa, New York.

Anthony Marguleas, philanthropist and Broker/Owner of Amalfi Estates of Los Angeles, California.

Nick Painz, Workman Certified Coach, Managing Broker at META Homes with Re/Max Alliance in Westminster, Colorado.

Corey Perlman, owner of Impact Social Media, speaker, author, consultant, and nationally-recognized social media expert.

Sam Richter, Chief Executive Officer of SBR Worldwide, LLC and the founder and creator of the IntelNgin | Business and Sales Intel Engine program. Hall of Fame speaker, bestselling author, and one of the world's leading authority on sales intelligence and digital reputation management.

Brooke Sines, Workman Senior Coach, team leader, and Broker/Owner of RE/MAX Executive Carolinas, and RE/MAX of Grand Rapids.

Tammie Slay, Workman Master Coach, team leader, and Broker/Owner at HIP Realty Group in Frisco, Texas.

Michelle Terry, Workman Senior Coach, and Broker/Franchisee of EXIT Real Estate Executives in Spencer, Massachusetts.

Stephanie Verderose, Workman Senior Coach, team leader, and Broker/Owner at EXIT Homestead Realty Professionals, in Vineland and Pitts Grove, New Jersey.

Ryan Young, CEO at Fello, CEO and team leader at The Young Team, in Cleveland, Ohio.

I'm confident I have missed acknowledging someone, but please know it was not intentional. There have been so many of you who have served willingly and without credit and if, for some reason, I missed listing you, please accept my apology in advance and know you are very much appreciated.

Finally, I would like to especially acknowledge the entire Workman Success Systems family, whose dedication and passion drive our mission forward every day. I could write an entire book on everyone who has influenced me,

ACKNOWLEDGMENTS

just giving credit to all of you. Please accept this acknowledgement as my effort to include everyone in our Workman family who has and continues to coach, mentor, inspire, and add to our work. Together, we are transforming the real estate industry and empowering professionals to achieve their highest potential. This book is a testament to the incredible work we do together. I am truly grateful for your dedication, support, and belief in our shared vision. Thank you all for being part of this journey.

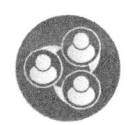

IMAGINE...

Have you ever wanted to make a more significant difference in the world? Now don't just skip past this question. Take a moment to give it some thought.

What would you do if your business was so successful that you suddenly found yourself with all the fortune and fame you've always dreamed of? What if you had flocks of Perfect Prospects and ideal clients flooding to your business because of your stellar reputation and superb service?

What if you were a recognized expert and respected authority in your field? What if other businesses paid you to travel the world sharing your knowledge and wisdom with their employees, partners, and clients?

How would you use your newfound influence and affluence? Would you simply retire and live out your days on some golf course or sunny beach? Or would you use your wealth and wisdom for good?

WE'RE ON A MISSION

We're asking you these questions because we're on a mission to impact and empower every person on the planet. You see, we believe every man, woman, and child deserves nutritious food, clean water, exceptional healthcare, empowering education, and opportunities for financial freedom.

Now, you may think the possibility of achieving that goal is entirely unrealistic, and you just might be right. But the one thing we know is that every time we share our purpose and vision with others, we experience a deep sense of fulfillment and satisfaction. And we're willing to bet you feel that same indescribable joy every time you make a meaningful difference in the lives of others.

As you read this book, mastering the strategies that unlock all the income and influence you desire and deserve, we hope that you will, in turn, positively impact and uplift your clients, customers, co-workers, employees, vendors, and referral partners as well as your friends, family, neighbors, and community.

Together, we can make a difference and change the world in meaningful ways.

Brandon and *Verl*

Table of Contents

Foreword	xix
Preface	xxi
Introduction	xxix
1. What's Your Referral Score?	1
2. The 7 Laws of Raving Referrals	9
3. Perfect Prospects & Lifetime Clients	31
4. Learn Why They Buy	47
5. Establish Your Expert Status	55
6. Engage Your Referral Champions	67
7. Referral Rewards	83
8. Master the Art of the Ask	93
9. Client Appreciation Events	107
10. Referral of a Lifetime	115
11. Wealth Through Workshops	127
12. Partner with Top Trusted Pros	135
13. Network Strategically	153
14. Create a Referral Alliance	161
15. Leverage LinkedIn	171
16. The Referral Partner Blueprint	181
17. Top 21 Cross-Promotion Campaigns	187
That Is My Excuse (TIME)	211
Time For ACTION	213
Success Scripts	217
Experts & Influencers	223
Industry Icons	243
Podcasts	263
Recommended Resources	275
National Networking Organizations	293
Top 20 Real Estate Referral Groups	299
Become a Raving Referrals Co-Author	305
Become a Raving Referrals Certified Trainer	307
About the Authors	309

Foreword

by Dr. Ivan Misner

Founder of BNI and NY Times Bestselling Author

Referrals are the lifeblood of any successful real estate business. As the founder of BNI, the world's largest business networking organization, I have seen firsthand how building strong, authentic relationships can lead to consistent, high-quality referrals. Yet, many real estate agents struggle to systemize and scale their referral business. That's why Raving Referrals for Real Estate Agents is such an invaluable resource.

This book provides a proven roadmap to generating a steady stream of high-value referrals. Inside, you'll discover powerful scripts, practical strategies, and step-by-step systems that take the guesswork out of networking and client engagement. Whether you're a new agent looking to establish a solid foundation or a seasoned professional ready to take your business to the next level, the insights in these pages will help you cultivate deeper connections, increase your referral flow, and ultimately close more deals.

One of the key principles in this book aligns perfectly with what we teach at BNI—Givers Gain®. The more you invest in providing value to others, the more opportunities will come back to you. Raving Referrals for Real Estate Agents shows you exactly how to build trust, create raving fans, and turn past clients and professional partners into an ongoing source of referrals.

If you implement the strategies in this book, you won't just grow your business—you'll build a thriving referral-based practice that serves you for years to come. I encourage you to read it, apply it, and watch your referral network expand like never before.

To your success,

Dr. Ivan Misner

Founder of BNI.com

New York Times Bestselling Author

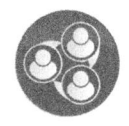

Preface

CONGRATULATIONS… for Investing in yourself and your real estate business, for pursuing a faster path to success, and for discovering the system to Raving Referrals!

Since you're reading this book, we believe we know a few things about you…

1. Your business may not be quite where you want it to be. You simply aren't getting the kind of leads, referrals, prospects, and clients you need to earn the income you want.

2. Most likely, you are skilled at listing and showing homes and just need a better system when it comes to bringing in more clients.

3. Perhaps you feel awkward and uncomfortable asking for referrals, so you don't receive them as often as you'd like.

4. You already know some of the principles and practices in this book. Still, you don't have a formalized referral system and sometimes rely on divine intervention—hoping new client opportunities will magically appear each week.

5. Most importantly, you are serious about changing all that, and you're looking for a system that will generate a steady stream of highly qualified and profitable prospects.

You Are On The Right Path!

This book will empower you with time-tested, proven strategies, scripts, and secrets we've used to close literally billions in real estate transactions and have created consistent income for everyone who works the system. We're sharing what we learned from over two decades of researching, refining, and perfecting the real estate referral process.

What we can give you goes far beyond simple theory. We've used these powerful principles and practices to build what we believe is the single most comprehensive and effective referral marketing system the world has ever known. Our clients are closing as many as 86 transactions a year, working with just 50 people, 1 hour a day.

We are passionately committed to helping you transform your business to create a consistent and dependable flow of Raving Referrals and profitable prospects that turn into lifetime clients. Our goal is that you start each week with a calendar full of new client appointments, so you never have to worry about where your next referral is coming from. Imagine meeting with people every day who already trust you because they've been referred by a loyal friend or professional that they have known for years.

I say "we" because "WE" IS THE KEY. This book is all about changing your mindset and approach when it comes to growing your business. Rather than being a lone wolf always out hunting for new opportunities by yourself, we want you to have a tribe of talented and trusted people you work with who are constantly helping refer clients back and forth, so everyone wins together.

As you apply the Raving Referrals process to your real estate practice, Perfect Prospects will flock to you, gift wrapped with trust, respect, and ready for the solutions and services you provide.

The Results Are In

Most real estate agents and business owners understand and agree that referrals are the best source of new business. After all, decades of research have proven this time and time again.

Empirical studies from major universities, publications, and research firms have concluded:

- People are 400% more likely to buy from you when they are referred
- 90% of people trust recommendations from people they know
- Referred clients are 16% more profitable than non-referred clients

PREFACE

So, if referrals are so profitable, why do so many agents, teams, and brokerages struggle to generate new client opportunities consistently?

What is it that Holds You Back?

If you're like most of the agents we serve, you may fit into one of the following categories:

- You're new to the real estate industry, or your local area and are just getting your business started
- You've never learned to build your business by referral, and you aren't really sure how to start
- You know a lot of people, but don't have many people who refer people to you
- You're always busy, but don't always get the results you want
- Sometimes you stare at your phone and think, "Who do I call next?"
- You give out a ton of referrals but don't seem to get many back

Does it feel like you grind away, day after day, and aren't yet getting the lead flow you want? Perhaps you've been studying referrals for years and even belong to an awesome networking organization like BNI, Master Networks, LeTip, your local chamber of commerce, or some other local leads group. You're likely getting referrals already and want to learn how to exponentialize your referrals expanding both the quantity and quality of the referrals you receive.

The good news is that if you simply follow the step-by-step process explained in this book, you can systematically build a strong referral business that will generate referrals for year to come.

Stop the Insanity

You've heard the definition of insanity is to do the same thing over and over and expect different results. Well, we want to commend you for investing in yourself and taking the time to learn these time-tested and proven referral tactics instead of just doing what you've always done.

What we're going to share with you can be a total game-changer for you, your business, and your family... but only if you take ACTION and implement the simple steps outlined in this book.

As author Og Mandino says "I will act now. Only action determines my value and to increase my value, I must act without hesitation." In my study of greatness, I have found that the biggest difference between average and exceptional is "the exceptional act" and "doing the task that everyone knows they should do, but don't." They act without hesitation.

If you follow this proven program and consistently take the quick and easy success steps we guide you through, your business and bank account will grow. As you expand your income, you'll unlock financial freedom and the time freedom you desire and deserve.

Our goal is to help you attract Raving Referrals quickly and consistently so you can spend more time doing what you love with the people you love. Whether pursuing your passions and hobbies, serving in your favorite charity or church, or traveling the world enjoying amazing experiences, everything you want can be achieved once you learn the secrets and the science of attracting Raving Referrals. So that's our vision for you. But what are your goals?

How Much Money Do You Want to Make?

Clarity is power, so take a moment and get clear on your Annual Income Goal and why you want to achieve it. Ultimately, the number one reason you are reading this book is that you want to earn more money. If that's true for you, it's imperative that you set a stretch goal that is beyond what you actually believe is possible for how much you want to earn over the next 12 months.

You can then use your financial target as motivation to stay on track and take the actions needed to achieve your goal.

What is your Annual Income Goal for the next 12 months? Are you stretching beyond what you believe is possible? We challenge you to push the limits and believe that if you put in the work the results will be there. Use our Income Goal Sheet to determine how many transactions you need to hit your income goal. Once you know that, the rest of your plan will fall into place as you learn the system.

Be sure to download your Income Goal Sheet and your Goal Achievement System at *ReferralChampion.com/toolkit*.

As a high performance coach helping thousands of agents go beyond what they believe is possible, I (Verl) have found that we often set our goals based on our previous experiences. If you could look into the future and set your goals based on the potential your greatest advocate sees in you, how would that change the goals you set for yourself? Could I suggest you take your best performance and simply double it? How would that impact your life? How would your double goal make a difference in your family dynamic, the home you own, the investments you are able to make, the lifestyle you can provide for your family, or the impact you can make on your community? I believe in my core that we are all sons and daughters of a greater being and that God doesn't make mistakes. That means that the potential you have is only limited by your belief in yourself and goals. So let's begin a new chapter and remove limiting beliefs that to this point have held you back and just go for it. Let's double!

What's Your WHY?

Now that you've declared how much money you want to earn in the next year, and regardless of what your double is, let's explore what really drives you. The following questions will help you gain clarity on your true reasons for achieving your Annual Income Goal.

1. Why is it important to you to increase your income and achieve your financial goal?
2. What would achieving your financial goal allow you to do that you can't do right now?
3. How will people benefit when you reach your goal?
    - Your Family (spouse, children, and grandchildren)
    - Your Friends
    - Your Company
    - Your Employees and/or Team Members
    - Your Church or Charities
4. How will your friends and family feel about you when you achieve your goal?
5. Beyond the money, how will you feel about yourself once you have achieved this level of financial success?

The reason it's so important to understand your WHY is that it is our WHY that really drives us as human beings. The clearer you are about WHY you want to achieve your desired outcome, the more driven and committed you will be to create those results.

Eliminate Excuses For Failure

What is it that you will use as an excuse for not hitting your goal? If you are willing to be real and honest with yourself and identify your excuses for failure before you begin this journey and then one by one eliminate them, you will find success much faster than you ever imagined. This process is part of our Goal Achievement System Workman coaches use with every single coaching client.

> "When I went through the exercise of setting my goals, determining my real WHY and really being honest with myself and my coach about what excuses I would use if I didn't hit my goals, I felt for the first time that I could do something special. Not only did I hit my goals, I have continued to double and have literally quadrupled my income to over 7 figures a year the past few years with Workman Success Systems."
>
> - Brooke Sines, RE/MAX Executive Carolinas and RE/MAX of Grand Rapids.

Enlist Others in Your Success

To achieve success faster, share your goal with others who can help you reach it. You might choose a business coach, business partner, manager, employee, or even one of your referral partners. Ask them to hold you accountable. Better yet, invite your referral partners to join you in this program so you both grow your businesses together.

After all, if you really want to lose weight, hiring a personal trainer committed to your success will dramatically increase your results. Just having a membership to the gym doesn't mean you actually show up and work out. Having a personal trainer that will hold you accountable ensures that when it comes to working out, you are doing what you should, when you should, exactly how you should. Granted, it takes time to see the results, but you will feel stronger, faster, and fitter over time. You'll see old fat transform into new muscle. You'll start to notice new lines and indentations on your stomach and problem areas where before there were only bulges and curves.

When it comes to building your business, the reality is you want as many people as possible invested in your success and cheering you on. The more champions you have for your business, the more business you will have.

Verl's Coaching Tip: When you engage others in your accountability and actually pay for that advice we have found that you are more likely to actually hold yourself accountable. Accountability is not something someone else does to you, rather, it's the most important choice you will make to yourself. As a lifetime member of the weightloss class, I have found that when I pay for personal training, I always show up to the gym rather than when I find a friend who wants to go with me. For me, I think it's the fear of wasting my hard-earned money and not showing up that motivates me to simply get up early and go meet the trainer.

From Success to Significance

What's exciting to realize is that the success you create throughout your life and career can impact future generations if you do it right. Not just for you and your spouse. When you achieve serious success, you can leave a lasting legacy that changes the lives of your children, your grandchildren, and generations to come. Not to mention the impact you can have on your community and the causes you care about.

Our mission is to transform the lives of real estate professionals around the world. That's why we are so committed to empowering and equipping you with the tools, the training, and the trade secrets that you need to succeed.

We want you to WIN. Our hope is that you feel so confident and driven that you take ACTION immediately and consistently apply what you learn in this program. If you do, you WILL get more referrals and clients, guaranteed!

We love what we do because we get to work with some of the best people and companies on the planet. There's nothing more rewarding than hearing stories of professionals worldwide who have gained financial freedom as a result of our system.

Our request is that as you put these practices and principles to work in your business, you will share your wins and success stories with us at RavingReferrals.com/success. We'd love nothing more than to spotlight your victories with our growing global community of people who are living a life powered by Raving Referrals.

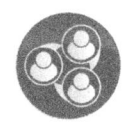

Introduction

Getting Personal

Welcome to what I know will be a transformative journey for you in mastering the art of referrals. As we walk this path together, I am thrilled to introduce myself as your new co-author, Verl Workman. With decades of experience in the real estate industry and as the CEO and co-founder of Workman Success Systems, I bring a unique perspective and a wealth of expertise to this book. My mission is to empower professionals like you to achieve unparalleled success through the power of referrals.

At Workman Success Systems, we believe that success is not just about closing deals; it's about building lasting relationships and creating a thriving business ecosystem. Our approach is rooted in the principles of collaboration, innovation, and continuous improvement. Our coaches and clients represent what I like to call the "wisdom of our crowd". It is that wisdom that separates us from all others. When great people get together and share what is truly working in their businesses, the results are almost always better than any one individual. The crowd always gets it right. As a result, we have helped countless professionals elevate their businesses by implementing proven systems and strategies that drive results. But it wasn't always that way for me.

The most important lesson I learned growing up in poverty was that if I wanted something I had to earn it. That simple, but profound, principle has led me to multiple business ventures, some of them more successful than others, but I am a true entrepreneur. I like to say that I'm "psychologically unemployable" and that mindset causes me to work harder and own the results for my actions: some of them great and others, well, they were failures. From each failure I can honestly say that the lessons I learned were critical to my next chapter of success.

From humble beginnings, my father was a high school history teacher and my mom a nurse. Sounds like a great family, however, my mother was a first generation immigrant from the Netherlands and my dad an only child from Marshalltown, Iowa. The significance of this is when you realize what they went through without any family near or even present in their lives. My mom and dad started off with the goal of having a big family. Mom had 12 pregnancies in 12 years ending up with seven children and endured five miscarriages. When I was just 11 years old my father, who was barely 40 at the time, suffered a brain hemorrhage. It left my father with severe brain damage and ultimately resulted in his going completely blind. Understandably, this caused tremendous stress for my mother who was trying to raise seven children on her own.

My father spent the next 25 years in a nursing home and each of us seven children got farmed out to the neighbors. I am so grateful for the community that reached out and took us all in. I can only imagine how hard it must have been to have these Workman kids move into their houses for a time - sometimes two of us, sometimes three of us, and sometimes just one of us, but I'll always be grateful for the neighbors who helped raise me after my father was disabled. When I look back at my childhood, I never think about how hard it was. I always think about how grateful I am that I was surrounded by so many people who were willing to share. And I know now that my role in life is to make a difference in as many lives as possible—just like others made a difference in my life. Some of the basic life lessons I learned was from one family who took us in. The father was a scoutmaster. He made sure that I participated in Boy Scouts; made sure I got my Eagle Scout; and served a mission for my church when I turned 19. This experience made me the salesperson, leader, and father that I am today. I learned that people don't reject you, they just don't know you, and I learned that when you do the right things, people tell others about it and your life is made better.

Without the hard things we had to go through as children, we wouldn't have the strength, tenacity, and fortitude to keep going. I love and cherish every hard thing that has made me stronger. And that brings me to where I am today.

Today, I lead an amazing team that includes three of my six children, many of my past clients who are now coaches, and an army of amazing individual clients and coaches who teach me everyday how to be better. I

INTRODUCTION

love and pursue the study of greatness. I am constantly looking for people who do things better than me or better than anyone in their field, and I want to know what makes them tick. What are their habits, what books do they read, and what is it that they do that we can duplicate. The key to predictable greatness is understanding how to create systems that, when followed, result in great things. I have spent my life in search of greatness and this book is the result of studying some of the greatest producers in all of real estate.

Join me as we explore the critical role that referrals play in building a sustainable and profitable business. Referrals are more than just leads; they are endorsements from satisfied clients and trusted partners who believe in your value. By harnessing the power of referrals, you can create a steady stream of qualified prospects who are eager to work with you.

Throughout these pages, you will discover actionable insights and practical tools that will help you cultivate a robust referral network. We will explore the strategies that have propelled top performers to success and consider how you can apply these principles to your own business. My promise to you is to share what really works - and avoid hypothesis and fantasy - using only proven systems that give predictable results. From understanding your referral score to mastering the art of the ask, each chapter is designed to equip you with the knowledge and skills you need to thrive.

Are you ready to learn from the masters of giving and receiving referrals? Are you ready to stop relying on the internet or paid leads to grow your business? Are you ready to build real authentic relationships based on trust?

As we journey together, I encourage you to embrace the mindset of a lifelong learner. The real estate landscape is constantly evolving, and staying ahead requires a commitment to growth and adaptation. At Workman Success Systems, we are dedicated to supporting you every step of the way, providing the resources and guidance you need to achieve your goals.

I am excited to share this journey with you and look forward to seeing the incredible impact that mastering referrals will have on your business. Let's get started on this exciting adventure and unlock the full potential of your referral network. Together, we will create a legacy of success that extends far beyond transactions, building a community of advocates who are eager to champion your brand.

Welcome to the world of Raving Referrals!

Congratulations and thank you for reading this Raving Referrals for Real Estate Agents book.

Unlock Your Toolkit for Maximum Results

This book isn't just about reading—it's about taking action. To help you apply what you're learning, we've created a Toolkit filled with powerful resources, templates, scripts, systems, and tools worth over $3,000 that you can access and use immediately.

How to Access Your Toolkit:

Scan the QR code below to access your personal Toolkit. In each chapter we introduce new tools and resources - all available in your Toolkit.

Why This Matters:

Think of this Toolkit as your secret weapon. The strategies in this book are designed to be implemented, not just read. By using these tools, you'll reach your goals faster and achieve real-world results.

Stay Updated:

New tools will be introduced as you move through the book, so keep coming back to your Toolkit. Don't skip this step! We don't want you to miss out on key resources specifically designed to make your journey easier and more effective.

ReferralChampion.com/toolkit

Chapter 1:
What's Your Referral Score?

As you begin your journey towards achieving your Annual Income Goal, it's crucial to understand precisely where you are starting from and what gaps you might have in your current referral business practices.

If you study the top performers and producers in the real estate industry, you'll likely find that they all exhibit the same daily practices. By making a few minor changes to your daily habits, you can reach the same level of financial success that the top performers in your company and industry have achieved.

We've developed a Referral Score assessment to help you understand how well you're currently performing in each of the top ten daily practices that drive referrals.

This tool has been designed to identify quick and easy improvements you can apply to your business processes that can drive referrals for years to come.

Let's look specifically at the top ten actions that drive referrals and see how you measure up. As you review each practice, write down your self-assessed score on each of these daily practices. This will give you your baseline Referral Score and identify simple, yet powerful opportunities for improvement.

#1 SERVING YOUR CLIENTS

When it comes to business, nothing matters more than serving your clients!

Providing exceptional service to each and every client, customer, guest, and community member should be the reason you do what you do. The money is simply the reward for a job well done!

The more exceptionally you serve your clients, the more referrals will flow your way. As people see how much you care about their success and satisfaction, they will naturally be more inclined to refer others to you.

On a scale of 0-10, how well do you score when it comes to serving your clients? Write down your score now.

#2 PLANNING YOUR SUCCESS

Every successful real estate agent, team, and brokerage has a detailed business plan for how they will achieve their goals and objectives. However, when it comes to referrals, this doesn't always hold true.

We're amazed how few real estate professionals actually have a written plan that details exactly what they are going to do this week, this month, and this year to grow their referral business.

Considering the fact that over 65% of new business comes by referral, you are leaving money on the table if you don't have a written plan and system to drive referrals for your business. Your plan should include your goals for the month, quarter, and year, along with a detailed promotional plan and communication calendar, so you can plan out your key offers and campaigns throughout the year.

How do you score when it comes to having a detailed business development and referral plan? Rate yourself on a scale of 0-10, where 0 indicates you have no plan at all and 10 means you have a detailed action plan with written goals, promotions, and a communication calendar.

#3 ENGAGING PEOPLE CONSISTENTLY

The most successful professionals ensure they engage and connect with their most important relationships consistently. As you invest time and energy in building strong relationships, you increase the number of people who know, like, and trust you enough to refer you to the people in their lives. The key is to engage them consistently while focusing on the things that matter most TO THEM. After all, people don't care how much you know until they know how much you care. The more consistently you engage others personally and meaningfully, the more consistently they will recommend and refer you to their friends, family, colleagues, and Social Sphere.

So how do you score when it comes to connecting with and engaging people? Are you skillful at following up and building strong relationships, or do people rarely hear from you after they've met you for the first time?

Write down your score, with 0 being awful and 10 being masterful.

#4 ASKING FOR REFERRALS

We're often amazed at how few professionals actually ask their clients for referrals. Most people in business understand that referrals drive their success, but often they feel awkward and uncomfortable asking for them. That's probably because they've never been taught when and how to ask for referrals in a way that makes your clients feel comfortable and happy to help.

We are going to help you master "The Art of the Ask" in Chapter 8. For now, be sure to write down your score of how consistent you are at asking for referrals from both your clients and professional colleagues.

#5 TRACKING YOUR REFERRALS

The most successful professionals always measure and track their results, especially when it comes to referrals!

We're surprised how few people actually understand where their business comes from. After all, if you aren't tracking and measuring where each and every client comes from, how can you expect to maximize your results? Business experts teach, "What gets measured, gets maximized," and that is absolutely true. By tracking your referrals, you focus your mind on the #1 driver of your business success. The information you gather allows you to concentrate your valuable time and energy on your most productive and profitable relationships.

Okay, it's time to score how good you are at tracking the referrals you give and receive. Go ahead and write down your score now.

#6 THANKING PEOPLE WHO GIVE REFERRALS

Thanking people is a critical practice that can dramatically impact your success...if you do it consistently. Every time you receive a referral, you should be thanking the person who made the recommendation or introduction. Not only does this help them feel good because you've recognized them, but it also demonstrates your professionalism, which reinforces their feeling that recommending you was the right move to make.

Thanking the people who refer business to you will dramatically boost their confidence in recommending you, and improve the probability they send you more referrals in the future. This is one of the fastest and easiest ways to get more referrals and grow your business, so make sure you thank people each and every time they give you a new referral.

So one a scale from 0-10, how do you rate when it comes to consistently thanking people who give you referrals?

#7 UPDATING PEOPLE WHO GIVE REFERRALS

Updating people who give you referrals is another important practice that builds trust. People are highly appreciative when you call, text, DM, voice memo, or email a quick update, letting them know if you were able to help their client, friend, or loved one.

This is especially true when the person giving you the referral is another professional. After all, they've entrusted their own personal credibility and relationship with their client to you.

Following up with a quick update gives you a natural and comfortable opportunity to ask if they know anyone else who would benefit from your service. If you've never even thought about updating people after they refer prospects to you, you may need to write down a score of 0 on this practice. On the other hand, maybe you are awesome at letting people know what's going on with the people they refer to you. If so, then write down a 10. Just be sure to write down your number so you can see your overall Referral Score.

#8 REWARDING PEOPLE WHO GIVE REFERRALS

Rewarding your referral sources is another excellent business practice and catalyst for referrals, whether you incentivize people or simply surprise them with a gift when they refer you. Of course, because of RESPA laws, you are not allowed to pay anyone Referral Rewards if they don't have a real estate license.

We've left this as a part of the referral score system of Raving Referrals because you can use this strategy to incentivize referrals from other licensed agents, as well as in other industries and businesses you may be involved in. Just be sure to research and follow the regulations and restrictions for the real estate industry and do everything by the book so you are always in compliance.

So, how good you are at rewarding people who give you referrals. Are you a 0, a 10, or somewhere in between?

#9 RECOGNIZING PEOPLE WHO GIVE REFERRALS

Most people love to be publicly recognized for doing good work and helping others. In fact, the human ego has a very strong desire and need for recognition, especially in today's social media obsessed world of likes, shares, tweets, and follows. That's why many businesses grow rapidly once they start publicly celebrating and recognizing people who promote and refer them. Whether it be in the public areas of the business or through a newsletter, website, or social media accounts, the social proof and credibility built by recognizing your referrers works quickly and effectively.

How about you? How well do you score when it comes to celebrating and recognizing the people who recommend and refer you? Write down your score so we can move to the final referral practice that drives your income and wealth.

#10 PROMOTING YOURSELF AND YOUR SERVICES

Nearly 90% of business success comes down to your marketing and lead generation. After all, if you have enough sales and revenue coming in the door, most other problems can be solved. On the other hand, if you don't have a consistent flow of new clients, leads, and sales opportunities for your business, you don't really have much of a business, do you?

After coaching, consulting, and working with over 250,000 real estate agents worldwide, we've found where most agents fail is in their self-promotion and marketing efforts. Rather than attending events, networking, mailing out offers, or running ads online and offline, many people simply do unprofitable "busy-work" that never gets them any closer to their Annual Income Goal.

Whether that be because they are too busy, too shy, or just don't know how, they simply don't invest enough time or money attracting new business opportunities.

How do you rate yourself in the marketing and promotion side of your business? If you are one of those people who always finds a reason not to invest your time or money promoting yourself and your services, you may need to give yourself a 1, 2, or 3 on this practice. If you are a super promoter who always stays top-of-mind with your clients, customers, fans, and followers, you should write down a 9 or a 10. Most people score between 3 and 5 on this one, so don't feel bad if you didn't score well on this important practice.

TIME FOR THE TALLY

Now for the fun part! Write down and add up each of your scores from the 10 best referral practices above.

1. Serving   _____
2. Planning   _____
3. Engaging   _____
4. Asking   _____
5. Tracking   _____
6. Thanking   _____
7. Updating   _____
8. Rewarding   _____
9. Recognizing   _____
10. Promoting   _____

TOTAL REFERRAL SCORE: _____

Your Referral Score ranges from 0-100 and works just like a standard school grade. That means...

If you scored 90 or higher, you get an A

We'll bet you dollars to doughnuts that you are in the top 5% of income earners in your company and industry. You're probably already earning a great 6 or 7-figure income and living the good life. You have solid systems in place that generate referrals consistently and automatically. Most likely, you take multiple vacations each year and share your abundance with everyone you love.

We hope every single one of our readers achieves this level of Referral Score after going through the training in this book and setting up your Referral Marketing System. If you scored in this range, we congratulate and celebrate you!

If you scored between 80-89, you get a B

Most people who score this high are in the top 20% of income earners in their industry and company. You likely have new referrals and opportunities coming to you on a weekly basis and are doing quite well financially.

If you got a B on this test, you should feel proud for mastering so many of the referral best practices. Business must be pretty good, and your income is increasing. You're on your way, and it's just a matter of time before you blast through your Annual Income Goal.

If you scored between 70-79, your grade is a C

In the Olympics, third place still gets you on the podium, so feel proud of what you've accomplished. Just know there's more work to do to reach gold medal status. This is still a passing mark. You are likely in the top half of the producers in your firm and are doing fine financially. You may have identified some opportunities for improvement as you reviewed these top 10 practices. Hopefully, you are now motivated to learn and apply the proven strategies, systems, and scripts we are sharing in this book.

If you scored between 60-69, that means you got a D

If you're in this category, you're not alone. The majority of professionals initially get a failing Referral Score before they go through our program and apply our strategies. The knowledge and wisdom in this book can help you identify quick tweaks that help ramp up your revenue and maximize profitability.

If you are serious about growing your business and generating more income, just work on each of these daily practices and take consistent action. Fortunately, our easy-to-use system can help boost your score significantly.

If you scored below 60, you know what grade you got...

The optimists in us would tell you that scoring in this range just means you have many opportunities for improvement.

The power behind building a business through referrals is that you actually compound your success once you start; new clients refer more new clients, who refer more new clients.

We're Here to Help

If you're feeling a bit stretched, stressed, or overwhelmed right now, we totally understand. Don't worry! We are committed to teaching you all you need to know to build a thriving business.

Remember, this isn't your final grade. It's just the beginning. Think of it as your baseline score before learning our Raving Referrals system and putting our strategies to work for your business. The truth is that there is a lot you can do to quickly boost your Referral Score and your income. Especially now that you are aware of these 10 best practices.

You'll be retaking this test at the end of this book, so just focus on putting these practices to work in your business, and you'll see your referrals and income start to rise.

If you haven't already taken your Referral Score Quiz online, scan this QR code or visit the link below to take the quick quiz now.

AgentReferralQuiz.com

Chapter 2:
The 7 Laws of Raving Referrals

According to marketing guru Jeffrey Hayzlett, Chairman of the C-Suite Network:

"Relationships have always been at the heart of business success. It's not a trend; it's the foundation. With strong relationships come referrals—the ultimate way to show trust and respect. Referrals are the cornerstone of great business relationships, and I've seen them drive billion-dollar deals and simple gestures alike. Be it a heartfelt thank-you note, a bottle of wine, or a simple handshake, the gratitude that follows a referral speaks to the ripple effect of value they create.

At the C-Suite Network, we focus on building trusted networks, where the spirit of giving—helping without expecting—is the driving force. When you approach relationships with a mindset of generosity, the rewards, both tangible and intangible, naturally follow."

When it comes to generating Raving Referrals for your business, there are seven laws you need to understand and master. When you build your business in accordance with these seven laws, you will attract a steady stream of new client opportunities for years to come.

Raving Referral Law #1:
Every Referral Starts with Trust

The first thing to understand when it comes to referrals is that every referral starts with trust. Think about the last referral, recommendation, or introduction you gave to a friend, client, or colleague. How well did you know and trust the person you recommended? Most likely, you trust them to some degree, or you would not have made that recommendation, right? If not, you gave the recommendation with a disclaimer saying something like, "I've never used them myself, but I hear they do a good job." The same is true for everyone you know. The more they know, like, and ultimately trust you, the more they will sing your praises and passionately endorse you to the people in their lives.

In fact, your income is directly tied to the amount of trust that you build with your clients, colleagues, and Social Sphere. The more trust you earn, the more money you will earn over your career.

Gallup has conducted polls over the past several decades that consistently show that the most trusted professions on the planet are also the most highly paid, including doctors, engineers, and accountants.

David Horsager, in his most recent book Trust Matters More Than Ever, states that "trust can be defined as a confident belief in a person to do what is good and right on a consistent basis."

The more people that trust that you are a person of integrity and an expert professional in your trade, the more confidence they will have in recommending you. Ultimately, it is their trust in you that gives them the confidence to refer people they care about to you and your business because they believe you will do the right thing consistently.

Raving Referral Law #2:
The More You Give, The More You Receive

Giving is the key that builds trust, deepens relationships, and unlocks referrals. The Bible teaches, "As you sow, so shall you reap." That timeless truth definitely applies to your referral business.

The more generous you are with your time, attention, understanding, and respect for others, the more liked and trusted you will become. In turn, people will go out of their way to help you win. In life, there are people who take more than they give and those who give more than they take. Those who are constantly putting their own wants and needs first are typically viewed as selfish, egotistical, and greedy. Those who give generously tend to be viewed as noble, big-hearted, and even charitable.

So which camp do you want to be in?

Can you imagine being a keynote speaker whose business model depends on live events when a worldwide pandemic hits? That was my (Verl's) business in 2019 and suddenly as 2020 started we watched over 7 figures of speaking and potential coaching revenue evaporate from my calendar in just a few short days.

Our motto has always been "Events Drive Revenue". My mastermind group in the National Speakers Association went from meeting monthly to meeting weekly as almost every speaker was watching their entire revenue stream disappear. Some of the greatest speakers on the planet were afraid of where the next dollar was going to come from as we all set up our home studios for virtual events and prayed that people would still hire us to speak, inspire, and help their teams navigate this new world.

I've had many discussions with Cleve Gaddis, a WSS Master Coach, team leader, and past coaching client on what we could and should do in the real estate industry to keep the business going. I remember the specific Zoom call I had with Cleve, and my daughter Brianne, President of Workman Success Systems. We had looked at our finances, our projections through the year, and realized that we were going to be okay if we did not do a single live event for a year. For the first time in my career we had saved enough to survive a downturn and not have to lay anyone off.

It was on this call that we changed one of our internal sayings from "Serve Before Opportunity", to "Serve Regardless of Opportunity", meaning, "How can we help others who are struggling and may find themselves in a place that is less fortunate than we were in?" We developed tools, resources, and systems for doing virtual real estate, we offered webinars to any company, brand, office, or board of REALTORs that would have us, all for FREE. We not only taught agents what they might be able to do, but gave them tools such as "How to Master Virtual Showings", "Master Virtual 'Open Houses on Steroids'" and other great tools.

All of these tools, systems, and virtual events were given out for free to anyone who was open to receive. The results were staggering. Not only did we help hundreds and then thousands of REALTORs sell and survive, many grew their businesses and had their best years ever in real estate through the following couple of years.

At Workman, when we believed we would suffer financially, we actually grew without doing any live or in person events for over a year—a true testament that the mission to Serve Regardless of Opportunity brought joy and returns we had never dreamed of. As a company, you will see this Serve Regardless of Opportunity often as we give away some of our best tools, trade secrets, and best practices throughout this book, on our website, and at events worldwide.

Raving Referrals in Action: Alvaro Erize's Early Encounter Serving Regardless of Opportunity

Alvaro Erize is the CEO of CINC - a leading provider of lead generation and CRM solutions. His unique journey early in his life and, essentially, at the beginning of his career, vividly illustrates the principle of serving regardless of opportunity. One defining moment occurred during his early entrepreneurial days in Argentina, while running a comic book import and distribution business. At just 16 years old, Alvaro was building a small, yet impactful, operation making international comics accessible to Argentine readers.

During this time, a retired Japanese diplomat, Kanji, approached him with an unusual request. Kanji, a fan of the niche Japanese comic Golgo 13, asked Alvaro to translate and publish the comic in Spanish. Despite the project offering no financial gain and holding limited commercial prospects, Alvaro agreed.

"There was no money in it... but I thought, this is a fun project, and it's for someone I respect. Why not put in the extra effort?"

His decision stemmed not from profit motives, but from a desire to help someone Alvaro admired. He secured the rights, completed the translation, and published the comic. While the endeavor resulted in a financial loss, it demonstrated his willingness to give time and resources to create value for others.

Many years later, the impact of his act of service became abundantly clear. Kanji, impressed by Alvaro's dedication and trustworthiness, recommended him for a critical role with Toyota. At the time, Toyota needed a factory in Argentina to replace a key supplier and turned to Kikuchi for help. Remembering Alvaro's earlier service, Kanji facilitated an introduction that completely changed the trajectory of Alvaro's career.

"That small, little thing I did as a 16-year-old turned into what launched my entire career. Translating a Japanese comic set me on a path to running a Toyota factory and, eventually, moving to the U.S."

This connection was, to say the least, transformative. Alvaro, then just 23, was entrusted with setting up and managing the factory, an experience that taught him invaluable lessons about leadership, resilience, and operational excellence. It ultimately paved the way for his admission to Stanford and contributed to his ongoing success in the U.S.

Lessons from Alvaro's Story

Alvaro's experience teaches that serving without expecting an immediate return can have life-altering consequences. By focusing on creating value and helping others, even in seemingly insignificant ways, he cultivated trust and goodwill that opened doors he could never have imagined.

"I didn't do that project to gain anything; it was just the right thing to do. But it came back to me in ways I could never have envisioned, especially during one of the toughest times in my life."

Alvaro's story reinforces the principle that acts of service, driven by respect and a willingness to give, can lead to opportunities far beyond what we initially foresee. His story epitomizes the concept of serving regardless of opportunity, proving that sometimes the most significant outcomes stem from moments of selflessness.

Think about the greatest givers in your life. Who are the top three most generous and giving people you know?

The 3 Most Generous People in My Life Are:

1. _____
2. _____
3. _____

How do you FEEL about the people you just identified? Does their generosity make you like them more? Most likely, the answer is a resounding YES! That's why when it comes to building trust, the more you give, the more you receive. Make it your mission to go out of your way to give your time, talents, attention, and best efforts in all you do.

Give your respect and attention to everyone you meet. Listen to them intently and ask probing questions about their passions and pursuits. Get to know what they really care about and help them achieve it if you can. Give praise and public appreciation when people help you.

Post a quick shout-out on social media or send them a thank you card, text, or testimonial for their business. The more you give, the more referrals you will receive. So, give generously in all you do.

Raving Referral Law #3:
Relationships Trigger Transactions

You've probably heard the saying that "people don't care how much you know until they know how much you care." As you build trust and give generously, you will strengthen and deepen relationships with people who have the ability to refer and recommend all the clients you will ever want or need. The reality is that trust only gets built through relationships.

This is why the third law of Raving Referrals is that Relationships Trigger Transactions. The quality of your relationships determines the quality of your life.

Before getting married, Brandon and his wife went through a premarital course with the pastor of their church. One of the lessons he taught them was that relationships were like bank accounts. Every time you show someone you care about them, you make a deposit in that account, and your balance with them grows.

The more often you connect with the people in your life, the greater your relational equity with them will be. The better they get to know you, the more they start to like you and trust you, which then leads to them recommending and referring you and your team. It makes sense, doesn't it?

Most banks charge service fees on inactive accounts, and the same thing happens with your relationships. The more time you let pass without communicating or connecting, your relational balance with that person declines. If you don't reach out from time to time, they may actually forget about you altogether. They certainly won't be on the lookout for clients for you, which is what you want for your business.

That is why it's so important to continually engage and nurture all your Referral Champions, including your clients, referral partners, and Social Sphere. Of course, it's always best to connect with people in person, because humans experience the strongest bonds when we are hanging out together having fun. That's why we recommend that you get together with your top relationships at least once every month or two.

One of Verl's favorite sales trainers is Tom Hopkins. His book, How to Master the Art of Selling, teaches that you should STP—See Twenty People belly to belly. This concept of getting out there and seeing people you want to do business with, or connect more deeply with, has played a significant role in generating more referrals, both given and received. Seeing people is the #1 way to build true relationships with trust.

What we call BRT, Building Relationships with Trust (BRT), is the center of our sales cycle. Without the true focus on relationships we are just sales people with a pitch. Slick dialog and fancy scripts will only take you so far, but deep relationships built on a foundation of trust will be the foundation your businesses, and lives, are built upon.

That said, you can always send a text, call them on the phone, or send a handwritten note to show you are thinking about them. When you do, you are making relational deposits that will pay off big time once you learn the secrets to generating referrals.

The Best Referral System Ever Created

In my study of predictable greatness, I (Verl) came across a great real estate agent by the name of Mike Parker. Mike was one of the top agents in the country. He was a Howard Britton Star Power Star, and one of the best referral givers and receivers I've ever encountered. I remember sitting down with Mike and asking him what is it that made his business so great. Mike shared with me, "Every day I go through my list of 50 people that I call my top 50 list to ensure I have a personal touch with every single one of them each month." The concept of having a personal touch with 50 people every single month created an environment where he was always at the front of their mind. When real estate came up, everyone on Mike's Top 50 list always thought of him first. That year Mike closed 86 transactions through referrals by interacting with his Top 50 list for just one hour each day. So we created a system around it. A Verlism, which you will hear often as you become acquainted with the way we think, is "anything you do 3 times in your business - whether daily or weekly. If you do it three times, you must create a system for it. Systems first!"

Another Verlism is, "That which gets measured gets done." Over the years, WSS coaches and clients have perfected the Top 50 system with a high level of execution on a basic fundamental system, creating the highest converted leads of all time. The Top 50 is simply defined as the top 50 people in your life who are most likely to give you one referral a year. Once you identify your list of the Top 50, you then use our Top 50 Tracker to have one personal touch with each one of them every month. A personal touch is defined as a face-to-face meeting or a conversation. It does not include an email or a text message. Having an effective referral business where you literally have hundreds of Raving Referrals requires you to be in a contact sport with your Top 50. Everything Brandon has shared to this point is so much in alignment with how we view referrals that adding the WSS Top 50 system to the Raving Referrals system was a natural addition to a great program.

Many of our clients over the years have improved and expanded their top 50 lists to include things like the top 50 agents outside their market who could refer business to them, or the top 50 vendors that they use and recommend when somebody needs help in and around their home.

Raving Referrals in Action: Tammie Slay's "The Sticky Factor"

The Sticky Factor – Defining Personal Connection

Before coaching, WSS Master Coach, Team Leader, and Broker/Owner at HIP Realty Group in Frisco, Texas, Tammie Slay's strength lay in her ability to connect deeply with people. Her interactions left lasting impressions, though she didn't fully understand why or how. Through coaching, Tammie was encouraged to study herself by recording her presentations and client conversations. This exercise revealed her unique ability to "stick" in clients' lives by focusing entirely on them—whether it was noticing subtle cues, engaging their children during showings, or giving personalized, meaningful gifts.

For example, Tammie once left a puppet with a child during a home tour, ensuring that the family associated her with that warm, thoughtful moment.

The coaching insight? Be a student of yourself to identify the moments when you truly connect with clients and replicate those experiences.

The Power of Intentionality – Outlawing the Word "Referral"

Tammie's results skyrocketed when she moved from organic, unstructured referrals to an intentional approach. One key shift was banning the word "referral" and replacing it with a simple, direct question: "Do you know anyone looking to buy or sell real estate?" This approach removed the pressure and awkwardness associated with traditional referral "asks", while still prompting her network to think of potential connections.

Impact:

- In her first year of intentionality, her referrals grew from 20 to over 40
- By the third year, she received over 100 referrals, leading to nearly 70 closed transactions

Tammie's strategy demonstrates that clarity, confidence, and consistency in your ask can create exponential growth.

Transformative Relationships – The Referral of a Lifetime

One of Tammie's most remarkable success stories started with a seemingly unremarkable lease listing. She showed the property to a tenant prospect who was initially hesitant to buy due to credit issues. Tammie connected that client with resources, helped repair her credit, and ultimately closed on her dream home.

The pivotal moment? Tammie gifted a bouquet of pink roses to the builder sales rep who went above and beyond during the transaction. This thoughtful gesture led to an incredible relationship, with the sales rep sending Tammie dozens of unrepresented buyers over the years, resulting in nearly 70 transactions.

Lesson: Every client and connection matters. Treat every opportunity as valuable, and you'll be surprised at the doors it can open.

Leveraging Systems – Top 50 Strategy

Tammie refined her business further by implementing the Top 50 strategy, where she focused on her most valuable relationships. This involved creating intentional touchpoints like regular calls and innovative gift programs, such as her "Hip Faves" boxes. These curated collections of her team's favorite items—ranging from honey to humorous spice grinders—kept her top clients engaged and loyal.

Key Insight: When her team struggled to ask for referrals, the gift program provided a way to naturally start conversations and build confidence in their outreach.

Conclusion: Be Easy to Refer and Build Relationships That Multiply

Tammie's success boils down to a few core principles:

1. **Study Yourself**: Identify what makes you unique and lean into it.
2. **Be Intentional:** Create a structured plan for engaging your network.
3. **Focus on the Client**: Make every interaction personal and meaningful.

4. **Ask the Right Questions**: Avoid vague referral requests; be specific and direct.
5. **Build Systems**: Implement tools like Top 50 lists and creative gifting programs to stay consistent.

Actionable Steps for Agents:

1. **Discover Your Sticky Factor**: Record your interactions with clients, identify moments of connection, and amplify those elements in your process.
2. **Create a Top 50 List**: Identify the most influential people in your network and engage with them consistently.
3. **Outlaw "Referral" Requests**: Replace them with specific, situational questions like, "Do you know anyone looking to buy or sell real estate?"
4. **Personalize Your Gifts**: Use thoughtful, tailored gestures that resonate with your clients.
5. **Leverage Coaching**: Work with a WSS coach to analyze and refine your strengths, creating repeatable systems for growth.

By following Tammie's approach, agents can transform their businesses into referral powerhouses, turning every interaction into an opportunity for lasting success.

Raving Referrals in Action: Christy Buck's "Intentionality"

Team Leader Christy Buck's journey in real estate is a testament to the power of boldness and intentionality in building a referral-based business. Starting as a WSS Coaching client, Christy is now a WSS Master Coach, team leader, and Broker/Owner with Infinity Real Estate Group in Pearland, Texas. Christy transformed her annual income from $250,000 to an impressive $3.4 million. Her success is deeply rooted in her fearless approach to asking for referrals and her strategic follow-up.

One of Christy's standout stories involves a simple, yet bold, question she posed to her car salesman and his team. She promised to purchase a Range Rover from them, however, they had to give her at least 1 referral over the next 12 months. This led to a series of transactions: a million-dollar home for the sales manager, a $1.5 million property for his father, and ongoing deals with her car salesmen. This single question has already paid for her car and continues to generate substantial business, illustrating the power of asking for and maintaining relationships.

Another remarkable story began with a woman who wanted to rent Christy's garage for her parents' 50th wedding anniversary. Instead of charging a rental fee, Christy asked for two referrals by the end of the year. This agreement led to the sale of a $475,000 home and a subsequent purchase of a $379,000 property, turning a $500 check into $18,000 in commissions.

Christy's approach to referrals extends beyond clients to include vendors and partners. She actively engages with her network, asking for referrals and creating opportunities through community events. By hosting up to 12 events a year, Christy keeps her database active and maintains strong relationships. Her events, like pie days and community gatherings, are not just about business; they're about fostering connections and creating a culture of giving and receiving.

Christy's story is a powerful example of how being intentional, asking boldly, and nurturing relationships can transform a real estate business. Her success is a reminder that opportunities are everywhere, and with the right approach, they can lead to extraordinary results.

Building your business is as Simple as: 3-2-1-1

Verl has always asserted that the top issue almost every agent experiences is how to generate more business and eliminate the peaks and valleys in their income. The answer lies in the question. First, do you honestly believe that the real estate business goes up and down every 2-3 months, where the universe sends you leads one month then takes a couple of months off?

The reality is that the activities you personally participate in or focus on that generate business go something like this: You need money so you prospect, call your sphere, work open houses, etc. While doing that you generate a few buyers or sellers so you stop doing those things and work on the transactions those activities created until closing happens, often several at once, or what we call a peak. After the 30-day celebration period of a great month, a shopping spree, or just getting caught up on your bills, you then look at the pipeline and realize that there is nothing coming in for the foreseeable future... the valley. So it begins again: you start calling your sphere, you prospect, do open houses, etc. You see, it's your activities that drive the peaks and valleys in your business, so to eliminate the peaks and valleys and have a predictable, sustainable revenue stream you must have consistent prospecting activities. There must be a regular system in place where you spend time looking for new business.

We have built that very system: our 3-2-1-1 System. Every day we ask our coaching clients to call 3 past clients with a focus on the relationship. You can use F.O.R.D. to engage with them; ask about their Family, Occupation, Relationships, and Dreams, and also offer something of value (e.g., an up-to-date graphic with new listings, pendings, closings, and price reductions). This is your opportunity to really reach out and share with them information that sets you apart from every other REALTOR. Once you've made your three calls to past clients or people in your sphere of influence, you now want to prospect until you add two new people to your database. Next, I want you to learn one new technology-oriented thing every single day (think AI, ChatGPT, or CRM short cuts) and, lastly, give one outbound referral per week from your business with no strings attached; nothing commission related. Just refer someone to your community because they've done a good job for you and you want to share that love. Let me rephrase it to 3-2-1-1. I want you to think about the math on this.

After just one month doing this five days a week you will have reached out and talked to 60 people in your database. You will have prospected out 40 new prospects. You'll have given away four referrals, and have learned 20 new things with technology you're implementing regularly so it makes a big impact in your business. In 90 days you will have talked to 180 people in your database and really focused on the relationship, getting to know them better, finding out how you can serve and give them something of value. You will have prospected 120 new prospects. You will have given out 12 referrals and learned 60 new things with your technology.

If you stop doing everything else in your business and you only focus on 3-2-1-1 you would never, ever have to wonder where the next dollar is coming from. You would eliminate the peaks and valleys in your business and have a constant flow of new business coming in. Are you ready to eliminate the peaks and valleys in your business? If so, then download the 3-2-1-1 System following the QR code at the end of this chapter.

Remember, nothing happens to you. Making the commitment and taking accountability are the most important choices you will ever make. The difference between average agents and those who are truly exceptional is the fact that the exceptional do the basic fundamentals everyone knows they should do... but most don't.

The more personal your interactions are, the more relational equity you are creating. Remember that every touch counts. Even a quick text, email, direct message, or voice memo will help you gain mindshare. Just remind your Referral Champions you are never too busy to help them and the people they care about. The more value you deliver to your relationships, the more frequently they will refer you.

Raving Referrals in Action:
Nick Painz's "It's the Relationship"

Nick Painz, WSS Coaching client and Certified Coach, shared this experience of simply doing the right thing and delivering real value.

> *"In June of 2022, I was given a referral from an agent that I stayed in contact with from Northern Colorado. It was for a townhome that had already been listed, but that was not having much success selling. After the client terminated their listing agreement with the original agent, I was able to secure the listing. I sold the property in under 10 days. During the sale of the house, I discovered that the owner was the CEO of a major home builder and after the sale was completed, I asked if I could have the opportunity to sell his new builds. Two weeks later, his VP of operations called to interview me about selling their homes. Just over two years later, I've sold over 20 of their new builds, for $11M+ in volume. A new community that they are building will have 350 homes, of which I will list and sell about 50 over the next two years. Being present in that moment when a referred client needed expert help has turned into hundreds of thousands of commission dollars. Agent referrals are a critical part of our business. But it's the relationship that precedes the referral that generates all of the opportunities."*

Raving Referral Law #4:
Stellar Service Creates Stellar Success

The fourth law of generating Raving Referrals is that Stellar Service Creates Stellar Success. It should go without saying that the better you treat your clients, customers, and especially your team, the more success you will experience—both in terms of your personal income as well as your personal satisfaction and fulfillment.

The more your clients and referral partners know how much you genuinely care about them and their success, the more they will care about you and your success.

Have you ever experienced a referral to a person or place that under delivered? I (Verl) have a favorite sushi place in Salt Lake City. They make special rolls, have fish flown in daily, and even create special dishes that I have personally named. I may be a bit of a food snob, but I love to eat, and I love sharing meals, creating memories, and forming bonds around great culinary experiences. I have talked about, referred, sent, and taken many people there over the years, and they get it right most of the time. They usually do a great job, but there was one time that stands out where I told my friend about this place, offered to take him there for lunch, and when we arrived the experience was, well, less than promised. The service was slow, the chef made no attempt to offer or create any of our "special items", and the experience was below average. While this may have been a day they were just off, I found myself trying other places and recommending different restaurants. Even after many great experiences, one off day changed the referral relationship. Now, to their credit, I have been back several times and they have done a great job re earning my trust, but it took time and probably cost them thousands of dollars in referred business by simply not creating stellar service.

The 5 Traits of 5-Star Service:

So how do you create a 5-star experience for your clients? There are five traits of 5-star service, and when you serve clients using these five traits people will go out of their way to help you. In fact, some will rave about you each and every chance they get.

1. Listen intently to understand their cares and concerns.

    One of the most difficult challenges in providing 5-star service is listening to understand instead of listening to respond. Becoming interested in where they are and how you can serve, rather than always wanting to be interesting, creates a culture and relationship based on authenticity.

2. Communicate clearly.

    Communicating openly and honestly is one of the core principles we strive to achieve at WSS. We like to say that we don't have people problems, only process problems and when we struggle or have a challenge or issue, it can almost always be traced back to open and clear communication. Provide 5-star service by keeping your client informed and updated on progress through their preferred communication style to eliminate issues, drive success, and open the door for a lifetime of referrals.

3. Meet and exceed expectations.

    Oftentimes, agents don't live up to the minimum standard for the fees they charge. This became evident in class action lawsuits that swept the industry. When you over deliver and do the right things regardless of how it impacts what you make, the money takes care of itself. There is always another level that can be achieved in providing amazing client experiences.

4. Be on time and on budget.

    This aligns with communication. By setting proper expectations up front and then delivering on those promises, you deepen relationships and foster results. Often, we have to make course corrections that change what was promised because of things out of our control. This is normal in business, but does not have to be catastrophic if you stay engaged, communicate instantly when there are issues, and focus on solutions. Many of our strongest relationships have been forged through adversity.

5. Always have integrity.

    Be intentional about building a community of clients that are grateful for your service, generous with praise, and quick to recommend you to others. After all, word spreads quickly when you deliver stellar service to your clients. Soon, the only possible outcome is stellar success for you and your business.

Raving Referral Law #5:
Delighted Clients Refer Delightful Clients

Wow your clients and referrals will follow. The fifth law of Raving Referrals is that when you go above and beyond to delight your clients, they will happily and consistently refer you to delightful clients.

Decades of empirical research shows that referred prospects:

- Trust you faster
- Refer more often
- Are more loyal
- Are more profitable
- Are more eager to meet with you
- Are often pre-sold on hiring you
- Are more enjoyable to work with

When you add all of these factors together, it's no wonder why delighted clients refer delightful clients! As your clients praise you to others, they actually transfer the trust they've built with you onto others. Every time that happens, your new prospect's confidence in you and comfort with you grows.

Your goal should be for your clients to rave about you and your business with so much reverence and appreciation that the people they recommend you to have already decided to do business with you... even before you've ever heard their name. Of course, attracting Raving Referrals to delightful clients can only happen when you follow law number 6.

Raving Referral Law #6:
The Fortune is in the Follow-Up

When it comes to your success as a real estate professional, your fortune will be made or lost based on how well you follow-up and communicate with people. In fact, follow-up is the single best way to double your referrals in a very short time. Why? Because so few people actually do it. That means it's easy for you to stand out from your competition. Plus, it's a great demonstration of how well you follow through and get the job done right.

If you really want a steady stream of Raving Referrals, become famous for your follow-up. Herbert True, a marketing specialist at Notre Dame University, conducted research that found:

- 44% of all salespeople quit following-up after the first call
- 24% quit following-up after the second call
- 14% quit following-up after the third call
- 12% quit following-up after the fourth call

That means 94% of all salespeople quit after the fourth call, yet 60% of all sales are made after the fourth call. Plus, the more you update people as you serve them and the clients they refer, the more trust and confidence you build and the more referrals you will receive. Even if it's just a quick text, voice message, email, or social media message. Follow-up and watch the money start flowing to you faster!

Mastering the Art of Lead Conversion

I've (Verl) always been a huge proponent of having a real estate-specific customer relationship management platform (CRM). Your CRM is the center of every relationship, and automates the follow-up process. After selling our company, Automation Quest LLC, to Homes.com, my partner and I embarked on a journey to sell 100,000 websites to real estate agents in 12 months. The leadership team knew what they were doing when they told me it couldn't be done and even tied stock options to hitting that goal.

At that time, Homes.com was changing from Homes and Land Magazine to a web-based portal that taught agents how and why they needed a website and digital marketing strategy. In the process of selling those websites and hitting our goal, we learned that generating leads is simpler if you give the consumer what they want. It was the conversion of those leads that made the difference between our success and failure. With the understanding that anything we do 3 times requires a system for it, I realized that lead follow-up and conversion are the same.

Understanding the nuances of lead conversion is crucial for success. The following will guide you through the ABC's of lead conversion, helping you categorize and manage your leads effectively.

Our ABC Lead Follow-up System works in every CRM and with any lead system.

A Leads: The Appointment Setters

An A lead is someone with whom you have a scheduled appointment. This is the most straightforward category, as no additional follow-up system is required. You don't need to bombard them with emails or drip campaigns; the key is to maintain the momentum by always scheduling the next appointment during your meetings. Whether you're showing a home or attending a listing appointment, ensuring that the next meeting is on the calendar keeps them in the A lead category.

B Leads: The Near-Future Prospects

B leads are those who are likely to transact within 30 to 90 days. The strategy here is to reach out to them twice a month, specifically during the weeks of the first and the 15th. This consistent communication involves checking in to ensure they are receiving the properties you're sending and addressing any questions they might have about their listings. The goal is to serve them proactively, regardless of immediate opportunities.

C Leads: The Long-Term Opportunities

C leads are prospects who are more than 90 days away from buying or selling a home. The approach for these people is to contact them once a month during the second week of the month. Consistency is key, using a standard dialogue to ensure you're not neglecting them. It's important to build a relationship by getting to know them and providing valuable information during each interaction.

The Power of Consistent Follow-Up

To create a robust referral process, it's essential to maintain regular contact with your entire database. Each month, during the third week of the month, reach out to everyone in your network. This consistent engagement keeps you at the forefront of their minds whenever real estate is mentioned. Whether they're past clients, friends, or business referral partners, staying connected ensures that referrals will flow your way consistently and in significant numbers.

By mastering these lead conversion strategies, you'll be well-equipped to nurture relationships and drive success in your real estate business. How long should you follow-up with someone in your database? The saying goes, until they buy, tell you to die, or until they file a restraining order. If you want to convert prospects into clients, consistent, organized follow-up utilizing the ABC's of lead follow-up systems flat out works. Our question to you is simply this: "How much better is this follow-up system than the one you currently are not using?" Remember that everything works, but nothing doesn't!

If you really want to drive sales, follow-up with everyone who gives you a...

- Referral
- Introduction
- Testimonial
- Rating or Review

The more valuable the gift someone is giving you, the more important it is to follow-up with them. Be sure to thank them and give them updates so they have all the information they need and want.

As we mentioned earlier, when calculating your Referral Score, this practice is especially important when you receive a referral from a referral partner or professional colleague.

When they trust you enough to serve their valuable clients, you have an incredible opportunity to deepen that relationship by following up with them. These updates demonstrate a high level of professionalism and continually build trust and collaboration.

The Appreciation Challenge

Giving is the key that unlocks receiving. The more you give, the more you will receive. Be on the lookout for ways to give to people you care about and those you're looking to build profitable partnerships with or attract referrals from. The more time and energy you invest in your key connections and meaningful relationships, the more relational equity you build, which will generate opportunities for years to come.

One of the fastest, easiest, and most powerful things you can do to add value is to simply appreciate them. That's why we challenge you to show some appreciation right now.

The Rules:

1. Look through your contacts.
2. Choose the top 10 people you want to build relationships with. Start with your Top 50 and do 10 each week.
3. Text or send a direct message or personalized video expressing your genuine appreciation for them.
4. Complete this exercise within 1 hour of reading these instructions.
5. Don't ask anything of them in return. Just give them some love.
6. Don't even ask them to respond to you. It's as easy as that!

Appreciation Examples:

- Been thinking about you and wanted you to know how much I appreciate you.
- Thanks for all you are and all you do. I appreciate you!
- Someone asked me to think of people I appreciate, and you immediately came to mind. Just wanted to let you know I appreciate you. Have a great day.
- Have I told you lately you inspire me?
- I just wanted you to know I was reading some of your social posts and really appreciate how you show up in the world.
- I thought you would like to know I was just thinking about the people I admire most, and you are at the top of my list. Thanks for being you.
- I just wanted you to know how much I respect and admire you. You inspire me.

As you text your expressions of appreciation, you'll be amazed at the response you will receive. People will be blown away because they don't hear unsolicited praise very often. As you show your appreciation for them, they will naturally thank you for your kind words. Often, this will lead to opportunities to connect and discuss the possibility of a profitable partnership.

So have fun and spread the love right now!

Seriously. Stop reading and DO THIS RIGHT NOW. It's one of the easiest ways to quickly start a conversation with someone you admire who can make a difference to you personally and professionally. It only takes a few minutes, so put a bookmark on this page and spread the love. You'll be glad you did, and so will those you reach out to.

Raving Referral Law #7: Everyone Wins, or No One Wins

The seventh and final law of generating Raving Referrals is that **everyone wins, or no one wins**.

When it comes to serving clients and building profitable partnerships with other professionals who serve your Perfect Prospects, it's important you ensure they always feel like they win every time they do business with you. That requires you to strategically design your business practices, operations, and communications to guarantee that people know you have their best interests at heart.

As I (Verl) have learned and engaged with Brandon, co-author in this book, this principle of "everyone wins" is not just a phrase or cliche' but rather part of his DNA. As a business leader his focus on doing the right thing and creating opportunities for all is evident in every single interaction. Creating win-wins can happen when you look at each party and ask, "What makes it great for them?"

Find Ways To Help Them Win

Offer to cross-promote and recommend your partners to your clients, colleagues, and Social Sphere to help them attract more profitable prospects for their business. Praise your clients, employees, and partners publicly whenever possible. People love recognition, so give them a shout out in your newsletter, website, email, or social media accounts. They will feel honored, valued, and appreciated which will boost the likelihood they will refer you again in the future.

The more people feel like they win every time they do business with you, the more business they will do with you... and the more Raving Referrals they will send your way.

To Review, The 7 Laws Of Raving Referrals Are:

1. Every Referral Starts with Trust
2. The More You Give, The More You Receive
3. Relationships Trigger Transactions
4. Stellar Service Creates Stellar Success
5. Delighted Clients Refer Delightful Clients
6. The Fortune is in The Follow-Up
7. Everyone Wins, or No One Wins

As you master these seven laws and integrate them into your business, you will generate a steady stream of Raving Referrals for years to come.

In your toolkit, you will find a PDF version of The 7 Laws of Raving Referrals, ABCs of Lead Management, and The Top 50.

ReferralChampion.com/toolkit

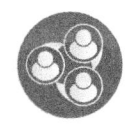

Chapter 3: Perfect Prospects & Lifetime Clients

Perfect Prospect Profile

Have you ever heard someone describe another person so vividly that you instantly thought of someone you know who's just like them? That's exactly what your goal is with your Perfect Prospect Profile, also known as your ideal client avatar. You'll use that profile to create your client avatar.

In this chapter you'll ask, "Who is your Perfect Prospect Profile? What are their dreams? What are their emotional challenges? What fears do they have?, and How can you serve them?" Using our worksheet we'll show you how to create your own client avatar.

To empower others with the ability to refer quality clients quickly and consistently, you must create a Service Statement that paints a clear picture of precisely who you help and how you help them. As you practice and perfect describing your Perfect Prospects and your Service Statement, you can start sharing a clear, concise statement that will stick in the minds of people you meet. They will have no choice but to think of you the next time someone is describing the challenge that you solve.

Quality Over Quantity

When it comes to referrals, it's better to have high-quality referrals to qualified candidates who actually need and want the service or solution you provide. After all, introductions to people who don't match your preferred profile can be a total waste of time and energy for both them and you.

Your goal is to describe your Perfect Prospects to clients and referral partners, so they easily understand, remember, and scout for people who match your target. Your Service Statement gives them the ability to retell your story to others so their desire to do business with you increases before you've even spoken with them.

Once you've accomplished that, you will have enlisted them as Referral Champions scouting for you and singing your praises to the precise people you are looking to serve.

The Two Parts to Your Perfect Prospect Profile are:

1. Who you help
2. How you help

Once you get clear on these two things, the final step is to write your Service Statement and start sharing who you help and how you help as a story. That way people can tell your Service Statement and story each time they are talking to one of your Perfect Prospects. The Service Statement is a description of your business you will share over and over in one-on-one meetings, at networking events, and professional functions.

Who You Help

Take a moment to think about the best clients you've ever had throughout your entire career. The type of client where if you could attract more exactly like them, you'd be beyond thrilled, and so would they.

Can you picture them right now? If we were to ask you the names of your five best clients, who would they be? Take a moment to write down their names now.

My 5 Best Clients Have Been:

1. _____

2. _____

3. _____

4. _____

5. _____

What Makes Them Your Best Clients?

- Why did these people come to mind?
- What do they have in common?
- Were they your most profitable clients, the most enjoyable, or somewhere in between?
- Is there a specific type of property buyer or seller who hires you most frequently?
- What common goals, needs, or challenges do they share?
- What type of people give you the most referrals and introductions?
- How often do your ideal clients use your services?
- How much revenue do your ideal clients typically represent to you?

The answers to these questions should start to reveal some commonalities you can use to build your Perfect Prospect Profile. The clearer that you are, the easier it is for others to refer you effectively and consistently.

Homeowners and Consumers

In addition to the fact that you serve homeowners and home buyers, how would you describe your ideal clients when factoring in their:

- Age
- Gender
- Income
- Location
- Stage of Life
- Marital Status
- Parental Status
- Homeownership Status
- Occupation, Hobbies, or Passions

Maybe your ideal client is a corporate executive in their 50s who loves yoga, cooking, and dancing. Or perhaps it is a grandparent over 60 who is getting ready to retire and is looking to downsize into an active senior living community. The more specific you are, the more clearly you can describe the type of people you are looking to serve. Your job is to make it easy for others to introduce and refer you to people who are a great fit for the services and solutions you provide. That will lead to more profitable prospects coming your way.

Businesses and Business Owners

If part of your business focus is selling commercial real estate, you may be looking for introductions to businesses and business owners. In that case, you may want to target specific prospects who meet certain characteristics, such as their:

- Title
- Industry
- Annual Revenue
- Years in Business
- # of Employees and/or Locations
- Type of Products or Services they Provide

Maybe you're looking to connect with a specific position within a company like the HR director, relocation manager, or sales manager. If so, be sure to let people know. They may have a friend, family member, or close contact who matches your Perfect Prospect Profile.

How You Help

Once you have clarity around what your ideal client looks like, you then need to define how you help them.

- What specific types of properties do you specialize in?
- Are there any specialized services you offer that are important to your ideal clients?
- What are your best client success stories?

These questions will help you get clear on how best to describe the challenges you solve and the solutions you provide.

Write Your Service Statement

Once you've gotten crystal clear on who you help and how you help them, it's time to write your Service Statement. Remember, this is a description of your business you will share over and over in one-on-one meetings, at networking events, and professional functions. Your Service Statement will help paint a clear picture in the mind of the person you are talking to so they immediately think of people who might need your services.

We recommend you follow our DREAM formula to ensure your Service Statement is:

- Descriptive
- Relatable
- Engaging
- Authentic
- Memorable

Descriptive: We specialize in crafting customized coaching programs that address the unique challenges faced by real estate professionals. Our proven systems are designed to enhance productivity, streamline operations, and drive sustainable growth.

Relatable: We understand the complexities of the real estate industry because we've been there. Our team of experienced coaches brings a wealth of knowledge and firsthand experience, ensuring that our clients receive guidance that is both practical and insightful.

Engaging: Our approach is interactive and collaborative. We work closely with our clients to identify their goals and develop actionable plans that inspire confidence and foster success. Through workshops, one-on-one coaching, and innovative tools, we engage our clients in a journey of continuous improvement.

Authentic: Integrity and transparency are at the core of everything we do. We believe in honest communication and building relationships based on trust. Our clients can count on us to be their reliable partners, committed to their success every step of the way.

Memorable: At Workman Success Systems, we don't just coach; we create lasting impact. Our clients remember us for our unwavering support, transformative results, and the positive changes we bring to their businesses and lives.

Example REALTOR Service Statement

To help you better understand what a powerful Service Statement looks like, here is an example of a REALTOR's Service Statement for one of our (Verl's) coaching clients:

"As a luxury real estate specialist, I help discerning clients buy and sell high-end properties that reflect their lifestyle and aspirations. With over 20 years of experience, I've built a reputation for delivering exceptional service, tailored strategies, and a seamless experience in even the most complex transactions.

Luxury real estate isn't just about the properties; it's about understanding the people and their unique needs. I take pride in offering a concierge-level approach—whether that means identifying the perfect home with unparalleled amenities, marketing a property to attract affluent buyers, or managing every detail with discretion and precision.

Clients often tell me they value my commitment to excellence, market expertise, and ability to negotiate successfully in competitive situations. I believe that luxury is in the details, and my role is to ensure no detail is overlooked.

Who do you know that's looking to make a move in the luxury market? I'd be honored to assist them in achieving their real estate dreams."

Workman Success Systems Service Statement

Workman Success Systems is a business coaching company that's the only one of its kind. We specialize in real estate teams and companies, and we do so in a very unique way. We know that Greatness is Predictable, and through decades of experience and the wisdom of our crowd, we've found a predictable and repeatable path to greatness in real estate.

Our unique approach has changed the lives of 1000s of agents, brokers, team leaders, and other real estate professionals by addressing the parts of their businesses where there are gaps, and tailoring our coaching to their specific business needs. We do that by helping them adopt our proven systems, processes, and tools that account for a real estate business in its totality and drive growth.

For over a decade, WSS has been helping agents build real estate businesses that thrive in any market and succeed where others fail. Every client who has adopted the Workman Way and the systems prescribed by their coach has outpaced the industry standard for revenue growth year-over-year, all while intentionally increasing their free time.

It isn't magic—it's Predictable Greatness. With the combined experience of our coaches, we've identified exactly what works to create lasting success in the real estate industry. We've learned the most effective ways to leverage a team to increase your income so you can build a business that supports your lifestyle instead of one that becomes your life.

This is possible because we're careful with who we hire to coach for us. All of our coaches ran, or currently run, real estate businesses in the high six, seven, and eight figures. Before becoming a coach with WSS, our coaches spend over 180 hours learning systems and processes that have been proven to make growth in your business inevitable.

Our coaches believe in giving back and prioritize community, legacy, and charity in their personal and professional lives. They coach with WSS because they have the same vision for their clients that the company does: Predictable Greatness. They keep coaching with us because of our shared values and because they've seen Predictable Greatness change the lives of their clients time and time again.

Above all else, WSS is a family business. We were created by a family who wanted to work together and create something the market was lacking. They've done that. Adding more members to the family isn't a minor thing. When you join WSS as a client, we're setting you a place at the table and inviting you to become a part of our family.

Get Started Now

Take a few moments to describe a challenge that your ideal clients face. Then, describe your solution in a way that tells a story the person will understand and remember. That way, they will immediately think of you and refer them to you.

Just fill in the blanks to create your Service Statement:

You know how:

(Describe Your Ideal Clients and the Challenges they Face)

Well, I help:

(solve/achieve)

Practice saying it out loud in the mirror once you've created a Service Statement you feel good about until it becomes completely comfortable and natural. Then, once you've mastered the mirror, ask a colleague or referral partner if you can share it with them. As you test it out on a few people, be sure to ask for their honest feedback.

Are there any refinements or improvements you want to make now that you've used it in a conversation and heard it out loud?

Was your statement clear as to who you help and how you help? Was it memorable? Ask them to restate what they heard so you can listen to how they describe your services.

Is there anyone they think of right now who matches your Perfect Prospect Profile? You might attract some Raving Referrals just by practicing your Service Statement.

As you practice and perfect sharing who you help and how you help with others, the more comfortably and powerfully you'll be able to share it. Over time, more and more people will understand exactly who you help and how you help.

Raving Referrals in Action: **The MVP Program** by Mike Coke, Broker/Owner of Terra Firma Realty, DeForest, Wisconsin – Building a Legacy of Loyalty and Referrals

Every great referral system has its foundation in authenticity and service. Mike Coke, WSS Coaching client and now Master Coach represents the pinnacle of what it means to elevate client relationships and build a business rooted in raving referrals. Mike and his team's MVP Program at Terra Firma Realty didn't just implement a referral program, they redefined how referrals could work, turning simple transactions into meaningful partnerships.

The MVP Program is his team's approach that transforms clients into long-term advocates while fostering a sense of community and loyalty.

The Genesis of the MVP Program

Mike Coke's journey with the MVP Program started with a foundational principle of real estate: your sphere of influence is everything. Drawing on strategies learned through WSS, Mike's team initially implemented the Workman Top 50 program—a structured approach to engaging the most influential clients and connections. This method kept Mike's team top of mind and generated steady referrals. But for a busy team leader, maintaining consistent touchpoints with such a large network became challenging.

Mike wanted more than a system that worked—he wanted a system that scaled. He dreamed of leveraging his team and administrative staff to build deeper, more meaningful connections with his clients. That dream became the MVP Program, where the acronym took on new meaning: Most Valuable Partners.

"Our clients are not just customers—they're our partners," Mike shared. "They do business with us, and they send us business. This program is about recognizing them for both."

How the MVP Program Works

The MVP Program is structured around consistent, intentional touches combined with a tiered referral rewards system. Here's how it's executed:

1. **Monthly Touchpoints**
   - Every month, MVP members receive a newsletter that includes real estate updates, upcoming listings, and details about the program's monthly giveaway. The giveaways vary by season but always feel personal and thoughtful. Examples include:
     - Customized cheese trays with a gift certificate to a local cheese shop.
     - Mother's Day flowers delivered to homes.
     - Tailgate kits with folding chairs and coolers for football season.
   - These touches ensure high email open rates and keep clients engaged.

2. **Quarterly (or More Frequent) Events**
   - The program includes in-person events designed to build relationships, such as:
     - A Halloween party with elaborate decorations and fun for the whole family.
     - A Thanksgiving Pie Day, where clients pick up a pie from the office.
     - Local baseball game outings, with food and beverages provided.
   - These events create lasting memories and deepen emotional connections.

3. Referral Rewards
   - Clients who make a referral to the team are recognized with thoughtful, tiered rewards:
     - **Initial Referral**: A $20 Starbucks gift card that's reloaded with $10 each month for six months.
     - **All-Star Level:** Recognition and elevated rewards for sending two referrals.
     - **Hall of Fame Club**: A prestigious tier for clients who send three or more referrals, with exclusive benefits.

Each referral triggers another thoughtful touchpoint—a thank-you email, a gift card, or an invitation to an event. These gestures reinforce the partnership and encourage continued referrals.

The Impact: Turning Referrals Into Results

The numbers speak for themselves. In one six-month period, Mike—no longer a full-time producer—generated $8 million in sales volume directly attributed to the MVP Program. Two-thirds of that business came from referrals cultivated through this system.

Most impressively, the program operates on a modest budget. Monthly giveaways cost $250–$350, and events are offset by sponsorships from local businesses and trusted partners. With an annual investment of roughly $12,000, the program delivers an ROI of 45X!

"What else can you do that consistently generates a 45X return?" Mike asked. "This program is the most consistent, reliable way to create opportunities."

Building a Community of Raving Fans

The true magic of the MVP Program lies in its ability to foster a sense of community. With 350–375 members, Mike's team focuses on the clients they genuinely enjoy spending time with—people who share their values and contribute to a positive, fun environment. By carefully curating the program's participants, the team has created a network of true advocates.

"We focus on people we want to hang out with," Mike explained. "These are our raving fans, and we treat them like family."

Lessons Learned From the MVP Program

Mike's experience with the MVP Program offers several key takeaways for anyone looking to build a referral-based business:

1. **Consistency is Key**: Monthly touchpoints and events keep the program fresh and engaging.
2. **Personalization Matters**: Tailored giveaways and themed events make clients feel valued and appreciated.
3. **Leverage Your Team**: By involving administrative staff, Mike freed himself to focus on relationships rather than logistics.
4. **Involve Sponsors**: Partnering with local businesses offsets costs and strengthens community ties.
5. **Focus on Relationships, Not Transactions**: The program's success stems from genuine care for clients and a long-term view of relationships.

A Legacy of Impact

The MVP Program exemplifies how referrals can transcend business. For Mike, it's not just about transactions, it's about connections, partnerships, and creating a legacy of trust.

As Mike puts it, *"The more we give, the more our clients give back. It's about showing up, staying top of mind, and genuinely caring about the people who support us. That's how you build a business that lasts."*

Like MIke, many Workman clients and coaches take the fundamentals of a great business and add their unique flavor, spin, and approach. We encourage this creativity and our culture is one where clients and coaches share with the group, elevating everyone's opportunities and performance. We call this the "Wisdom of our crowd", and as you can imagine, the crowd almost always gets it right. By following Mike's lead, you'll have clients for life… bringing with them a lifetime of value.

Lifetime Client Value

Each client you serve is worth far more than the value of that single transaction or service call. After all, when you service your clients exceptionally well, they will do business with you for years to come and refer you to others frequently.

Brandon learned that first-hand back in the mortgage business. Although he would earn an average of $3,000 per loan funded, he realized each client was really worth over $10,000 on average throughout the lifetime of each client relationship. Clients would come back to him for multiple loans over time, whether it be to buy a new home, refinance their existing home, or invest in a vacation or rental property. Plus, they would refer Brandon to their friends, family, co-workers, and clients who he was happy to help. By viewing each client as a minimum of a $10,000 relationship rather than a $3,000 transaction, Brandon learned to view and value each client on the total potential of the relationship.

Knowing that a real estate client is worth many times more than this to your business, how would you treat a prospective client if you thought they were worth $100,000 to your business? As you will see in the following calculation, that is exactly what each client can be worth to your business.

Calculate your Lifetime Client Value:
Understanding the Lifetime Value of a Real Estate Client

In your real estate business, understanding the lifetime value of a client is crucial for long-term success. Let's take a close look into the calculations and key metrics that reveal the true worth of a client to your business.

After helping clients close billions of dollars in transactions, Verl has come to learn that the average real estate transaction typically earns an agent between $7,000-$10,000. So for the purpose of this example, we will use the low end of that commission range.

When you sell a home, your relationship with a client doesn't end after the initial transaction. If you maintain honesty, integrity, and consistent communication, clients are likely to return. Statistics show that people tend to move every five to seven years. Thus, five to seven years after the initial transaction, you might receive a call from the same client wanting to sell their house. This leads to two more transactions: listing their current home and helping them purchase a new one.

At this point, you've completed three transactions with the client, totaling an average of $21,000 in commissions ($7,000 per transaction). Fast forward another five to seven years, and the cycle repeats. The client lists their house and buys another, resulting in two additional transactions. Now, you've completed five transactions, accumulating a total of $35,000.

But is $35,000 the full value of a client? Not quite. The lifetime value of a real estate client extends beyond direct transactions. Consider the power of referrals. If you provide exceptional service and remain at the forefront of your client's mind, they are likely to refer you to others.

The average person knows over 200 people. While it's unrealistic to expect 200 referrals from one client, let's conservatively estimate that you receive two referrals over the client's lifetime. Each referral is worth $35,000, just like the original client. Therefore, the total value of these referrals is $70,000.

Adding the initial $35,000 from direct transactions, the total lifetime value of a client becomes $105,000. This figure underscores the importance of nurturing client relationships. Every new client represents a potential $105,000 in value, while losing a client equates to an opportunity cost of the same amount.

Understanding these metrics transforms your approach to client interactions. When a client contacts you or sends a referral, recognizing their $105,000 potential value influences how you greet and serve them. Embracing the full monetary value of a real estate client can significantly impact your business strategy and success.

Referrals are the accelerator that really drive your revenue and business. If each client refers you just one additional client and your average Lifetime Client Value is $105,000, your initial client has now delivered an additional $105,000 in projected revenue to your business.

Understanding the total value that each new client represents to your business over time can change your perspective and appreciation for them in a hurry. It also determines how many marketing dollars you can afford to spend to acquire each new customer. After all, if you could spend $100 to gain a client worth $105,000 to your business, how many times would you like to do that? As often as possible, right?

The key lesson here is to view each client not just by the one-time revenue you will earn from servicing them today. Through the perspective of the Lifetime Client Value, you will earn by serving them and their referrals for years to come.

Raving Referrals in Action: Charles Furlough's Transforming Lives

No matter the industry, the power of a referral can transform lives and careers. I (Verl) had the pleasure of speaking with Charles Furlough, president and CEO of Pillar To Post Home Inspections, whose story is a testament to the profound impact one simple referral can have.

Charles shared a remarkable tale about a man named Jim, who was working a labor-intensive job. Recognizing Jim's potential, Charles referred him to a sales position in his business, despite Jim lacking any formal sales training. This referral became a turning point for Jim, who not only excelled in his new role, but eventually became the top salesperson for Charles' heating and air conditioning company. Jim's journey didn't stop there; he continued to thrive, moving on to sales training and management roles, ultimately crafting a successful career spanning over two decades. This story underscores the importance of recognizing talent and the transformative power of just one well-placed referral.

In another instance, Charles recounted his own journey from running a small family business in Raleigh, North Carolina, to becoming the president and CEO of Pillar to Post Home Inspections. His path was paved with strategic referrals and opportunities, including the chance to purchase a master franchise for North and South Carolina; a chance he took. This opportunity allowed Charles to grow a successful home inspection business, leveraging the power of referrals to build a robust network of franchisees and clients.

His stories highlight the essence of what we teach at WSS: the importance of building a referable business through exceptional service and strategic networking.

The key ingredients to creating a business that's referable include delivering an outstanding brand experience, consistent sales and marketing efforts, and building a fantastic team to support growth.

If you're looking to harness the power of referrals, try these action items:

1. **Recognize Potential**: Look beyond the surface and identify individuals with untapped potential. A well-placed referral can change lives.
2. **Deliver Excellence**: Ensure that every client interaction is exceptional, creating a brand experience that stands out.
3. **Network Strategically**: Build and maintain relationships with trusted advisors and partners who can refer business to you.
4. **Invest in Your Team**: Develop a team that can deliver on your brand promise and support your business growth.

By following these principles, you can create a business that not only thrives on referrals, it can also transform lives.

Do You Have Any Gaps?

Danny Creed is the six-time #1 global business coach for Brian Tracy's Focal Point Coaching company. In Danny's book, Thriving Business, he states the five most common marketing mistakes are:

1. No idea who the ideal customer is
2. No idea what the ideal customer wants
3. No idea as to what business you're really in
4. No idea why anyone should buy or what sets you apart from the competition
5. No idea how to explain your business in 30 seconds or less

If any of those is a gap for you, take a few minutes to get clear on each of these five areas of your business. Before long, you'll have Raving Referrals and introductions coming in consistently.

Creating your Perfect Prospect Profile is an important step towards success.

In your toolkit, you will find a copy of The Lifetime Value of a Client Calculator as well as The Perfect Prospect Profile that you can share with your clients and referral partners to attract more Raving Referrals.

Chapter 4:
Learn Why They Buy

For many agents, closing clients can be a challenge. So, what if there was a quick, easy, and effective way that has been proven to increase conversions of listing appointments by an average of 123%, and to increase converting buyers to signing your buyer broker agreement by up to 300%? That's exactly what happens when you learn people's "BANKCODE" and understand how each person thinks and how they make buying decisions.

The truth is that we human beings have 24 very different personality styles. Some people are naturally outgoing and friendly, greeting everyone they meet with a smile and a hug. These people excel in sales, customer service, and other positions where relationships matter.

Others are more shy and introverted, preferring to have as little human contact as possible. You probably know a number of these people, and perhaps that is how you were created. These people tend to be computer programmers, accountants, mechanics, electricians, plumbers, and in other professions where they can excel working with things more than with people.

Take It to The B.A.N.K.

When it comes to the buying process, the same is true. When working with prospects and selling your products or services, some will use their intuition to assess your offer quickly. Others need time to analyze information on their various options to select the optimal solution before moving forward.

It's important to recognize people think differently based on their personality style. So, if people process information and make decisions much differently, why do most businesspeople use the exact same presentations and conversations for each prospect they meet?

This was a question I (Brandon) had never considered until October 14, 2017, when I was leading a 2-day event called the Profit Partner Summit where I was teaching this Raving Referral system to an audience of over 200 in Phoenix, Arizona. After walking off stage, a woman named Sandy approached me, introduced herself, handed me four colored cards, and said, "Do me a favor: read the information on these cards and sort them in the order of what's most important to least important to you. That will help me serve you better, and save us both time."

After reviewing the cards, I quickly sorted and handed them back. What happened next blew me away. As Sandy reviewed the order of the cards that I handed her, she started describing my personality. I was shocked at how accurate her assessment was, and all I had done was sort four cards. I've taken at least a dozen different personality assessments, including Myers Briggs (MBTI), DiSC, The Harrison Assessment, and StrengthsFinder, to name a few. Each time, I had to go online and tediously answer 60-100 questions which typically take between 10-20 minutes. With B.A.N.K., it was nearly instant, and there was no technology needed.

Sandy went on to explain how this B.A.N.K. system helps you close more sales in less time, increasing closing rates to as much as 300%. She also shared a white paper scientifically validating B.A.N.K. as the world's only sales methodology that accurately predicts buying behavior in real-time.

Can You Really Close More Sales in Less Time?

The key to increasing your sales conversion rates is to identify your prospect's personality type. Once you understand their BANKCODE you can customize your conversations and presentations to be most effective based on how each person processes information and makes buying decisions. In just seconds, this easy and reliable system can help you:

- Supercharge Your Sales
- Transform Your Communications
- Make Lifelong Connections

Science long ago determined that four distinct primary personality types explain how we think, make decisions, and interact with the world.

LEARN WHY THEY BUY

B.A.N.K. uses this personality science to help you improve interpersonal communication for better personal and professional relationships.

In 1992, the Chally Group conducted a research project known as the World Class Sales Project. They concluded that only 18% of buyers would buy from a salesperson who doesn't match the buyer's personality type. That's much lower than the 82% success rate when personality types are aligned.

The four BANKCODES are: Blueprint, Action, Nurturing, and Knowledge. As you look at the list, which would you choose as your top choice if you could only choose one?

BLUEPRINT	ACTION	NURTURING	KNOWLEDGE
Stability	Freedom	Relationships	Learning
Structure	Flexibility	Authenticity	Intelligence
Systems	Spontaneity	Personal Growth	Logic
Planning	Action	Significance	Self-Mastery
Processes	Opportunity	Teamwork	Technology
Predictability	Excitement	Involvement	Research & Development
Responsibility	Attention	Community	Science
Duty	Stimulation	Charity	Universal Truths
Rules	Competition	Ethics	Expertise
Credentials	Winning	Harmony	Competence
Titles	Fun	Morality	Accuracy
Tradition	Image	Contribution	The Big Picture

1. Blueprint (B) – Structure, Systems, and Stability

Blueprint personalities value order, rules, and predictability. They prefer proven systems, well-defined processes, and a clear plan before taking action.

2. Action (A) – Results, Speed, and Winning

Action personalities are driven, competitive, and thrive on fast-paced environments. They seek excitement, big opportunities, and love to take bold risks to achieve success.

3. Nurturing (N) – Relationships, Connection, and Community

Nurturing personalities prioritize people, relationships, and making a positive impact. They value trust, collaboration, and authenticity, always striving to support and uplift others.

4. Knowledge (K) – Logic, Research, and Mastery

Knowledge personalities are curious, analytical, and driven by data and expertise. They thrive on deep learning, intellectual challenges, and making well-informed decisions based on facts.

Now that you've identified your first choice, what would you choose next? Complete that process until you have your four-code combination and write that in the lines below:

_____

_____

_____

_____

Unlike other personality systems that are based on psychology, B.A.N.K. is the only values-based assessment that measures a person's "buyology." My fascination grew after Sandy emailed my 24-page BANKPASS report, which explained my personality in great detail. It outlined the triggers which get me to yes and the tripwires that lead me to say no in a sales setting. Beyond that, it helped me understand how to better connect and communicate with the other codes I had struggled with before.

Instant Empathy

The market researcher in me needed to test the system and see what results it delivered. As I started using the cards at networking events and one-on-one meetings, I found people were as fascinated as I was. Each person I handed the cards to was happy to participate because the exercise was all about them. They were excited to share why they chose each card. It was amazing to watch these colorful cards quickly identify each person's personality in under 90 seconds.

What I soon realized was that B.A.N.K. gave me instant empathy. Within seconds of meeting someone, I cracked their code and immediately understood how their mind works. Best of all, it's fast, fun, and fascinating. People love talking about themselves, which creates the space where people open up, helping you understand them rapidly. I call it a "magic trick" because everyone wants to see a magic trick. The best part is, it's all about them so they are fascinated by the process and you build rapport faster than any other method I've ever seen. Business aside, the most important code I ever cracked was for my daughter Ella. While we are incredibly close and have great daddy-daughter dates, our conversations have felt more like debates ever since she entered her teen years.

After cracking her BANKCODE and watching her select the Knowledge card first, everything suddenly clicked. Our codes are complete opposites, which helped me understand the space between us. Instantly I saw how my way of expressing myself completely repelled her because it didn't match the way her brain processes information. In the past, sometimes when we would talk, her scientific mind would go to work analyzing for accuracy and application. If I made a grandiose or generalized statement, her natural response is to question or challenge, which left me feeling criticized and judged.

Because of B.A.N.K., I now understand my daughter much better. Rather than trying to change her, I embrace and celebrate her strengths. Seeing her choose the Nurturing card last helped me understand why she rarely shows affection like she did when she was young. Now that I understand how her brilliant brain works, I truly appreciate the woman she was created to be. It's been five years since cracking Ella's code, and our relationship has never been better. I'll be forever grateful for the understanding and empathy B.A.N.K. has given me.

To unlock the secrets, the science, and the system to supercharge your sales in less than 90 seconds, visit KnowYourCode.US. You can also get great training on this powerful sales methodology at The Champions Institute (TCIChampions.com).

Referred to a Rockstar

Since this book is about generating Raving Referrals, I have to share that I was thrilled when Sandy called offering to introduce me to Cheri Tree, the creator of the program and author of the book, Why They Buy. Over a series of phone calls, Cheri and I became fast friends and mutual admirers. Before long, we were collaborating and creating a strategic alliance to empower more people with B.A.N.K. We scheduled an interview and promoted her to my tribe. Then, as our respect and relationship grew, Cheri invited me to teach the Raving Referrals system to her audience at the international B.A.N.K. conference in Vegas. The following month, I invited her to join me at an Oscars after party at Universal Studios in L.A. with Ashton Kutcher and Matthew McConaughey as guests of Honor. Over the years that have followed, my respect and admiration for Cheri have grown immensely, and I believe the feeling is mutual. In my opinion, B.A.N.K. can help everyone improve their relationships and live better lives. That's why I am committed to supporting Cheri's mission to crack the code of every person on the planet.

To that end, I dedicated ten months of my life to helping her build and launch Codebreaker Technologies, including Codebreaker AI back in 2019. That revolutionary technology enables you to crack personality codes in just one click using a LinkedIn profile. It's an amazing tool that I recommend to anyone looking to close more sales and build better relationships.

BANKCODE For REALTORs

While working with Codebreaker Technologies, I commissioned a research study to determine how using BANKCODE could impact success for REALTORs, and the results were staggering.

What we found was that on average, using B.A.N.K. to customize conversations and presentations to prospective sellers helped REALTORs increase listing appointment conversions by an average of 123%. That means you have an opportunity to teach REALTORs how to more than double their listing conversions using this simple methodology.

In addition to the impact on listings, B.A.N.K. also helps real estate agents increase buyer-broker agreement conversions by an average of 300%. This truly is a tool you can use to offer massive value to the real estate agents you are building referral partnerships with. The best part is few REALTORs have learned the B.A.N.K. sales methodology so you have a secret tool for your mutual success.

One of the reasons I share this example is that being referred to influencers is a strategy you want to master. This will help you gain access to people you may otherwise never meet. In today's hyper-social world, just one referral can change your life.

The key is to follow up and follow through. Add value and help achieve whatever mission, dream, or goal they are passionate about. Then, when you earn an influencer's trust and have given them tremendous value, they will feel indebted and naturally offer to promote. When they do, their celebrity endorsement elevates your expert status, which in turn, boosts your referrals and revenue.

The question is, are you ready to boost your expert status? If so, you'll love what's coming next.

Raving Referrals in Action:
Nick Painz: The Highest form of Respect

Nick Painz, a seasoned real estate professional we've talked about previously, has really mastered the art of leveraging relationships to create a thriving business. His journey is a testament to the power of referrals and the impact they can have on both personal and professional levels.

Nick's story began with a simple connection that blossomed into a lucrative partnership. Simply by introducing two individuals who shared a passion for real estate, Nick inadvertently set the stage for a series of transactions that would yield significant financial returns. This partnership not only brought in close to half a million dollars in revenue but also opened doors to new ventures, including sourcing funds for real estate deals. Nick's ability to connect people without an agenda, purely based on the potential for mutual benefit, has been a cornerstone of his success. Nick believes the highest form of respect is to adapt your style to the person you are in front of so they are comfortable in the conversation. Whether it's B.A.N.K. or DiSC, acknowledging someone's behavioral style is critical to your success.

As far as vendor partnerships go, Nick's approach is refreshingly straightforward. He believes in the quality of work and integrity of his partners, referring clients to them without expecting anything in return. This philosophy perfectly aligns with the HOA.com model, where trusted advisors collaborate to create community events and cross-market to each other's databases. By fostering an environment of trust and collaboration, Nick has built a network that not only supports his business goals, it also enhances his clients' experiences.

Nick's journey is also a powerful reminder of the importance of setting ambitious goals. When challenged to think beyond his current financial targets, Nick was encouraged to envision a future where his earnings could reach $10 million! This shift in perspective is not just about numbers; it's about redefining what is possible and pushing the boundaries of what can be achieved.

To emulate Nick's success, consider these action items:

1. **Cultivate Genuine Connections**: Focus on building relationships without expecting immediate returns. The value of a connection often reveals itself over time.

2. **Leverage Trusted Networks**: Collaborate with trusted advisors and partners to expand your reach and create mutually beneficial opportunities.

3. **Set Ambitious Goals**: Challenge yourself to think bigger and explore new avenues for growth. Use creative tools like ChatGPT to model different scenarios and inspire innovative strategies.

4. *Embrace a Collaborative Mindset*: Engage with your community and industry peers to share resources and knowledge, fostering an environment of collective success.

Nick's story highlights the power of referrals and the limitless potential that lies in nurturing relationships. By adopting a similar mindset and leveraging the tools and systems available, real estate professionals—just like you—can unlock new levels of success and fulfillment in their careers.

The WSS team has taught behavioral style messaging as a critical part of relationship building for over ten years. Again (and it's worth repeating), we believe the highest form of respect is to adapt your style to the person you are in front of so they are comfortable in the conversation. This is easy to say but not always easy to do because you don't actually know each person's behavior style. Using the cards is fun, simple, and it works.

It was the first meeting with Brandon when I (Verl) was introduced to BANKCODE. Brandon simply asked me if I wanted to see a magic trick. (sound familiar?) He then handed me the cards and asked me to sort them as described above. It was the first time I had ever seen something so complex be delivered with such amazing simplicity. We had some fun with the styles and compared other systems, but the fact remained that I had never seen such a simple system clearly identify who I am and how to best communicate with me. Our coaches and clients now use this "simple magic trick" to better serve clients, understand customers, and communicate effectively in every aspect of their lives and business.

Leveraging personality science is not just about understanding others—it's about creating authentic, lasting connections that inspire trust, loyalty, and enthusiasm. By tailoring your communication and approach to match your clients' unique preferences, you'll not only close more sales but also foster deeper relationships that naturally lead to raving referrals.

The more you align with your clients' needs and styles, the more they'll see you as the go-to professional they can't help but recommend. In today's competitive market, mastering personality science isn't just a strategy—it's your competitive edge for achieving more success in less time while leaving a lasting impact on the people you serve.

As you put this system and these strategies to work in your business, you will build a growing group of referral partners and loyal clients who will gladly refer profitable prospects to you quickly and consistently.

Your free Raving Referrals toolkit contains an advanced BANKCODE assessment as well as a whitepaper showing the impact of using BANK in real estate transactions.

Chapter 5:
Establish Your Expert Status

Establishing yourself as an expert is one of the most influential and strategic ways to build your business. It increases your credibility and visibility, which helps attract new clients and referral partners. Plus, if you don't share your expertise online, your competitors will be happy to step in and win over your clients.

When you look up the word "expert" in the Oxford dictionary, you'll find the definition reads, "a person who has a comprehensive and authoritative knowledge of, or skill in, a particular area."

While you may not feel like an expert, the truth is you have specialized knowledge that can help people improve their lives. You have mastered systems, strategies, tips, and tricks that can help them save money and buy their dream home. When you realize that the purpose of your business is to make a difference to others, you can stand strong in your power, confidently sharing your wisdom with others.

One of the many inspiring authors Brandon has had the pleasure of knowing is Debbie Allen, author of the book, The Highly Paid Expert. Debbie truly is an expert on becoming an expert. In her 2019 book, Success Is Easy, Debbie shares, "What's great about being an expert is that while you are fulfilling your life's mission, you are also influencing and teaching others. As the expert, you can go deeper with your knowledge than the average person in the industry and develop a step-by-step blueprint, program, or system that can be duplicated by other people."

In creating and uncovering your unfair competitive advantage, consider A.R.U.B.A. Cleve Gaddis, team leader, Workman Master Coach, and critical contributor to many of the Workman's processes and systems, along with Workman writer and editor, Harry Katcher, created an amazing system for identifying your unique selling advantage called A.R.U.B.A. While this was built specifically for our proprietary recruiting program called JOLT - High Voltage Agent Attraction, A.R.U.B.A. works to help you identify what really makes you different and how to articulate that to potential clients and partners.

A.R.U.B.A. is an acronym. It stands for Available Resources that are Unique, Better than your competition, and provide Actual benefits. The ARUBA Process for developing your unfair competitive advantage is a relatively simple matrix whereby you'll list your available resources, and then articulate why each resource is unique, why it's better, and then you'll list the actual benefits. The ARUBA Process is a simple, points-based matrix. It is a reflective, self-discovery tool that will guide you through the process of assessing what you have to offer. But most importantly, it will help to identify the aspects of your organization that are so truly unique that it becomes unfair to your competition for you to use them.

To establish your expertise, consider posting and promoting the following on your website and social media channels, as well as displaying them throughout your office:

- Affiliations with Chambers of Commerce or the Better Business Bureau
- Articles or blogs you have written
- Associations to which you belong
- Awards you have received
- Boards on which you serve
- Books you have written or have been featured in
- Charities for which you volunteer or committees on which you serve
- Endorsements from industry leaders
- Media interviews or coverage you have received
- Partners who have chosen to do business with you
- Photos with celebrities, authors, and influencers
- Podcasts you've produced or been featured on
- Testimonials from clients and customers

In addition to posting and displaying these examples of your expertise, you can also go live on social media, sharing quick tips for your Perfect Prospects. While it may seem intimidating at first, here's a simple formula you can follow to share your expertise:

- Introduce yourself, stating your name and company
- Describe the challenges you solve
- Emphasize the pain of not taking action
- Outline top options and solutions
- Share success stories
- Suggest next steps

Here's an example script to give you some ideas

"Hello, this is Amy Andrews with Andrews Realty, here to give you my top five tips for new homeowners. I love helping clients buy their first home because there's nothing more satisfying than helping a family achieve the American dream of homeownership.

The challenge many people face is that as first-time homeowners, they often find themselves overwhelmed with all the new choices and responsibilities that come with owning a home for the first time. That's why I wanted to share my top five tips for first-time homeowners to help make your life a little easier as you move into your first home.

1. Change the locks (share a sentence or two as to why they should follow each tip).
2. Do a deep clean.
3. Perform a home energy audit.
4. Replace air filters regularly.
5. Paint and make upgrades before you move in.

These tips are great reminders even if you have owned your home for years. Recently, I helped a client named Sarah buy her first home, and she was so grateful for these tips because she scheduled a home energy audit, which reduced her energy bill by $500 per year. She even qualified for an energy efficiency tax credit.

If you ever need introductions to any REALTORs or home service professionals, I have a vetted, trusted network of professionals I am happy to recommend. That offer goes for your neighbors, friends, and family too. I'm always here to help and am never too busy to take care of the people you care about. Just have them call or text me at (123) 456-7890.

Thanks for watching, and remember, at Andrews Realty, we're committed to helping you reach your real estate goals. Whether you are looking to buy, sell, invest, or refinance, we're always here to support your success."

Become A Reporter

As an avid sports fan I often get drawn in when a commentator who played the sport I'm watching shares their insights. This insight from having been at the highest level provides a different perspective than from someone who has never played the game. As a real estate agent, the best teacher of how to be great at this business is to get into the game and do it well. Here are a few key steps in learning to be an expert.

Put yourself in a position to do a lot of transactions. Join a team or brokerage where they have mentorship and high volume. As a full time agent you should be doing at least 24 transactions a year and really closer to 48 after a couple years of experience.

Be your own best client. What I mean by that is to put yourself in the role of a client looking for different things: locations, neighborhoods, residential, town homes, commercial, etc. Then set yourself up in the MLS on auto hot sheets and run the numbers and different scenarios to find the perfect fit for that imaginary client. By doing this you will see properties, understand what is selling and what is not selling, and begin to add expert advice to your clients.

This is not a "fake it, until you make it" business. If you put the work in and develop a real knowledge of neighborhoods, construction, luxury homes, commercial, investment real estate, 1031 exchanges, or whatever you want to focus on as the trusted expert, you will not only find success in that arena but your clients will be better served because of your skills specific to their need. Referrals come as a result of: #1 Doing a great job with a level of skill, and, #2 Asking for them. #1 earns you the right to ask for #2.

If you're not sure where to start, simply search online for articles related to the real estate industry. You will find countless books, blogs, strategies, and tips you already know and can easily teach your clients.

Now it's time to share that wisdom with the world. As you post your golden nuggets, you'll find that your clients and your Social Sphere will engage, ask questions, and request more information about your services. As if by magic, new client opportunities will appear as if they are drawn to you like a magnet. People you've never met will also share what you do with others, especially as you tell stories of the impact you make.

You can establish your expert status by creating a blog, podcast, video, special report, workshop, webinar, or book. The key is to constantly share your knowledge and wisdom online so you stay top of mind and elevate your status with everyone you can.

Social Media shouldn't be hard! But we know it's not always easy creating content. We designed this system to make it a little simpler for you! This strategy is proven and used by top producers from all around the country!

Video Content

Schedule one hour on Mondays to record long form videos (about 3-5 minutes each) for your YouTube channel. Start with frequently asked questions, cover new programs and industry trends, or highlight new technologies that will help your clients. The sky is the limit for topics. Just commit to recording these videos each Monday. These will help your footprint when someone is searching about these topics on Google and other search engines.

After recording your long form content, the next opportunity is turning those videos into engaging, bite-sized pieces for other social platforms. A great way to do this is with REDX's Brand Builder. This tool helps you create and share high-quality videos across multiple platforms. With features like AI-generated scripts and professional editing, Brand Builder enhances your YouTube videos to make them more engaging. It then takes your long form videos and creates shorter clips and distributes them to platforms like Facebook and Instagram. This allows you to get in front of more potential clients without spending hours editing.

Go Live!

Take 15 minutes on Tuesday afternoons to go LIVE! This should have an informal, unpolished, yet personal feel. What to talk about? Start with storytelling! Talk about what's inspiring you, how you recently helped a family get into their dream home, or just what's going on in your life. These posts will help you show your personality to your past and new clients and show them why they want to work with you.

Webinars

Schedule one hour every Wednesday to do a FREE webinar series for your clients and community. Invite other industry experts, i.e., contractors, interior designers, lawyers, mortgage lenders, financial advisors, or other local business owners from your community to join you and talk about what's going on in their business. Not only will this help your viewers learn what's happening, it will help you build relationships with key people in your community. Plus…they will share it in their social communities as well!

Client Call Out

On Thursdays, highlight magical moments for your clients! Wishing them a Happy Birthday, congratulating them on closing on their new home or new jobs. Create a 'Favorites' timeline featuring only your clients and referral partners so you can make sure you don't miss any of their life moments. Make sure to "like" or comment on their posts to stay top of mind!

Culture Is King!

Take time on Fridays to post about the culture you are building with your brand. Post about fun events happening at your office or with your team. Did you attend a charity event or get tickets to your favorite sports team? Share it! This is where you create the personal connection with your community and stay top of mind! Most of the time people would rather work with someone they like, so show them why they should like you!

One of the most significant benefits of sharing your expertise on social media is that other influencers and business owners will ask to interview you to help their clients and Social Sphere. As they do, you may find some of them make excellent guests sharing their expertise with your audience.

This is one of the most powerful strategies you can use to grow your referrals, which is why we will cover it in detail in Chapter 16 of this book as we outline the 21 Top Cross Promotion Campaigns.

Be Easy to Refer

To maximize the quality and quantity of Raving Referrals coming your way, it's critical you make yourself easy to refer. Giving your clients, customers, referral partners, and Social Sphere an easy way to recommend, refer, and promote you is one of the fastest ways to grow your business. When you think about your business, why would someone tell another person about you?

The answer is likely different than you imagine. The fact of the matter is most people don't care about you or your business the way you do. Their motivation for recommending you is primarily to solve the problems and challenges for the people they care about. Your job is to make it quick and easy for them to spread the word about you far and wide so you can attract as many prospective clients as possible. When people have a referral for you, what are you asking them to do? If you're sitting there stymied by that question, that means you have a big gap in your business. You are making

ESTABLISH YOUR EXPERT STATUS

them do all the work and creating barriers between you and your ideal clients.

The simple truth is that business development is your job. It's not your client's or customer's job. So why do you make them work to give you business?

Just check out this rack card we give out for HOA.com. This is a great leave-behind that gives people our website, toll-free phone number and even a QR code they can scan with their mobile phone. One of the biggest gaps we see when coaching clients to get more referrals is that they have no system in place for their referrals.

Your Referral Kit

Your Referral Kit is something tangible you give your clients and referral partners to share when recommending you. Simply package your expertise as a special report, book, video, or brochure that explains the challenge you solve, the possible solutions clients should consider, and a specific call-to-action, so they can contact you for assistance. This elevates your authority in the mind of your prospect, which instantly boosts trust. Using this strategy, you can dramatically increase your revenue per client too. That's because your Referral Kit will increase the number of prospects you attract while simultaneously boosting your average revenue per client once they view you as a trusted expert.

The good news about creating your Referral Kit is that you only have to do it once, and you can use it for the rest of your career. The easiest way to create your Referral Kit is to compile blogs you've written into a book or special report. If you haven't written any blogs, you can use the Frequently Asked Questions section of your website to get started. Another great option is to record an interview and have the audio recording transcribed. Simply coordinate a conversation with one of your business or referral partners via zoom or Facebook Live. Then download the video file and upload it to one of the many online transcription services like Temi.com or Otter.ai.

Once you package and publish your expertise through your Referral Kit, you boost your influencer status, which will lead people to seek you out. After all, your Referral Kit elevates your status from being seen as a salesperson to an industry expert.

That was my (Brandon) experience after Mark Victor Hansen and Robert Allen featured me in their best-selling book, Cracking the Millionaire Code, back in 2005. Once that book was published, I had prospective clients calling and contacting me from around the world. They were eager to do business with me because these global authorities and influencers had established my expertise before I had ever spoken with these people. Nearly 20 years later, people still reach out to me from time to time after reading that book.

Give the Gift of You

The goal of your Referral Kit is to give your Referral Champions a turn-key tool they can use to promote your services easily, effortlessly, and effectively. When they share your Referral Kit, you educate your audience, elevate your status, and reduce sales pressure. These factors all attract profitable prospects who will schedule with you quickly and consistently.

You can even present your Referral Kit as a gift. Once you package your expertise in a special report or book, your referral partners can give it as a gift for each of their clients and customers. They are looking to help and add value to their clients, so if you give them a way to do that by introducing your expertise, it creates a win–win–win scenario where everyone benefits.

That's exactly what Brandon did with Cracking the Millionaire Code. That book became his personal brochure. Every time he met a new prospect, he gave them a copy of the book along with his business card inserted on page 42, where his three-page bio began. Even if they never read a word of the book, the simple fact that these literary giants had endorsed and written about Brandon established his expertise and trustworthiness. Plus, it became an easy way for people to recommend him to their clients and contacts.

Creating your own Referral Kit and establishing your expertise will elevate your status and accelerate trust. The key is to make it easy for others to refer you in a way that makes you the most trusted option in the eyes of your partners and prospects. Once you do that, you are on your way to attracting Raving Referrals for years to come.

Truth be told, that was one of my (Brandon) primary drivers for writing this book. Although I've been teaching these strategies for over a decade, I needed a better way to pass on my knowledge and give people a better way of sharing my message with the world. Not only that, writing this book gave me an opportunity to connect and collaborate with over 100 experts and influencers we are featuring in this book, training courses, and social promotion campaigns.

The power behind establishing your expert status cannot be overstated. After creating our Raving Referrals system, we have expanded the book into a Raving Referrals for Real Estate Agents video course and continuing education (CE) class taught by our Raving Referrals Certified Trainers. Having experts teaching our curriculum all over the world allows us to expand our influence and impact empowering more REALTORs who are eager to learn more about our system and coaching services.

So how can you establish your expertise and get others sharing the lessons they've learned from you?

Become a Certified HOA Specialist™

One of the best ways to elevate your expert authority is by earning designations and certifications. Designations showcase your specialized knowledge and give you a competitive edge that sets you apart from other agents.

RAVING REFERRALS FOR REAL ESTATE AGENTS

As you think about your business and look back over the listings and sales you closed last year, what percentage of your closed transactions were located in a homeowner association or HOA?

Considering that 53% of all homes in the U.S. are located in HOAs, your answer is probably either most of them, or all of them.

If that's true for you, consider becoming a Certified HOA Specialist so you stand out in the competitive real estate market, and win more listings in top HOAs.

When choosing which agent they are going to hire, homeowners prefer agents who understand their community's unique rules and can effectively market their properties.

When you become a Certified HOA Specialist, you position yourself as an expert in navigating the complexities of HOA transactions. This helps you become the go-to agent for sellers and buyers in highly sought-after HOA neighborhoods.

This also helps you establish credibility and relationships with HOA boards and professional HOA management companies. Considering they serve homeowners as well as real estate investors, each community you serve can generate substantial deal flow for your business.

Once you become a Certified HOA Specialist, HOA.com gives you a simple step-by-step system to activate HOA communities. Best of all, they promote their Certified HOA Specialists positioning you as a top trusted real estate agent in the HOAs you farm.

If you are ready to grow rich in this niche, scan the QR code below or go to *HOA.com/CHS* to learn more.

Raving Referrals in Action: Corey Perlman's "Referral Success"

Harnessing the Power of LinkedIn

Corey Perlman, owner of Impact Social Media, has long championed LinkedIn as a powerful tool for generating referrals. His approach is not just theoretical; it's backed by real-world success stories that demonstrate the effectiveness of his strategies. One such story involves Nancy, a client who owns a Dale Carnegie franchise in Huntsville, Alabama. Nancy was eager to establish a partnership with a major manufacturing company in the area. Corey advised her to leverage LinkedIn's unique features to make this connection.

Nancy followed Corey's guidance by visiting the company's LinkedIn page and identifying Jamie, the head of HR, as her target contact. Although she didn't know Jamie personally, LinkedIn revealed a mutual connection—a dedicated Dale Carnegie graduate. Nancy reached out to this mutual contact, rekindled their relationship, and asked for an introduction to Jamie. The result was a decade-long partnership with the company, a testament to the power of LinkedIn referrals. "It's magic when you get that mutual connection to refer you."

For real estate professionals, Corey outlines a clear strategy to replicate this success:

1. **Connect with Your Network**: Actively build your LinkedIn connections to expand your sphere of influence.

2. **Be Referable**: Utilize LinkedIn's QR code and personalized URL to make it easy for others to connect with you.

3. **Engage with Others**: Participate in conversations and add value to your network by engaging with their posts.

4. **Ask for Referrals**: Be proactive in seeking referrals and provide clear instructions on how you wish to be introduced.

5. **Add Value**: Establish yourself as a thought leader by consistently sharing valuable content.

Corey also developed a thoughtful and personalized approach to expressing gratitude for referrals, which goes beyond the typical thank-you note. He believes in the power of personalization to make the gesture more meaningful. "In the dawn of social media and the age that we're in, we can go beyond just a box of brownies."

When someone refers business to Corey, he and his team strive to tailor their gratitude to the individual's interests. For example, knowing that a client is a diehard tennis fan, Corey might send a gift card to a tennis store, allowing the recipient to choose something they truly value. This personalized touch shows a deeper level of appreciation and recognition of the individual's preferences.

Corey's team, led by Halina, excels at this personalized approach. They leverage social media insights to understand what would be most meaningful to the person receiving the referral gift. This strategy not only strengthens relationships but also reinforces Corey's commitment to going the extra mile for those who support his business.

By focusing on personalized gratitude, Corey ensures that his appreciation is not just heard but felt, creating a lasting impression and encouraging ongoing referrals.

Now that we've covered the Raving Referral basics, it's time to give you the secrets and the science to engaging and activating your referral network, so they become your Referral Champions.

In your toolkit, you will find a copy of the A.R.U.B.A Process Spreadsheet.

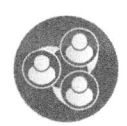

Chapter 6:
Engage Your Referral Champions

As a real estate professional, you likely refer business to a lot of different professionals and don't get many referrals back. We're here to help you change that once and for all. After all, when you refer clients to a contractor, painter, plumber, or mortgage lender, they should be proactively scouting for clients to refer back to you so a client for one, becomes a client for everyone.

The level of your success is mainly dependent on your ability to attract Raving Referrals. The more recommendations you receive from your Top 50, your clients, and your Social Sphere, the faster your business will grow and the more prosperity you will achieve.

That's why it's so important to engage your network systematically in a way that transforms them into Referral Champions for you and your team. Then, the more you celebrate, thank, and reward your Referral Champions, the more Raving Referrals you will receive.

The introduction of the internet and online leads has created a generation or two of what Verl calls "lazy agents". If you have a little bit of money you can generate leads for real estate. If you have a lot of money you can generate even more. The ability to generate leads online by purchasing them or subscribing to lead sources has become addicting to many agents and they either have never learned to prospect or they have stopped doing it all together.

Another Verlism states that we "lead with revenue, not expense". The job of a real estate agent, team leader, or broker is to provide stability and security for the people they lead—and that includes their families. The only way I know to do this is to have, and run, a profitable business.

How do we lead with revenue? It's more simple than it seems. First, we identify the areas of business we have access to like our database or Top 50 or our social sphere, and we ask the following questions:

- Do I have a Top 50 list, and do I contact each of them once a month with a personal contact?
- Am I closing 80+ deals a year from my Top 50?
- Am I receiving all of the referrals that are available to me in my database?
- Do I follow the 3-2-1-1 system?
- Do I work "Open Houses on Steroids" and turn every listing into 1.5 buy-side opportunities?
- Am I marketing to my database whenever I have a new buyer to see if any of the homes in my database meet the criteria of the buyer and reach out to see if they might be interested in selling?

This specific list of activities has a zero cost factor and generates the most profitable leads. Let me rephrase that, "It generates the most leads and costs nothing." Before you spend a bunch of money on attracting strangers, let's get our house in order and make sure our free or low cost systems are in place to generate more business than we have ever done in the past. It simply works!

Tammie's coach, WSS Master Coach Paul Sessum, played a pivotal role in helping her understand and harness her unique strengths in real estate. When Tammie first started coaching with Paul, she was already successful but couldn't quite articulate why. Paul challenged her to become a student of herself, encouraging her to record and analyze her interactions with clients to identify what made her "sticky."

Through this process, Tammie discovered that her success was rooted in her ability to connect deeply with clients, leaving a lasting impression that went beyond the transaction. Paul helped Tammie realize that her confidence and adaptability, honed from moving frequently as a child, were key assets in her real estate career. By studying herself, Tammie was able to build a system around her natural talents, which not only elevated her business but also allowed her to coach others in finding their unique "sticky" factor.

Paul's guidance continues to be instrumental in Tammie's journey, helping her transform her innate abilities into a structured approach that has led to significant growth and success in her massive referral-based business.

The 4 Sources of Raving Referrals:

The vast majority of referrals come from one of the following four groups of people:

1. Your Clients

2. Your Social Sphere

3. Complimentary Businesses and Professionals

4. Your Top 50

Each of these groups can be an incredible source of referrals. While each group needs a slightly different approach to activate them into Referral Champions for your business, the overall strategy is very similar.

1) Your Clients

Current and past clients can be your #1 source of referrals because they have personally experienced and benefited from your product or service. When they share their story and testimonial about the difference you made for them, the people they recommend to you automatically trust you more, which increases the likelihood they will use your service.

The key here is to consistently communicate to your clients through phone calls, text messages, email, direct mail, social media messages, and client appreciation events, so they feel the love over and over. Then, when they hear someone is looking for the service you provide, they will naturally and passionately recommend you and your company.

The success stories involving our referral relationships are a testament to our commitment to maintaining trust and providing tailored solutions for our clients throughout their journey as homeowners. Fostering meaningful, long-lasting relationships with clients, vendor partners, and REALTORs alike can generate more opportunities than ever. Agents inside and outside of your market can be an amazing source of referral business.

WSS Coaching Client, Workman Certified Coach, and Founder, CEO, and Managing Broker of META Homes, in Westminster, Colorado, Nick Painz, shared this story of how fostering meaningful, long-lasting relationships really can be a prime source of referrals:

> "In my second year of real estate, I started teaching a weekly class to the new agents at RE/MAX Alliance to help them succeed in their first year. One of the agents came to my class every week, and about 6 months into her business, she came to me with a small

commercial deal that she didn't know how to handle. She asked me how to handle it, and offered to refer it to me. I countered with an offering to co-list with her so she could learn the process.

After going to the listing appt., I realized I had met a buyer and soon developed a relationship. Long story short, this buyer, who was not my client at the time (they already had an agent), bought the property from me (we double ended the transaction). The deal was so transformational for the buyer, they began using me as their agent in 2020. Both of us greatly benefited from the relationship. The referring agent learned a new part of doing real estate, and chose to stay in residential, and I made a new friend who has become one of my best, long-term clients. The agent joined my team and we continue to do deals together.

Since then, I've done over 40 transactions with this buyer for over $15M in volume, and north of $250k in commission."

2) Your Social Sphere

Your Social Sphere includes all the people you interact with in your life, including your friends, family members, co-workers, and contacts. The truth is you should be promoting your services to everyone who is in your customer relationship management (CRM), email programs, phone contacts, and social media connections. Imagine how many more referrals you would attract to your business if you just stayed in touch with all the people you have met and hired for various services in your life.

You are literally three feet from gold, and it's time you started mining it. As you look over the list on the following pages, start thinking about people you know in each of these industries and categories.

ENGAGE YOUR REFERRAL CHAMPIONS

Accountants
Account Managers
Advertising Managers
Appraisers
Appliance Repair People
Architects
Athletes
Attorneys
Authors
Auto Mechanics
Babysitters
Bakers
Bankruptcy Attorneys
Bartenders
Bookkeepers
Business Brokers
Business Coaches
Business Development Managers
Business Managers
Business Owners
Career Coaches
Carpet Cleaners
Car Salespeople
CEOs
Charities
Chefs
Church Members
College Alumni
Concierges
Consultants
Contractors
Copywriters
Counselors
Credit Repair Experts
Cyber Security Experts
Daycare Providers
Dentists

Divorce Attorneys
Dog Groomers
Drycleaners
Drywallers
Engineers
Entrepreneurs
Escrow Officers
Estate Planning Attorneys
Event Managers
Executives
Family Members
Financial Planners
Firefighters
First Responders
Flooring Installers
Florists
Franchise Consultants
Friends
Fundraisers
Furniture Salespeople
Golf Pros
Graphic Designers
Hair Stylists
Handymen
Healthcare Professionals
Health Coaches
High School Friends
Home Builders
Home Healthcare Providers
Home Inspectors
Hotel Managers
House Cleaners
Human Resource Managers
Influencers
Insurance Agents
Interior Designers
Investors

RAVING REFERRALS FOR REAL ESTATE AGENTS

Jewelers	Property Managers
Goverment Employees	Public Speakers
Grocers	Real Estate Agents
Landscapers	Relationship Managers
Leasing Agents	Rental Agents
Life Coaches	Reporters
Manicurists	Restaurant Owners
Marketing Consultants	Roofers
Mediators	Salespeople
Mortgage Loan Officers	Sales Trainers
Movers	Secretaries
Musicians	Security Guards
Nurses	Software Designers
Nutritionists	Swimming Instructors
Optometrists	Seminar Attendees
Office Managers	Skin Care Specialists
Painters	Social Media Consultants
Paramedics	Surgeons
Pastors	Tax Advisors
Pediatricians	Teachers
Personal Trainers	Technology Experts
Pest Control Technicians	Tennis Pros
Pharmacists	Travel Agents
Photographers	Waiters and Watresses
Plumbers	Web Designers
Police Officers	Writers
Politicians	Veterans
Pool Cleaners	Veterinarians
PR Agents	Virtual Assistants
Printers	Yoga Instructors
Programmers	Youth Sports Coaches
Project Managers	

As you look over this list, you're undoubtedly thinking of people you know who should know about your business. If you have their contact information, start communicating with them regularly about the products and services you provide.

After all, you never know when they or someone they know will need what you offer. If you aren't marketing to them consistently and staying top-of-mind, someone else will be glad to serve them and win their business.

You may be looking at this list thinking, "I would never want to approach these people about my business." If so, that may be part of the reason you don't yet have the results you desire and deserve. Don't let your ego get in the way of your success. This is not the time to be shy. Your family's future success is at stake. Be confident and bold, knowing you provide great value to everyone you serve.

We learned long ago that you can either be right, or you can be rich. It's your choice, so choose wisely. If you are committed to success, spread the word far and wide about the services you provide. After all, nothing ventured, nothing gained. You have absolutely nothing to lose. If you email or contact people and they aren't interested in doing business with you, they will simply ignore your message and move on. That said, by keeping your name and brand top of mind, they are much more likely to use your services and recommend you in the future.

3) Complementary Businesses and Professionals

While your past clients and Social Sphere are incredibly important, in our experience, you can build your business exponentially faster and larger by partnering with complementary business owners and professionals who serve homeowners and real estate investors. This strategy is so powerful that over half of this book is dedicated to teaching you how to achieve wealth and prosperity by partnering and cross-promoting with people who are serving your Perfect Prospects each and every day.

Brandon personally closed over $500 million in business using this strategy, so we are here to tell you emphatically that it works when you work it. As a single dad back in his twenties, Brandon was earning over $50,000 per year from just one referral partner alone. Imagine what you can achieve for your business when you follow the Raving Referrals system and Referral Partner Blueprint to create ten or more referral partnerships over the next year or two.

By collaborating and co-marketing with these people, you will help them grow their business while they help you grow yours. Best of all, as you prove yourself to them and their clients, you will become an invaluable ally they can't live without. You will earn more and more of their business over time until, eventually, you will become the number one go-to expert to which they refer all of their clients and colleagues.

4) Your Top 50

We have, and will continue to, refer to the Top 50. To recap, the "Top 50" refers to a list of 50 people who already know, like, and trust you, and who you believe will send you at least one referral each year. This list is crucial for maintaining and growing the referral side of your business. The idea is to focus on a manageable number of people with whom you can maintain a personal connection, as opposed to trying to manage a much larger database. Consistent, meaningful communication with these 50 individuals is key, with the goal of ensuring each person receives a personal touch from you every month. This can include phone calls, handwritten notes, face-to-face meetings, or thoughtful messages. The Top 50 list is about building and nurturing relationships to generate referrals. Having an effective referral business where you literally have hundreds of Raving Referrals requires you to be in a contact sport with your Top 50.

Your Network Drives Your Net Worth

We will teach you everything you need to know about creating profitable partnerships in Chapter 11 of this book. Then, in Chapter 16, we will outline the Top 21 Cross-Promoting Campaigns you can deploy with your referral partners. First, let's cover how to build your database and stay top of mind with each of the three sources of Raving Referrals.

Compile Your Database

If you're serious about success, building a database of your past clients, complementary professionals, and Social Sphere is paramount. All of your contacts should be centralized in one contact relationship management (CRM) system to make it easy for you to consistently communicate with your network. That means importing your contacts from your phone as well as your Apple Mail, Gmail, Outlook, Yahoo Mail, and LinkedIn connections into one centralized communications command center. You also want to ensure you have all of your current and past clients as well as any and all prospects in your CRM.

Create Lifetime Clients

If you are serious about winning clients for life, it's imperative you keep your brand top-of-mind. Your goal is to become the top-trusted solution in the real estate industry, so people always use your services and tell everyone they know to do the same.

Once your contacts are centralized, be sure to schedule a regular message to your market every month at a minimum. Consistently keep your brand and services in front of your database through regular printed or emailed newsletters as well as through your social media channels.

Here are some great segments and ideas for what to feature in your newsletters and social posts:

- Articles and Blogs
- Awards and Recognition
- Charity Collaborations
- Client Appreciation Events
- Client Success Stories
- Community Impact Campaigns
- Company Announcements
- Holiday Highlights
- Industry Updates
- Inspirational Quotes
- Membership Opportunities
- New Employee Introductions
- Podcast Interviews
- Product and Service Announcements and Training
- Referral Partner Spotlights
- Referral Rewards
- Referral Shout-Outs
- Special Offers
- Technology Innovations
- Testimonials
- Tips and Tricks
- Training Events
- Trends and Statistics

We will go into detail on how to communicate and cross-promote to your network in a later chapter. For now, the key is to get all of your contacts into one centralized location and schedule a regular message or newsletter to your database at least once per month.

Survey For Success

One of the fastest and easiest ways to uncover opportunities for your business is by sending out a Referability Survey to your clients, colleagues, and Social Sphere.

Surveying your clients and professional network will help you:
1. Spread the word about your business.
2. Gain valuable feedback and insights into how people view you.
3. Capture testimonials you can use in your marketing.
4. Uncover opportunities to create profitable partnerships.
5. Generate referrals right on the spot.

Best of all, a Referability Survey will help you achieve all of this quickly. In fact, you can send out your survey in as little as ten minutes.

Creating Your Referability Survey

Surveying your Social Sphere is easy using the survey tools in Facebook, LinkedIn, or wherever you have a social following. There are also some great free software tools to help you quickly and easily send a survey. JotForm.com and Qualtrics.com allow you to survey your clients and customers to capture ratings, reviews, and testimonials.

Creating a Referability Survey is as simple as asking people to rate you on a scale from 1-5 on how they view your:

- Trustworthiness
- Subject Matter Expertise
- Quality of Work
- Professionalism
- Responsiveness

Sending a survey is super easy and only takes a few minutes. Follow the simple instructions, import or sync your contacts, and then select the specific people you want your survey sent to. Once your list is ready to go, customize your questions and message, then press send.

Your message should include the fact that your business is in growth mode, so they know you are looking for additional clients.

You can simply say something like:

"As one of my valued connections, I'd like to ask for your help. I'm working on growing my business and have a quick survey I'd like you to complete. It's totally anonymous and should only take about 30 seconds. This will give me some important feedback, so I'd really appreciate it if you would take a moment to do it now."

Then, for best results, add a thank you message that says,

> "Thanks for sharing your feedback. Before you go, if someone you know was asking about me or the services I provide, what would you tell them?"

That last question is specifically designed to capture testimonials. Hopefully, you will get some great feedback and client success stories or quotes you can use on your website and in your marketing collateral. You may even find people recommend or refer you right then and there because someone they know needs your services now.

Once your message says what you want, just press send, then sit back and watch the results roll in. If you send your survey to a large list, you should start seeing some completed surveys within minutes.

Value Your VIPs

You likely have some VIP clients who use you often, refer you regularly, and account for a large percentage of your overall revenue in your business. After coaching and consulting thousands of entrepreneurs and professionals over the years, we can tell you that the 80/20 rule is very real. What we mean is that for many people, 80% of their business comes from 20% of their clients and referral partners. These people should be treated like gold because they can represent tens or hundreds of thousands of dollars to your bottom line.

After my second year in the mortgage business, I (Brandon) analyzed all of the loans I had closed and commissions I had earned to that point. I was surprised to find that just one of my REALTORs, named Dana Berry, had referred 25% of my total income for the year. That one relationship alone brought me over $50,000 in annual income which made her my #1 VIP from that point on. Once I had identified just how lucrative that relationship was, I happily invested into co-marketing advertising campaigns with Dana in The Real Estate Book because I knew that every client that she attracted would be referred my way. Even though I rarely got a single call from our joint ads, buyers who called Dana about one of her listings would consistently be referred to me to be prequalified before she would take them out to tour properties. Best of all, Dana was an awesome woman who I loved spending time with. We would regularly go out to lunch, happy hour, movies, and concerts. That's part of the beauty of building referral partnerships. You get to build your business with people who become some of your closest friends and allies.

Take a moment to think about your business. Over the past year, who has referred you the most business or the best clients? Do you have some past clients who refer you more than others? If so, make sure you show them some appreciation.

Thank and Update Your Referral Champions

When people refer you, be sure to communicate with your customers throughout the process so they are always up to date. It's better to over-communicate rather than leave them wondering what's going on.

I (Brandon) learned this lesson back in 2005 after receiving a mortgage refinance referral from John Jones, a VP at Intel. John was definitely a VIP client. I helped him finance, and then later refinance, his primary home, as well as a vacation home he acquired. In addition to the thousands of dollars in commissions I earned from serving him personally, he regularly referred other Intel employees and executives to me. That's where I made one of my all-time biggest business blunders.

A couple of months after referring one of his colleagues to me, John called and asked how things had gone with his associate. Excitedly I said something like, "Just great. We closed on his loan two weeks ago, so he is a happy camper." To which there was a long uncomfortable silence, after which he replied, "Let me give you a tip. When someone refers business to you, it's a really good idea to thank the person who gave you the referral, and it's also good to follow up with the person and let them know what happened with the person they referred to you."

My stomach dropped, and I felt like a total idiot. I couldn't believe I had been so dumb as to not update my VIP on the status of the client he had referred to me. If the referral had come from one of my referral partners, I absolutely would have kept them updated, but because it came from a client, the thought never even crossed my mind. Needless to say, I apologized profusely and thanked him for the lesson. Then I quickly printed branded thank you cards with my company logo and a "thank you for your referral" message on the front with a pre-written message and blank line inside to fill in the name of the client they had referred.

We quickly trained our 30 loan officers to send these out every time they received a referral from anyone. Our goal was to thank them for the referral, so they felt the love. We also made sure our team kept them updated throughout the entirety of the transaction.

In the years since, I've asked thousands of professionals if they've ever given a referral to someone and never heard back from the person to which they referred their clients. Unfortunately, nearly 100% of the people I've surveyed have had that same experience. It doesn't take long to make a quick call or even just send an update by text or direct message. Alerting the people who refer you business will make them grateful for the update in just a few seconds. It gives you a great reason to reach out and add value. Plus, this leads to more people viewing you as a dependable professional worthy of sending their clients, colleagues, family, and friends to.

Send Video Messages, Voice Memos & GIFs

When it comes to following up with people, one of the best ways to make a great impression is by recording and sending them a personalized video or audio message. When you do, people will see your smiling face or at least hear the smile in your voice, and be impressed that you are connecting in a way they likely haven't seen before. This personal touch takes only a few seconds and is much more impactful than sending a text, email, or direct message through a social platform. Simply record a quick video on your cell phone and text it to them like you would with a photo. If you are connected to them on Facebook or LinkedIn, you can record your video right on the messaging app and send it over in seconds. The beauty of this strategy is that people can truly feel your spirit and will feel much more connected to you and served by you.

Another way to help your message stand out is to send them a voice memo or an animated or video GIF. These are entertaining, quick, and easy to send. Plus, they help you stand out and can make your contact smile or laugh, feeling emotions they rarely experience through a simple text message. If you've never sent a video GIF, just find the GIF icon in your text messaging app and search for an image that conveys the message you want to send. For example, if you want to send someone a Happy Birthday message, search the term "Birthday." Then review and select the video GIF you think would best express the emotion you want to convey.

Your message will make a lasting impression that will help you stand out from the crowd and build relationships faster.

Depending on the industry you are in, here are a few ways you can update your Referral Champions:

1. Call and thank them once their referred party contacts you.
2. Send a thank you card naming the person they referred.
3. Text or email an update whether the person moves forward or not.
4. Share a photo of the home that the client they referred chose to buy (with the client's permission of course).

5. Post the client's testimonial on social media, thanking and tagging your Referral Champion (again, with the client's permission).
6. Call your Referral Champion after the transaction is closed, showing your appreciation, and asking if there is anyone else you can help.

The amount of time, energy, and money you spend thanking your Referral Champions will vary based on your Lifetime Client Value. If the client is worth over $100,000 to your business, you may want to go the extra mile to make sure your Referral Champions feel celebrated and rewarded.

The First Is the Worst

Do you remember the first time you tried to ride a bicycle? If you are like us, it felt scary, and you had visions of a disastrous painful crash. Most likely, you had a parent or family member assure you they would hold onto you, and everything would be fine. So, you pushed past the fear, grabbed the handlebars tight, and got up on that seat to face your fate. As you anxiously started pedaling, you pleaded with the person teaching you to not let go so you wouldn't fall and fail.

They assured you everything would be fine, so you started your way down the street, sidewalk, or parking lot. After a few seconds, you started figuring out how to adjust your weight and balance the bike. One minute in, you had already learned the basics of riding a bike.

Then you had that joyous moment when you actually felt you were in control of the bike and would soon be racing down the street. That was likely the moment you looked up to realize you were riding by yourself, and no one was holding on to your bike any longer.

For me (Brandon) that was the point when I over adjusted the handlebars and quickly crashed on the pavement. After realizing the pain of colliding with the concrete hurt far less than I imagined, I got up, dusted off my scraped knees, and got back up determined to win. Needless to say, every other time I got on a bike after that experience, I was more confident than the first time because I had learned what to do and what not to do.

The lesson here is that typically the first time you do anything will be the absolute worst you will ever be at performing that task. After doing something new for the first time, you get wiser and better because you will know what you did not know the first time. It will feel easier and you will be more comfortable because you will have learned some tips and tricks to improve your performance the second time around.

When it comes to engaging your Referral Champions, you just need to TAKE ACTION and get started. Fail forward as John Maxwell would say. The faster you TAKE ACTION, the faster you will find success. Just give yourself grace knowing the first is the worst and that every time after will get better and better.

Sometimes It's A Winding Road

A key thing to keep in mind is that not every referral is going to turn into cash, however the relationship may be worth more than the monetary value of a client.

Life is full of unexpected moments that can change everything. For Rob Leggat, WSS Coach and Associate Broker at EXIT Realty Premier in Massapequa, New York, one of those moments came through a pivotal referral from a childhood friend—a connection that would ultimately shape his future in ways he never anticipated.

Rob was in Canada, navigating his career as a CPA, when his friend introduced him to a prominent entrepreneur with a vast network of retail stores. The entrepreneur had recently acquired a real estate project in New York and needed someone to oversee it. Without hesitation, Rob accepted the opportunity, boarding a plane to Tarrytown, near the legendary Sleepy Hollow. This decision marked the beginning of a new chapter, leading him to the United States.

The move was more than a career shift; it was a life-altering journey. In the U.S., Rob met his wife in a serendipitous encounter. This referral not only opened doors professionally but also personally, leading to a family and a life he cherishes deeply.

Rob's story is a testament to the power of maintaining relationships and the unexpected paths they can open through referrals. It underscores the importance of consistent communication with those who matter, as these connections can lead to opportunities that shape our destinies. His journey from Canada to the U.S., sparked by a single introduction, exemplifies how a referral can be a catalyst for profound change, both in business and in life.

Engaging your Social Sphere is one of the best ways to attract more Raving Referrals. The good news is we are going to teach you how to create a Referral Rewards program in the next chapter.

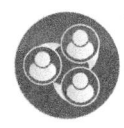

Chapter 7: Referral Rewards

The Power of Agent-to-Agent Referrals

One of the best ways to expand your real estate commissions and income is by leveraging agent-to-agent referrals. By partnering with other agents locally, nationally, and internationally, you can earn commissions on transactions you don't even have to manage.

Whether you're sending business to another agent or receiving referrals yourself, a well-structured referral strategy can generate consistent, passive income and expand your reach beyond your local market.

How Referral Commissions Work

The National Association of REALTORs® (NAR) encourages licensed real estate agents to legally pay each other referral fees, typically ranging from 20% to 35% of the commission earned on a closed deal. This means that if you refer a client who purchases a $500,000 home and the agent earns a 3% commission ($15,000), you could receive anywhere from $3,000 to $5,250 just for making the connection and giving them a Raving Referral.

On top of that, there are several real estate companies who have integrated agent recruiting revenue sharing and agent-attraction models that allow licensed agents to earn commissions by enrolling other real estate professionals into their companies. These models create passive income opportunities, providing REALTORs with an additional revenue stream beyond their own transactions.

Refer Clients to Other Agents

Receiving mailbox money is a beautiful thing. Is there a better feeling than getting a check for thousands of dollars just for connecting a buyer or seller with another agent who does all the work and manages all the details?

While many agents hesitate to pass on business, there are several key scenarios where making a referral is the best choice. The goal is to ensure the client gets the best possible service while you maintain credibility and earn generous referral commissions.

Here are some situations when referring a client to another real estate agent is best for everyone involved:

1. Out-of-Market Transactions

One of the most common reasons for referring a client is when they are buying or selling a home in a location outside your licensed area or expertise. If you live and work in Texas and have a client relocating to Florida, find a great agent who is an expert in that local market. This ensures the client gets top-tier service while you earn 20-35% of the final commission earned by the agent doing the work.

2. Specialization Needs

Real estate is highly specialized, and some transactions require niche expertise. Referring a client to an agent with specialized knowledge can lead to better results.

If you are a residential agent and you hear about someone looking to buy an office building, apartment complex, or industrial building, offer to find them an expert who can help them with their specific commercial transaction.

Not only will the client benefit from having someone who specializes in that type of property, you will earn a lucrative referral fee. The client will be grateful for the help, and you can get a slice of the pie just for being a connector. Plus, people will think of you as a trusted real estate professional with a vast network of people who can help them, their clients, and their social sphere regardless of what type of property they need help with.

3. Conflict of Interest

Sometimes you may face a situation where working with a client could create a conflict of interest. In that case, referring the client to another agent ensures transparency and ethical compliance.

For example, if you have a close friend, family member, or business partner and want to avoid any personal emotions and financial interests that could complicate negotiations, referring them to a third-party agent may be the best course of action. Conflicts of interest can also occur if you have two different clients interested in the same property. In a case like this, you can bring in an objective, outside agent and earn a nice commission while they do all the work.

4. Overwhelmed with Clients

If you have more clients than you can effectively serve, referring some of them to trusted colleagues ensures that every client receives top-notch attention. You can focus on giving great service to your most important clients and entrust a first-time homeowner to a team member who loves helping families find their first home.

If you haven't yet built a team of agents you are mentoring and referring clients to, partner up with another agent in your office or company and create a partnership where they help some of your clients and you receive a referral fee. Enrolling someone from your office or company allows you to communicate that this person is part of your team. That keeps the referrals coming your way and communicates that you are expanding your team because your business is booming.

Going on vacation. Enroll another agent to take over in your absence. Works well when life gets in the way of business too. The key is to choose someone you know, respect and trust to give your clients five-star service.

5. Personality or Preference Mismatch

Not every client-agent relationship is a good fit. If there are personality differences or clients with unrealistic expectations that may make a transaction difficult, a referral may be the best solution.

Perhaps you attract a high-demand client who insists on specific luxury property features that are outside your area of expertise. If so, you may want to enroll a luxury market expert who specializes in that niche and client personality. This helps you avoid any unnecessary frustration while ensuring the client is well-served by someone better suited to their needs.

6. Client Requires Bilingual or Cultural Expertise

Some transactions require agents with language skills or cultural knowledge to best serve a client's needs. If you have a client who speaks primarily Spanish or Mandarin and prefers to work with an agent fluent in their language, refer them to an experienced agent familiar with their culture, customs and communication style. This ensures seamless communication, preventing misunderstandings that could impact the transaction.

Position Yourself as an Expert

You've probably heard the expression, "Grow rich in a niche", but are you putting that strategy to work for your business?

Agents want to refer people to specialists who guarantee great service in a niche market. One of the best ways to stand out from the thousands of other agents offering services in your market is to specialize in a specific niche or type of property.

- » Become a Certified HOA Specialist at HOA.com/CHS. Considering the fact that 53% of all homes in the U.S. are located in homeowner associations, this certification and designation will help you win more listings in top HOAs. When you feature this designation in your marketing and online profiles, you elevate your expert authority when serving people looking to buy or sell in top HOA communities and neighborhoods.

- » Another attractive certification you should consider is earning a LUXE Luxury Listing designation. This helps you attract more luxury listings showing you have expertise when listing and selling premier properties in exclusive neighborhoods.

- » If you like working with investors, you may want to earn a Real Estate Investing designation. Offered by the National Association of REALTORs, this certification program helps you master the ins and outs of working with investors and those who are establishing themselves as real estate investors. The courses provide insight into 1031 exchanges, REITS, net operating income models, tools, and more.

Specialize in Referred Clients

Now that you see some of the scenarios where referring clients makes sense for everyone involved, have you ever thought about specializing in helping other agent's clients? Few people do. Yet, as you can see, solving the issues we just discussed for other agents facing those situations can lead to a substantial stream of clients and income for your business.

Building strong relationships with other agents is a crucial step in growing your referral business. Networking with professionals in different markets and specialties increases your chances of receiving referrals.

International Referral Success

One of the most powerful examples of leveraging agent-to-agent referrals comes from John Turley, who became the #1 RE/MAX Agent in the world in 2014 thanks to his building a global referral business.

After moving to the Caribbean island of Ambergris Caye, Belize, John quickly realized that almost all the buyers of Belizean properties were people living in the U.S. Being the savvy businessman he is, John started proactively identifying target markets and agents, and reaching out strategically. John would attend real estate conferences throughout the U.S. and Canada, to connect with real estate agents who wanted to earn commissions for referring people who purchase a vacation or investment property in Belize.

John would also do a deep dive to find which agents key markets (i.e. direct flight cities to Belize) already had the IRES (International Real Estate Specialist) or CIPS (Certified International Property Specialist) designations. These are agents who had already self-identified as having an interest in international real estate, and it didn't take much effort for John to connect the dots for them to become a strategic referral partner.

With real estate commissions in Belize typically at 10%, referring agents earned lucrative commissions simply by referring people to John. John set up monthly real estate investor tours over a 3-day weekend, where he would host 15-20 people at a time for a fully educational immersive experience to learn all about the market and investing in Belize.

John charged clients for their 3-day weekend experience, with the understanding that it was purely educational, and there was to be no selling during the field trip. (John would only work with qualified clients, and qualified meant that they had enough education to be able to make a qualified, educated informed decision about the market and the property they were looking at.) But at the conclusion of the weekend, John would take off his educator hat, and put on his real estate agent hat, now that his prospective clients were educated to make an informed investment decision.

As John toured people around the island of Ambergris Caye, he showed them all the best properties and taught them all the intricacies and benefits of investing abroad. As a result, John's weekend tours were full of Americans who were thrilled to have the opportunity to buy their dream home on a tropical island. There was no sales pressure because John let them know up front that nothing was for sale and he wouldn't write up any offers until Monday at noon when their tour and education was complete.

Agents loved referring people to John because clients were thrilled with the experience and results John delivered. For top producing agents in key markets, John would even fly them down to Belize and put them up on his own dime and let them audit his field trip experience at no charge, to motivate and impower them to unlock their network of clients and become outbound referral specialists to John in Belize. Over a 2-year period, John paid to fly and host over 50 top producing agents (minimum GCI of $1M US) from key markets across the U.S. and Canada to audit his field trips in Belize. Many of these agents became outbound referral specialists to Belize and earned great commissions with some earning over $100,000 per year just for sending clients to John.

This strategy was so successful for John that he achieved his goal of becoming the #1 top selling agent worldwide for RE/MAX in 2014, and finished in the top 3 worldwide for 3 consecutive years. And all from the Ambergris Caye, Belize market with a population of just 24,000 people!

After achieving his goal, John was thrilled when RE/MAX recognized his leadership and prowess, and offered him the opportunity to purchase the Master Franchise for RE/MAX throughout the Caribbean and Central America (35 countries and territories).

John is now the CEO and co-owner of RE/MAX Caribbean and Central America with nearly 100 offices and he leads 1,000 agents who educate and tour clients who are excited to buy property in exciting tropical destinations.

How John Turley Attracted Referrals:

- Built relationships with, and trained U.S. and Canadian agents to become international outbound referral specialists.

- Offered generous referral fees to incentivize agents to send him clients and to add international outbound referrals to their core business.

- Educated agents on the Belize real estate market, making them comfortable referring their clients. Even going so far as to fly top producing agents to Belize, to build a global referral pipeline.

- Provided turn-key marketing materials so agents could promote luxurious properties under their own brand and identity.

By focusing on agent education and strong referral incentives, John created a global referral pipeline that drove his record-breaking success. His strategy is proof that any agent can use referrals to increase income – locally or internationally.

According to John, to build a strong referral business, you must understand the three key types of referrals:

1. **Inbound Referrals (Clients Coming to Your Market)**

    - **Novice Level:** Passive referrals fall into your lap—maybe an agent from another city sends you a relocation client.
    - **Intermediate Level:** You take a proactive approach, identifying target markets and agents, and reaching out strategically.
    - **Expert Level:** You become an international local expert, actively attracting and managing global clients in your market.

2. **Outbound Referrals (Clients Seeking Properties in Other Markets)**

    - **Novice Level:** A client asks for help finding an international property.
    - **Intermediate Level:** You ask your network if they have international real estate needs, creating opportunities instead of waiting for them.
    - **Expert Level:** You become a local international expert, known in your community as the go-to agent for global transactions.

3. **"InterLOCALNational" (Mastery Level)**

    - This is a term John coined to describe the full integration of inbound and outbound referrals. At this level, international referrals become a primary part of your business model.

Where To Find Referral Partners

If you are ready to serve more clients, consider joining a real estate agent referral network. One of our favorites is RESAAS.com, a global real estate technology platform that connects over 700,000 residential real estate agents across 160 countries.

RESAAS helps you expand your referral network and generate more business opportunities. By providing a centralized hub for agents to showcase their listings and connect with professionals worldwide, RESAAS increases exposure and facilitates seamless referral exchanges.

The platform uses automated targeting technology to match referrals with the most relevant agents in a given area, ensuring timely and appropriate connections. With a focus on streamlining communication, RESAAS enables you to discuss client needs and transaction details with other agents efficiently, fostering stronger professional relationships and boosting referral success.

To simplify and manage the referral exchange process, RESAAS offers referral tracking, which helps you monitor the progress of referrals from initiation to deal closure. This transparency ensures accountability between referring and receiving agents. Additionally, their RESAAS Pay payment system facilitates quick and secure commission payments between agents.

By leveraging these features, RESAAS helps you grow your business through efficient, tech-driven referral management, making it easier than ever to generate passive income from agent-to-agent referrals.

Top 20 Facebook Groups for Real Estate Referrals

In addition to the RESAAS global agent network, there are numerous Facebook groups that help you network with other agents and exchanging referrals.

Here are the top twenty Facebook groups you can join to share referral opportunities:

1. Real Estate Agent Referral Network & Marketing Tips
2. Real Estate Community
3. REALTOR Networking & Social Media Tips
4. Let's Talk Real Estate
5. Inside Real Estate Discussion Group
6. Real Estate Conversations
7. Real Estate Lead Gen Scripts & Objections
8. All Things Real Estate
9. Real Estate Connections
10. Real Closers
11. Real Estate 101
12. Real Estate Agent & Loan Officer - Referrals, Leads & Networking
13. Real Estate Agents Group

14. Lab Coat Agent Referrals
15. Pop-Bys For REALTORs®
16. California Agents and REALTORs
17. All REALTORs and related Professionals
18. Real Estate Agent Referrals Group
19. The Preferred Real Estate Referral Network
20. Real Estate Agent Referral Network

*For more information and site links, see page #331.

Turn Referrals into Passive Income

Referral commissions can help fill your client funnel and also offer you an incredible passive income stream. This can supplement and even surpass traditional real estate transactions if you do it right.

Whether you're helping local clients relocate to other markets, supporting luxury sellers, international buyers, commercial investors or simply sellers in HOA communities, the opportunities are limitless.

Action Steps:
Steps to Earn Referral Commissions:

1. **Build a Network of Trusted Agents** – Connect with agents in key markets where your clients may be moving, investing, or purchasing second homes.

2. **Grow Rich in a Niche** – Stand out from the competition by specializing your services. When people see your profile online, designations help them know you have expertise in areas their clients are looking for.

3. **Formalize Referral Agreements** – Use written referral agreements to outline commission splits and expectations.

4. **Stay Engaged with Your Clients** – Ensure a smooth transition and keep in touch for future referrals.

5. **Track and Follow Up** – Confirm that the transaction closes and that you receive your commission.

RAVING REFERRALS FOR REAL ESTATE AGENTS

Following these steps will help you start attracting more referrals, increase your income, and expand your real estate business beyond your local market.

In your toolkit, you will find a copy of the 5 Steps on How to Ask for a Referral from your Top 50, as well as The Referrals Partner Agreement.

Chapter 8:
Master the Art of the Ask

The number one reason some professionals receive more referrals than others is that they simply ask for them. Many people feel uncomfortable and awkward asking their clients for referrals. However, once you are prepared and you have a strategy for when and how to ask, it will feel natural and comfortable for both you and the other party.

In their book, Selling Professional Services, Chuck and Evan Polin write,

"Most professionals do not ask for referrals because they are afraid they have nothing to offer in return. They are often surprised when they discover that the referring party's only expectation is that their client or friend receive the best service. When you ask for referrals, the other party typically expects less in return than you would think."

SRO - Serve Regardless of Opportunity. This simple phrase allows us to create an emotional bank account that has greater value than even our physical bank accounts. Relationship capital is, in my (Verl's) opinion, the most important kind of capital in our lives.

When my daughter, co-founder and President of Workman Success Systems, Brianne Ika, and I, sat down recently for a mastermind and business, we started by making a list of our assets—the tools, systems, and resources we had available to us that allow us to operate, serve others, and grow our company. This list was impressive, but in the middle of the conversation and list building we stopped and asked this question, "What do we really have that is an unfair competitive advantage? The answer to this question was relationship capital. The relationships that have been developed over the last 15-30 years span real estate, professional speakers, coaches, consultants, entrepreneurs, and so many more deep thinkers and givers.

The ability to recommend a great speaker at any price point to any size or type of company and know they would knock it out of the park is true relationship capital. These amazing relationships refer business, share insights, and sometimes are simply great sounding boards that have more value than anything else we have built or own. The question is how do you build relationship capital so that when it comes time to give or receive a referral you are at the front of mind in each relationship and they know you want to, need to, and will serve the referred client.

As I reflect on what created this capital, I can honestly say that many opportunities have presented themselves where we could serve, instead of selling something or someone, and the result of that has been multiplied in the raving referrals we have received from these relationships. When it's time to put your referral business on steroids, then you move from serve to ask. This is a simple transition that comes as a natural part of a relationship that is based on mutual trust and respect.

Most people ask for referrals after doing something great or delivering exceptional service and they tie the referral to a job well done. While this is good, there is a proven way to open referral conversations up before you ever deliver any service. You simply ask how you can refer them and if they are open to referring to you as well. Sounds simple, but it may not be that easy. We often overthink the ask. Let me give you an example of the exact dialog that works time and time again and is proven to give a positive and predictable response.

Start with "Will you do me a favor?" This question, whether spoken or delivered in text or even the email subject line, almost always receives a positive response. Most people are good hearted by nature and if you need something they would be more than happy to help. When you start with "will you do me a favor"? it opens up the next opportunity to ask for referrals.

As a real estate agent we recommend you learn this conversation and customize it in your own words:

> *"I know that everyone knows lots of people who might also do real estate. As you know, it's my full-time job and we specialize in creating amazing experiences for our clients so they are the most informed in any real estate situation. Here's the favor, when real estate comes up from time to time at work, with friends, or family, would you do me a favor and share my contact information with them as a professional option, and then simply shoot me a text with their contact information*

so I can follow up and give them the same kind of services you have come to expect? I would really appreciate it, and you know I'll do the same for you."

The answer is almost always "sure". But you can't leave it at that. You now need to give them an easy referral link, a contact card, or a simple pre-prepared email template that does the heavy lifting for them. We must make it easy for people to do business with us.

Raving Referrals in Action: Denise Klein's Scalable Awakening

Denise, a seasoned professional with over four decades of experience, Team Owner at eXp Realty - The Klein Team, in Las Vegas, Nevada, and a current Senior Coach with WSS, found herself at a crossroads. Despite her success, she was working tirelessly, seven days a week, with a mindset that hard work alone was the key to success. It was during a pivotal conversation with Verl Workman in a hotel lobby that her perspective began to shift. Verl's candid observation that her business wasn't scalable struck a chord, leading Denise to reevaluate her approach.

Reflecting on that moment, Denise shared, "I went to my room that night and I cried. I was overwhelmed by how Verl could see so clearly what I was unable to see about my business. It was a revelation that I needed to change my approach to achieve true success."

The next day, Denise attempted to recruit a promising producer to her team. Fresh from a transformative conversation with Verl she felt confident and ready to expand her business. However, the encounter with the potential recruit didn't go as planned.

As Denise sat across from him, contract in hand, she was taken aback by his candid response. "You know, you're not the right leader for me," he said. Despite his admiration for her achievements and character, he pointed out a critical issue: "If I still have to work seven days a week, all those hours, that's not what I'm looking for."

This feedback hit Denise hard, like a "Mike Tyson punch from every direction," as she described it. It was a stark realization that her work-life balance was not only affecting her personal life, but also her ability to attract and retain talent. The recruit's words echoed Verl's earlier insights about the need for scalability and balance in her business.

This encounter was a turning point for Denise, prompting her to reassess her approach and prioritize creating a more sustainable work environment. It underscored the importance of aligning her business practices with the evolving expectations of the real estate industry and the professionals within it.

Denise's journey with WSS began with a realization that success could look different. She embraced the idea of scaling her business, not just in terms of financial growth, but also in creating a sustainable work-life balance. This transformation was catalyzed by a significant referral opportunity that came her way.

The referral story unfolded when Denise, driven by newfound courage, approached Terry, a financial planner with connections to the Clark County School District. Despite years of knowing Terry, Denise had never asked about integrating real estate into his offerings. Finally, during a leadership class exercise, she mustered the courage to ask, "Why don't you have a real estate side?" Terry's response was simple, yet profound: "Because no one's ever asked."

This conversation opened doors to a contract with the Clark County School District, leading to over 300 transactions. Denise's ability to leverage WSS, along with her background in title and escrow, allowed her to scale this opportunity effectively. The systems and tools provided by Workman, including the Top 50 program and KV Core, enabled her to maintain a database of thousands of teachers, ensuring continued success even after her exclusivity ended.

Denise's story is a testament to the power of asking and believing in oneself. Her journey highlights the importance of WSS tools and coaching advice in transforming a business. The key action items from her story include:

1. **Embrace Scalability**: Recognize the importance of scaling your business to achieve sustainable success and work-life balance.
2. **Leverage Relationships**: Don't hesitate to ask for opportunities and leverage existing relationships to create new avenues for growth.
3. **Utilize Systems**: Implement WSS tools like the Top 50 program to maintain and grow your client base.
4. **Believe in Yourself**: Trust in your abilities and the resources available to you to seize opportunities and drive success.

Denise's journey is a powerful reminder that with the right mindset and tools, real estate professionals can transform their businesses and lives.

To download our proven referral generating scripts, go to *ReferralChampion.com/toolkit*.

If you've ever felt uncomfortable asking for referrals, it's likely because you are more focused on what you are asking to receive rather than what you are offering to give. When you shift your mindset from receiving to giving, you will feel comfortable and confident asking for referrals knowing that you are really offering to take great care of the people who are fortunate enough to be referred to you.

Energetically, it's the difference between selling and serving. When you approach conversations focusing on serving people, they can feel the generosity of your spirit and feel that you are truly out to help them and those they care about.

With that in mind, there are three steps to the Art of the Ask that will lead to many more referrals coming your way:

1) Set The Stage
2) Listen For Referral Triggers
3) A-S-K to G-E-T

Once you learn this simple yet powerful framework, it will forever change how you approach asking for and getting all the referrals you desire and deserve.

Step 1) Set the Stage

While most people ask for referrals once they have finished serving their clients, we recommend having a conversation about referrals and introductions at the end of your first client meeting once your new client has decided to move forward and hire you to help them sell or buy a home or commercial property. This sets the stage for a referral conversation later in your client service cycle.

Earl Kemper is a referral master and has been recognized as the #1 coach for ActionCOACH five times for the Americas region and twice globally. Earl is truly skilled at helping companies grow and create predictable profitability. A cornerstone of Earl's system is the ability to grow the business by systemizing their referrals.

Earl primarily coaches top-producing financial advisors to help them dramatically increase assets under management. He teaches them to weave a pre-referral request into every new client conversation saying:

> "Thanks so much for meeting with me today. Before you leave, I'd like to ask for your help. I love helping families like yours buy and refinance their homes. Once I prove myself to you and deliver a 5-star experience, would it be ok if I ask you for referrals at that later date?"

You'll find people are extremely receptive to this question because everyone likes to help other people. Also, you haven't asked them for a referral at that moment in time. You've simply gotten their permission to ask them for referrals and introductions in the future once you've provided your services and earned their trust.

Step 2) Listen for Referral Triggers

After your client has given their approval to ask for referrals and introductions in the future, you need to be on the lookout for expressions of appreciation. These Referral Triggers let you know when it's time to ask for a referral or introduction because your clients are in peak referral state.

- Thank you so much!
- You are so good at what you do!
- You did a great job!
- I couldn't have done it without you!
- You're the best!
- This was way easier than I expected!
- Wow, I love my new home. Thanks so much for helping us!
- I can't believe how much I'm saving each month!
- I can't believe how much I made on this investment property!
- I have a friend who owns a lot of rental properties/AirBNBs.
- I have a friend/neighbor/client who might need your services.
- I should introduce you to…

Listen closely, and whenever your clients say any of these Referral Triggers, it's time to ask for referrals.

Step 3) A-S-K to G-E-T

When you hear any of these Referral Triggers, immediately smile and say,

> "I'm so glad to hear that. I love helping clients like you buy and sell real estate. By the way, I may have mentioned before that I am expanding my business, so if you know any {describe your Perfect Prospect} who might need help {share your Service Statement}, I'd love to connect with them and see if I can help them the way I helped you.

Do you know anyone right now who is looking to {share your Service Statement}?"

Be ready to ask for referrals when opportunities arise and when trust has been established in the relationship. Actively listen for the Referral Triggers and be prepared to deliver your ASK confidently and naturally.

Never miss a prime opportunity to ask. Even if they don't have a referral for you now, you've planted a seed and set the stage so they refer you later when they hear of someone that might benefit from your services. What you'll find is that when people voluntarily express their appreciation for your work, they are much more likely to introduce you to others who need your services. Plus, you get the added benefit of your Perfect Prospects hearing a passionate testimonial about you and the services you provide.

One of the greatest lessons I've learned from Mark Victor Hansen is to A-S-K to G-E-T. If you've never read his book with Jack Canfield called, The Aladdin Factor, take a moment and order it now either in printed form, eBook, or as an audiobook.

The key concept of the book is that the more you ask for what you want, the more you will get it. If you are in sales, are self-employed, or make a living selling products or services, the more often you ask for the sale, the more often you will get it. The beauty is, we're going to teach you how to generate referrals and introductions simply by asking questions that lead people to the Referral Triggers we just described. By asking clients questions about their satisfaction with your products or services, you set the stage for an expression of appreciation which often leads to opportunities to ask for referrals.

When meeting with your clients, try inserting the following questions into the conversation:

- I hope you're pleased with the service I've provided. Is there anything I can do to make you even happier?

- Now that we've been working together for a while, I'm wondering if you can tell me what you have found most valuable about working with me?

- I'm committed to growing my business through exceptional service. On a scale of 1-10, how happy would you say you are with my services? What would make it a 10?

- Do you mind if I ask what you have liked best about working with me?

- If you don't mind me asking, if you knew someone who was looking for a {insert your profession} how likely would you be to recommend me? What would you say?

If the client responds positively, you can follow up by saying,

"I'm so glad to hear that. I hope you'll recommend me any time you hear any {describe your perfect prospect} mention that they are looking for a good {insert your profession} or need help {share your Service Statement}. Is there anyone who comes to mind who might need my help?"

Not only will these questions lead to more referrals, but they will also give you testimonials you can use to market your services. Just be sure to capture what they say and ask for permission to use their testimonial on your website and promotional materials.

Another way for you to comfortably ask for referrals is by saying:

"By the way, if you ever have a friend or family member you think might benefit from my services, I would be happy to meet with them for free to see how I might be able to help them."

Teach How To Give a Great Referral

Ideally, you should describe your Perfect Prospect Profile and Service Statement, so they know exactly what type of clients you are looking to serve and how you help them. You might simply say that one of your specialties is working with recent retirees, first-time home buyers or whatever describes your Perfect Prospect and ideal client. Adding this detail into the conversation gives them clarity so they will be on the lookout for clients they can refer you.

There are no limits as to how to start the referral conversation. Just make sure you end with "And, as you may or may not know, a lot of an agent's business comes from personal referrals. Just out of curiosity, do you have anyone that you refer real estate to?"

This is when you will find out if someone will or will not refer to you. You will only have to do this on your initial call. For follow-up calls, skip "A" and "B":

A. If the person says "no," "I have someone else," "well, ya know..." etc., you do not attempt to convince the person to use you as that is not someone who would be on your Top 50 list. This person will be "downgraded" to a "regular sphere or general past client." Politely finish the call... and move on.

B. If they don't have anyone, then ask them: Will you please send all your real estate referrals to me?

When you get the YES, thank this person and go immediately to: "Teach how to give a GREAT referral"

You must reiterate this section over and over and over... on every call. This is critical!

Not all referrals are created equal... What is a GREAT referral? Ok, let me help you with what makes a great referral.

"Unfortunately, people 'just giving out my name and or business cards' rarely gets me a call. It's a nice gesture, but I just don't hear from the person you gave my name to very often. I receive and sell the most number of referrals when I receive a name and cell number of the referral directly from you... so I am able to call the prospective buyer or seller directly.

So please give me their names and cell numbers... and permission for me to call them directly! You don't have to attempt to convince your referral to "absolutely use me." Just convince them to speak to me and to provide me their names and cell phone numbers. That's all I need! I'll take it from there. It should be much easier for you to get their information if you are not attempting to convince them to make a snap decision right then and there to use me. I just need the opportunity to speak to them. Will you please commit to getting me just ONE of these types of referrals this year? I would really appreciate it!

I not only sell real estate in [City] or [City] where we have our office, but all over [County], [County], [County], [County] and [County] Counties as well. I am able to refer out to any other area, State or Province in North America too. If I am not able to assist the client directly, then I will refer them to a great agent who works in that location. Will you please commit to sending me ONE referral this year?

Thank you so much! I appreciate the help! It means so much to me and my family!"

Practice and Perfect

I (Verl) believe that every conversation can unlock the door to your next successful deal. Mastering the art of communication is paramount. Practicing scripts and dialogs allows agents to refine their language, tone, and approach, ensuring they can handle any situation with confidence and poise. By rehearsing various scenarios, agents become adept at navigating objections, building rapport, and closing deals.

Role-playing is a powerful technique that enables agents to simulate real-life interactions in a controlled environment. By partnering with colleagues, mentors, or even friends, agents can practice their scripts and dialogs, receiving valuable feedback and insights. This collaborative approach not only enhances their skills but also builds a supportive community of professionals striving for excellence.

For years, as we teach teams to create a culture of productivity, that process includes a daily huddle, 30 minutes of role playing specific scripts and dialogs, and a minimum of one hour of prospecting as a team. This process guarantees success in each of those areas.

At WSS we are constantly investing in technology that helps our clients automate every possible process. This includes role-playing. Enter the new role-play bot inside Coach Simple, a revolutionary tool that has transformed the way agents practice. This AI-driven platform offers agents the opportunity to engage in realistic, interactive role-play sessions anytime, anywhere. The bot simulates various client scenarios, providing instant feedback and suggestions for improvement. Agents can practice overcoming objections, perfecting their pitch, and adapting to different client personalities, all within a virtual setting.

The role-play bot's convenience and accessibility have made it an indispensable resource for agents seeking to elevate their skills. By integrating this technology into their daily routine, agents can consistently practice and refine their scripts, leading to increased confidence and success in real-world interactions. Across the industry, agents who have embraced the power of practicing scripts and dialogs are reaping the rewards.

Take Sarah, a once-nervous newcomer who struggled with client interactions. Through diligent practice and regular sessions with the WSS role-play bot, Sarah transformed into a confident, articulate agent. Her ability to handle objections and build rapport with clients led to a significant increase in her closing rate and referrals.

Similarly, Nick Painz (referenced earlier), a seasoned agent, found new vigor in his practice routine by incorporating the role-play bot. Despite years of experience, Nick discovered areas for improvement and fine-tuned his approach. The result? A surge in client satisfaction and a growing network of raving fans eager to refer him to others.

The journey to becoming a top-performing real estate agent is paved with dedication, practice, and the willingness to embrace new tools and techniques. By committing to regular practice of scripts and dialogs, and leveraging innovative resources like the WSS role-play bot inside Coach Simple, agents can unlock their full potential and create lasting impressions on clients.

Real estate is competitive, and those who invest in their communication skills stand out as trusted advisors and industry leaders. As agents continue to refine their craft, they not only enhance their own success but also contribute to a culture of excellence and professionalism within the industry.

While you've probably spent thousands of hours practicing and perfecting your trade or profession, you most likely haven't spent much time learning and practicing how to attract referrals and make introductions. Since practice makes perfect, we recommend you partner with another professional and roll-play these conversations, so they become second nature to you both. As you master the art of the ask, you will find that clients refer you without even being asked as you build a business that is powered by referrals. In addition to asking for referrals, start asking for anything and everything you want in life.

- Ask for an appointment
- Ask for an introduction
- Ask to take the next step
- Ask when they would like to get started
- Ask if they would like to move forward
- Ask if they would like to know their current homes value
- Ask if they would like to know more about creating income/wealth through real estate

Asking for what you want dramatically increases the likelihood that you will get it. Best of all, you have nothing to lose because if the answer is no, you are in the exact same position you were in before you asked. If they say yes, you will have achieved your desired outcome and have moved your business forward.

When it comes to charitable giving, I found in our Serve Regardless of Opportunity shift in the way we look at giving, we were introduced to a gentleman by the name of Anthony Marguleas, Broker Owner of Amalfi Estates, who lives, sells, and serves in Los Angeles, California. Asking clients to give back and make a difference in the community propelled Anthony from $110 million to over $400 million in sales in just a few short years. Here's Anthony's story in his own words.

"Back in 2014, I was a solo agent, working crazy hours with two assistants to achieve $110 million in sales. The hours were long, often stretching beyond 80 hours a week. But everything changed in 2015 when I saw an advertisement in RIS Media that led me to hire Verl Workman as my coach. This decision was pivotal. With Verl's guidance, I expanded my team to 15 agents, and by 2021, we were closing $471 million in sales. My business grew and I found myself working fewer hours and enjoying a better work-life balance.

One of the most significant moments in my career came from a referral that I received through my guest lecturing for a UCLA Real Estate Principles class. This connection led me to a bankruptcy attorney handling the sale of "The Beverly House", which I rebranded as "The Hearst Estate". After rebranding and selling it, the estate became the most expensive home sold at auction in the country, closing at $63 million. The publicity was immense, with 488 articles in most major publications. This opportunity was a testament to my belief in the law of reciprocity—giving without expecting anything in return. This principle has opened doors to incredible opportunities throughout my career.

Philanthropy is at the heart of my business. We donate 10% of our commissions to charity—a practice that sets us apart and positions us as community leaders. Over the past nine years, our charitable efforts have touched 107,000 families, far exceeding the 1,500 families we've served through real estate transactions. This legacy of giving has inspired other real estate companies to adopt similar practices, creating a ripple effect of positive impact.

To maintain strong referral relationships, I use systems like Client Giant, a gifting platform which provides personalized touchpoints for clients and top referral sources. This approach has been incredibly effective, enhancing client relationships and generating referrals. My goal is to receive at least one warm referral per week, a target I encourage my agents to pursue as well.

In essence, my journey in real estate has been about building a referral-based business through genuine relationships, philanthropy, and strategic systems. By focusing on these principles, I've created a thriving network and made a meaningful impact in my community."

One of the things that impresses me most about Anthony and his story is his desire to not only give back, but to create a movement around the world of agents who have gained so much from their communities by challenging them to find the giving amount that is consistent from every transaction.

Mastering the Art of the Ask is one of the top practices that creates more success. Scan the QR code or visit the link below for a quick video message on how to A-S-K and G-E-T.

While we're on the subject, we're asking you to share this video with your network. Together, we can help them get clear on what they are asking for in their personal and professional lives.

I hope you take these to heart: serve regardless of opportunity. Develop relationship capital through making a difference without any strings attached, then simply ask. "Will you do me a favor?" You'll find these are very powerful concepts.

Teach your referral partners how to improve their asking skills with the "Art of the Ask" PDF found in your toolkit.

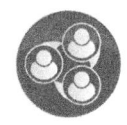

Chapter 9:
Client Appreciation Events

Back in 1999, Brandon learned the value of client appreciation parties from a REALTOR named Mikalan Moiso. Each year, she held her annual New Year's Eve party at a swanky downtown hotel in Portland, Oregon. It was the event of the year, and in order to get an invitation to the black-tie event, you simply had to give Mikalan at least one good referral throughout the course of the year.

"My wife and I will never forget ringing in the new millennium of 2000 playing poker, listening to the Frank Sinatra crooner, and tasting delicious eats and treats.

Months after the event, I asked Mikalan how impactful the event was on her business. I was shocked to hear that her annual event is the single biggest source of clients for her. In fact, she had shifted the vast majority of her annual marketing budget to the event because her clients and Social Sphere wanted to make sure they gave her referrals so they received their golden ticket to the event. The event was so successful, it led to Mikalan being named the 2004 Portland Metropolitan Association of REALTORs Broker of the Year.

After learning this strategy from her, I went on to host several client appreciation events, including private concerts, movie showings, wine tastings, holiday parties, and charity events. Everyone loves a great party. That's why a great way to show your clients and customers how much they mean to your business is to throw a customer appreciation party. A client event can be an impactful way to celebrate your customers, recognize milestones, and say "thank-you" for all the business they have done with you and your company."

Not only will you bring clients together for a fun and festive event, but you also create a culture of community that unites your team as you create an evening your clients will never forget.

- **Art Showings** – Partner with an art gallery and host a private showing
- **Awards Parties** – Invite your clients to a hotel, bar, restaurant, or private theater to watch the Oscars, Grammys, Golden Globes, or other awards show
- **Bowling Parties** – Rent an entire bowling alley or just a few lanes and give prizes for the bowlers who get the most strikes or spares as well as the top individual and team scores
- **Casino Night** – Hire a party company to bring casino tables and dealers giving out chips and awarding prizes for the top chip stacks
- **Charity Fundraising Events** – Create your own event or buy a table at a fundraising dinner inviting your top clients
- **Cigar Night** – Host a party featuring cigars and whiskey tasting for your high-action clients
- **Concerts** – Buy tickets for your VIP clients to an upcoming concert or host a private party with an 80s cover band or local musician
- **Cornhole Tournaments** – Host a cornhole tournament inviting top clients to register their own teams
- **Golf Tournaments** – Produce your own golf tournament or simply buy a foursome and invite VIPs to join you on the greens
- **Holiday Parties** – Throw a private party for Valentine's Day, Independence Day, Halloween, Thanksgiving, Christmas, or New Year's Eve
- **Private Movie Showings** – Rent out a theater and have your own private showing of the latest blockbuster film
- **Sports Events** – Host a tailgate party, rent a private box, or simply buy tickets and invite your best clients and customers for a sporting event

CLIENT APPRECIATION EVENTS

- **TopGolf Tournaments** – Rent a few private bays at TopGolf and give prizes for top scores

- **Wine Tours and Tastings** – Host a private party at a winery or tasting room

Become a Charity Champion

Of all the events and campaigns that we've used over the years, the most fulfilling and rewarding have been charity events. In my opinion, one of the absolute best ways to build goodwill with your clients and customers is to support charities and causes you are passionate about.

Cause-related marketing has evolved from a short-term tactic used to spike sales into a powerful positioning discipline used to build brand equity and elevate corporate perception. It's not only good for the community, it's good for business.

The Results Are In…

There have been numerous research studies over the years that prove consumers want to know about the impact your company makes in their community and in the world. The more you communicate what you are doing to make a difference, the more loyalty you win with your clients and customers.

Just take a look at what research companies have learned after surveying Americans nationwide:

- 93% of consumers want to know what companies are doing to make the world a better place

- 90% of consumers want companies to tell them the ways they are supporting causes

- 83% of U.S. consumers want more of the products and services they use to benefit causes

- 80% said they'd be "likely to switch brands, about equal in price and quality, to one that supports a cause"

- 66% of people believe it's no longer enough for corporations to merely give money away, but that they must integrate good causes into their day-to-day business

While this research is a few years old, we believe this is a trend that will continue to grow, especially with Millennials and Generation Z having been raised in this new era of corporate responsibility and social impact. Bottom line, the more you show you care, the more you inspire your community to care about you and your company. So, choose a charity or cause that you are passionate about that is in alignment with your brand and your community. Get involved and design ways that your company and your community can make a difference –together.

Early on in my coaching career I (Verl) met a fun REALTOR from rural Utah: Brooke Gardner. He grew up on a small dairy farm. Brooke called himself the "Mooving REALTOR". All of his marketing and his advertising on his postcards, everything he did had black and white cow spots on it. He did a great job positioning himself as the "MOOVING REALTOR". I remember the first time we suggested doing a client appreciation event and he was like, "I don't have enough clients to make it valuable". So I said, why don't you do a backyard barbecue? So his very first client event was the Backyard Barbecue. The next event got too big so he moved it to the city park, then he started renting the city's movie theater and eventually moved it to a much bigger venue. It was interesting that the simple act of doing a small event, a backyard barbecue, generated so many referrals that his business continued to grow year over year. I watched over 100 houses a year, in the center of his business, as coming from referral-based events. One of our Verlisms, or quotes, we like to use is "Events Drive Revenue".

I've seen agents donate a certain amount of their commission to Children's Miracle Network, to local food shelters, and so many more! One of my favorite events is when one of our clients took the Pie Day concept of selecting your pie for Thanksgiving, and when you receive one we donate one; basically it's a "to get one, give one" promotion that gives a pie to a first responder on Thanksgiving. Clients are excited to get their choice in an apple, pumpkin, or berry pie and then choose to give a pie to the police station, firehouse, or even a hospital. We've seen local news cover the events and clients use their social media channels to promote the event.

It's amazing to see what a small group of REALTORs can do when they choose to start making a difference in their community.

Raving Referrals in Action: Christy Buck's Formula for Success

Speaking of impact and the power of referrals, I watched the Christy Buck Team, Infinity Real Estate Group in Pearland, Texas, led by Samantha Knoer, go from $250,000 in Gross Closed Income to $3.4 million over just a few years. It was fascinating to watch them go from doing one or two events

CLIENT APPRECIATION EVENTS

a year, to changing their methodology and their strategy and then doing an event every month.

Christy states that events are so important because they give you multiple non-real estate sales reasons to reach out to the people that you serve, to all the people in your top 50, your database, and your community.

Then there's the invitation assembly to participate in a community event - whether it's Pie Day or booing for Halloween or pictures of Santa Claus or any other events. Think about this for a minute. When you decide to do an event you have an invitation that goes out initially announcing the event, then you have a personal invitation to your top 50 and your referral clients who you want to participate in the event. Then you send a reminder out the week prior to the event, another one the day before the event, and yet another one the day of the event. This shows excitement that you're going to see them that day. Then you get to have a face-to-face touch with them at the event where you literally get to give hugs, shake hands, and "kiss the babies", if you will.

Christy recommends hiring a photographer whose job it is to shoot video and great photography to create a collage and to record any client testimonials or raving fans who happen to be at the event. The follow-up email from the event shows pictures of people having a great time, individual pictures of you with your clients shaking hands, and the difference it makes in the community when the donations are made or the giveaway is executed.

The beautiful thing is you've had six to eight non-sales related touches with everyone in your database around each event. You have heard it said that agents don't receive many referrals from people they do business with, even though the clients are happy. It's simply because they're practicing "Secret Agency" - where they show up, do the transaction, kick butt in the negotiation, follow-up, and execute the close, and then they head off into the sunset never to be heard from again. Brandon calls it going into "Ghost Mode". I call them "Kung Fu closers" :) Events eliminate Secret Agency and are guaranteed to create more Raving Referrals.

As Christy's story continues, she is now a 7-figure team leader, broker/owner, and Master Coach with WSS. She has crafted a formula for hosting successful events that not only generate referrals but also strengthen community ties. Her approach is a blend of strategic planning, Workman tools and systems, personal engagement, and meticulous follow-up, creating a seamless experience that leaves a lasting impression on attendees.

Christy's formula begins with careful planning and theming of each event utilizing the Workman Agile to ensure that every detail is tailored to resonate with her audience - including her Top 50, past clients, and vendors - from the choice of venue to the activities offered. This thoughtful preparation sets the stage for meaningful interactions and creates an inviting atmosphere where guests feel valued and appreciated.

A critical component of Christy's strategy is the personal touch she adds through her team. Prior to the event, each agent reaches out to their clients with personalized messages and videos, building anticipation and ensuring a strong turnout. This direct communication not only reinforces relationships but also demonstrates Christy's commitment to her clients' experience.

During the event, Christy, along with her COO Samantha, who is also now a Master Coach with Workman, emphasizes the importance of engagement. She and her team are present, shaking hands and having genuine conversations with attendees. They utilize check-in sheets to gather information about guests' real estate needs, ensuring that no opportunity is missed. This proactive approach allows Christy to identify potential leads and maintain a comprehensive understanding of her clients' interests.

The final piece of Christy's formula is intentional follow-up. After the event, her team diligently contacts attendees to thank them for their participation and inquire about any real estate needs. This systematic follow-up reinforces the connections made during the event and keeps Christy top of mind for future opportunities.

Through this well-orchestrated process, Christy Buck has mastered the art of hosting events that not only generate referrals but also cultivate a sense of community and trust. Her formula is a testament to the power of personal engagement and strategic planning in building a successful referral-based business.

Hyper-Local Social Farming

Another way to utilize this strategy is by farming specific communities and hosting community impact events. By focusing on specific HOA communities, you can develop deep relationships with residents, establish yourself as the top trusted real estate expert, and ultimately win more listings.

The key to success in hyper-local farming is consistent engagement, offering value, and fostering connections that go beyond transactions. HOAs are naturally unified by shared rules and amenities, making them ideal for REALTORs to create targeted campaigns that resonate with residents and build long-term trust.

A highly effective way to implement hyper-local social farming is by using some of the 100+ Community Impact Guides available at HOA.com/impact. These guides and checklists provide you with the blueprints and tools to host meaningful community events, share local resources, and highlight services that benefit HOA residents. Hosting events such as neighborhood clean-ups, family fun days, or educational workshops not only brings the community together but also positions you as a Community Champion and advocate for the neighborhood. By serving as a community concierge who adds value and builds connections, REALTORs can strengthen their relationships with HOA boards and homeowners, creating a steady stream of referrals and listings.

Beyond winning listings, hyper-local social farming helps create unity through community. When you organize events, you're fostering a sense of belonging and pride among residents. This unity not only improves the quality of life within the neighborhood but also makes it easier for you to market the area to potential sellers and buyers. By embracing a community-first mindset, you can differentiate yourself, strengthen your reputation, and create a sustainable business model centered on relationships and referrals. Hyper-local social farming isn't just about real estate—it's about building thriving, connected communities.

The Ultimate Wishman

One of the favorite people Brandon had the pleasure of meeting was Frank Shankwitz, co-founder of the Make-A-Wish Foundation. Changing lives and granting wishes is what Frank dedicated his life to. If you haven't seen the movie Wishman about Frank's life, you owe it to yourself to watch this heartwarming film. You'll be glad you did.

While serving as an Arizona Highway Patrol officer, Frank had the honor of granting a wish for a 7-year-old boy named Chris who was battling leukemia. Turns out this boy had a dream of being a Highway Patrol Motorcycle Officer like his heroes, Ponch and John, from the television show, "CHiPs". After hearing of Chris' desire, Frank and a few of his fellow officers sprang into action and made Chris' dream come true. They had a uniform custom-crafted for Chris and gave him an old police badge and a "Smokey Bear" hat so he would feel like a real cop. Frank even set up a special course so Chris could drive a battery-powered motorcycle and qualify for the officer's wings he so deeply desired. A few short days later, Chris' body gave up the fight, and on May 3, 1980, he passed away.

This event led Frank to found Make-A-Wish to grant wishes for other sick children. Not long ago, I asked Frank what helped the charity become the global force for the good that it is today. Frank's answer was simple and powerful, "Disneyland." Turns out the first official wish the start-up charity granted was taking 7-year-old Frank 'Bopsy' Salazar to Disneyland.

This powerful partnership created massive visibility for both organizations and inspired millions of people to donate and do more for others in need. What started as a simple way to help a dying boy fulfill his wish, has led to over 450,000 children having their dreams fulfilled.

Over the years, Disney has invested millions of dollars promoting the impact they have made by granting wishes for Make-A-Wish kids. Every time a mom watches a commercial or story of a dying child's wish being fulfilled at Disneyland, it boosts loyalty and wins Disney another fan of the brand.

Starting Small Makes a Big Difference

The good news is that you don't have to create your own charity to tap into the power of cause-related marketing. You can simply raise awareness, funds, and support for great causes and charities already doing good work.

If you're curious how I (Brandon) got started as a Charity Champion, you're going to love the next chapter.

Everyone loves to have fun. That's why client appreciation events are a great way to recognize and reward your best clients and referral partners.

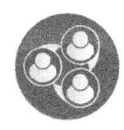

Chapter 10:
Referral of a Lifetime

Brandon's Story

My favorite referral of all time was to Mark Victor Hansen, co-author of the best-selling book series Chicken Soup for the Soul. Mark is an amazing man who has appeared on Oprah, CNN, and The Today Show, as well as in Time Magazine, U.S. News & World Report, USA Today, The New York Times, and Entrepreneur Magazine.

Among Mark's many achievements is his Guinness book world record for selling the most non-fiction books in the history of the world, with over 600 million books sold. That's a staggering number that still blows my mind.

I was referred to Mark by one of his closest friends back in 2004 when I was serving as a volunteer on the Corporate Industry Council for the charity Northwest Medical Teams, which has since been rebranded to Medical Teams International (MedicalTeams.org). This faith-based charity provides emergency medical relief in response to floods, famine, and other natural disasters.

I got involved after hearing one of their volunteer doctors share his story of taking what I call a "voluntour" trip over to Africa. The doctor recounted his story of 18-hour days spent caring for countless patients. No matter how many patients he treated, each day ended with a mother chasing the van crying, "What about my child?" The doctor's heartbreaking story stirred my heart into action, so I accepted the invitation and started raising money and awareness for the work they were doing.

The Perfect Choice

The biggest fundraiser of the year for Northwest Medical Teams was their annual Spirit of Life Awards, where they would honor a local titan of business for their impact on the community. Knowing I was a fan of personal development training, I was asked to help secure the featured speaker for the luncheon. Having just read, The One Minute Millionaire - The Enlightened Way to Wealth by Mark Victor Hansen and Robert Allen, I knew their message of doing well while doing good would be a perfect fit for this audience and might encourage the attendees to give more.

As fortune would have it, a financial advisor friend named Al Sizer had known Mark for over 30 years. It turns out Mark and Al came up together on the public speaking circuit back in the 1970s and had built a special friendship forged over three decades of traveling together and speaking at the same events.

After working up the courage to ask Al to ask Mark to speak at the event, I was beyond excited when Al called back, saying Mark's calendar was available that day and he was interested in helping.

After learning Mark's speaking fee, it was clear the charity couldn't afford him. After all, any fee NW Med paid would reduce the total impact the charity made, which was the entire reason for the event. That's when I made the courageous step of committing to cover Mark's speaker fee myself. Fortune favors the bold, so I gave my financial commitment and took a deep breath of faith, knowing that paying it forward always has a high ROI.

Two for the Price of One

What happened next was amazing. When coordinating the details with Mary, Mark's Vice President, she was so inspired by the cause we were supporting that she generously offered to have Mark speak in the evening at no additional cost in addition to the lunch event. This meant we were able to put on two events while he was in town.

Again, I said "YES" and quickly went to work producing an additional evening event we called "Success with Integrity," with my company, Integrity Lending, as the event's premier sponsor. I invited my loan officers to invite their top clients and referral partners to join us for this fun, feel-good, celebrity event. I have to tell you, the pride and unity this event brought to my team was immeasurable and was celebrated for months.

The morning of May 18, 2004, I had the honor of joining Mark Victor Hansen and Al Sizer for breakfast, along with three representatives of NW Med, including the CEO Bas Vanderzahn, the development director Brad Thomas who I had been working with for months, and the Chairman of the board Tom "TC" Crawford who I'm good friends with to this day.

During our breakfast, Mark asked about my companies and nonchalantly shared, "I can easily refer you a billion dollars in commercial loans," at which point quick calculations of the commissions and income that represented flashed through my head. That was the moment it hit me just how influential this man was and how impactful his endorsement could be for both my companies and me personally.

Throughout the two events of that day, Mark inspired and entertained over 500 people, helping us raise donations that delivered over $1.2 million worth of medical aid and supplies to those in need. As you can imagine, it was a day I will never forget.

As he closed his final presentation of the night, Mark made an offer for those who wanted to learn more. I immediately went to the back of the room and bought every CD and book he had for sale, including *Dreams Don't Have Deadlines, The Power of Focus,* and *The Aladdin Factor – How to Ask for and Get Anything You Want.*

The following week, as my wife and I traveled to Maui, I spent much of the trip listening to Mark mentor me through his audios. Mark's masterful training expanded my thinking and helped me reframe what was possible for my life.

During each of Mark's talks, he challenged the audience to make a list of 101 goals, including the date each person planned to achieve every goal they set. Since my wife goes to bed early, I spent hours each night on the beach, under the stars dreaming of all I hoped to achieve over my lifetime. By the end, I had created 338 short and long-term goals.

One of my top ambitions was to enroll Mark Victor Hansen to become my personal mentor. After returning from Maui, I gathered my nerve and made what felt like the scariest call I had ever made, asking Mark to be my personal mentor. He graciously agreed and has impacted my life in countless ways since I stepped out in faith and asked for what I wanted.

Mark had no idea, but one of the goals I wrote on that beach was, "To have Mark Victor Hansen write about me in a book by May 28, 2005." A few months after writing down that goal, Mark called and said, "Robert Allen and I are writing our follow-up to The One Minute Millionaire which will be called

Cracking the Millionaire Code. We'd like to feature you in the book. Would you be okay with that?" Excitedly, I said "YES," and almost as if by divine design, Cracking the Millionaire Code was published on May 31, 2005.

Dreams Fulfilled

Within 12 months of following Mark's system and writing down my goals, I had traveled to Asia, Europe, Africa, and South America for business. These were foreign lands I had only dreamt of traveling to before soaking in Mark's Mentorship. Before meeting Mark, the largest transaction I had been involved with was a $10 million development loan. Now, I was working on international financings of $200 million; twenty times larger than any transaction I had been involved in before Mark telling the world about me!

You can just imagine the clients and opportunities that the book brought because of the credibility and social proof of Mark's endorsement and promotion. When a celebrity or company with massive authority and influence endorses and promotes you, it creates tremendous credibility that unlocks lucrative opportunities. It also expands your vision for what's possible.

Within weeks of writing out my goals, Mark invited me to be a VIP guest of his MEGA Book Marketing, MEGA Info-Marketing, and MEGA Speaking Empire conferences. He routinely had me stand and introduce myself and share how I could help the audience. He later asked me to teach finance to his Enlightened Millionaire Institute Inner Circle both in the U.S. and abroad.

Around the World in 30 Days

That book became a turning point in my career, not only because of the business opportunities that came from readers of the book, but more importantly because the experience was powerful proof of our human ability to create and manifest anything we want. The key is to get clear on exactly what we want to achieve, accomplish, or experience. Of the 338 goals I wrote on that beach, over 100 were achieved in the first 12 months alone, a few of which included:

- Enroll Mark Victor Hansen as my personal mentor by 7/7/2004
- Have Mark Victor Hansen write about me in a book published by 5/28/2005
- Have Mark Victor Hansen invite me to his private home in Kona, Hawaii, by 5/28/2005
- Start a 501(c)3 charity by 5/28/2005

- Travel to New York City, London, Hong Kong, China, and Africa by 5/28/2005
- Hike the Great Wall of China by 5/28/2005
- Meet U2's lead singer Bono by 5/28/2005

Prior to meeting Mark, I had barely left the country. Within one year of his mentoring, I took a 30-day around-the-world trip Eastward from Portland, Oregon to London, England then off to Hong Kong, Macau, and Guangzhou, China, before taking the final leg to Caracas, Venezuela and Bucaramunga, Colombia.

As I met new clients and prospective partners, I gave them a copy of the Cracking the Millionaire Code book with my business card inserted on page 42 which featured my personal, professional, and charitable pursuits. That book elevated my status with my clients, team, and referral partners while simultaneously attracting new clients from around the world – just as Mark had predicted.

Mark taught me the power of specificity in goal setting, including writing down the exact date you plan to achieve each goal. In case you missed it, Cracking the Millionaire Code was published three days after the goal date I had typed on my laptop less than one year prior, a fact that astounds me to this day.

My purpose in sharing this story with you is two-fold. First, I want you to truly understand that you can create anything you want in your life when you get clear, put it in writing, and commit yourself to achieve your desire or dream. You will have to take massive action and ask others to assist you, but you can quickly transform your life simply by transforming your thinking.

Second, I hope to give you a vision for the power of getting endorsed, recommended, and promoted by people and companies that have the ability to take your business to an entirely new level.

The key takeaway here is that just one key referral partner can transform your business and your life.

Raving Referrals in Action: Cleve Gaddis and the Power of Genuine Service and Community Engagement

In Johns Creek, Georgia, Cleve Gaddis has become a beacon of genuine service and community engagement. As a WSS Master Coach, team leader, business consultant, radio show host, renowned speaker, and Co-Owner of

Modern Traditions Realty Group, in Atlanta, Georgia, his journey into the world of real estate began with an unexpected twist. As a teenager, Cleve discovered his knack for sales while running a small landscaping business. His ability to connect with people led him to a unique opportunity with Electrolux, where he honed his skills selling vacuum cleaners door-to-door. This foundation in sales taught him a valuable lesson: referrals don't have to be a forced endeavor if your purpose in business is to serve others beyond their expectations.

Cleve's philosophy of service was put to the test when he became involved in the zoning committee of his community association. Despite often arguing against a local developer's projects, Cleve's unwavering commitment to the community earned him unexpected respect. After a developer's passing, his widow, Linda, sought Cleve's expertise for a significant real estate deal. She remembered Cleve's dedication and integrity, saying, "I need somebody who knows how to fight for me like you were fighting for the community." This trust led to two multi-million dollar transactions, showcasing the power of serving with integrity.

Cleve's community involvement didn't stop there. As the co-founder of Johns Creek Beautification, he helped transform the city's medians and right-of-ways into beautifully landscaped areas, fostering a sense of pride among residents. His leadership in the Community Association and also on the Economic Development Committee further solidified his reputation as a dedicated community advocate. These efforts not only beautified the city and encouraged economic growth, but also created lasting connections that fueled his real estate business.

In addition to his community work, Cleve hosts a real estate radio show and podcast. This platform allows him to educate and engage with the Atlanta community, sharing insights about the local market and highlighting the city's unique features. The show has become a powerful tool for building relationships, as listeners often feel a personal connection with Cleve. One client who was also an appraiser even remarked, "I feel like I know you. I know everything about you because I hear you every Saturday on the radio."

Cleve's success is a testament to the WSS approach of Serving Regardless of Opportunity. By focusing on genuine service and community engagement, Cleve has built a thriving business with a significant portion of his transactions coming from referrals. His story exemplifies the power of authentic connections and the impact of serving others with integrity.

Action Items:

1. **Embrace Genuine Service**: Focus on serving clients beyond their expectations to naturally generate referrals. This is especially important when things get tough.
2. **Engage with Your Community**: Get involved in local organizations and initiatives to build lasting relationships and enhance your reputation, but not to build business. As your reputation grows, so will your business.
3. **Leverage Media Platforms**: Use radio shows, podcasts, or other media to share your expertise and connect with a broader audience. Again, genuinely serve your audience with whatever you're sharing.
4. **Systematize Follow-Up**: Implement a structured follow-up system for past clients, including regular mailings, newsletters, and client events. Your face-to-face time with past clients and people from your sphere is the most valuable time you spend.
5. **Celebrate Challenges**: Embrace difficult situations as opportunities to strengthen client relationships and demonstrate unwavering support. Change your perception of struggles being "inconvenient or uncomfortable" to those struggles being a great opportunity to forge an even deeper connection with your client.

You just have to A-S-K to G-E-T

After eight years in retail, selling satellite dishes and hot tubs, I (Verl) realized that that business wasn't going to be my future. Massive changes in the industry, the introduction of a 18-in satellite dish replacing the 10-ft satellite dish where we made all of our margin, and a series of unexpected events caused us to find ourselves in a situation where we couldn't financially or physically climb out of the hole we were in. The decision was made to close our business. It was heartfelt and there were tears shed and I felt like I was letting my family down.

During my going out of business sale that lasted 6 months (by the way it was the best sale I ever held), a gentleman walked into my store on his way to the new Ultimate Electronics they just opened up down the street. He saw my going out of business sign and everything must go and popped in on his way to make a purchase. I greeted him with enthusiasm and asked how I could help. He simply said, "I'm looking to buy a home theater and would like to know what my budget needs to be." I sat down with him and gave him a full demo showing him all of the amazing things a home theater could do. I remember I played a couple of Laser Discs (that will give you an idea how long ago this was). When I got done demonstrating the home theater he asked, "how much is it?" Knowing that I needed to sell something in the worst way, I simply asked the question, "What's your budget?" He answered with "I don't want to spend more than $10,000." That was an easy answer for me, $9860.00. He smiled and looked up at me and said, "What if I bought more than one could you give me a little better deal?" I asked him what he had in mind and he said, "I'd like to buy seven $10,000 home theaters."

If you can imagine, my leg started to bounce up and down like a sewing machine because I was nervous, now feeling like I had a $70,000 sale on the line that I couldn't screw up. I thought about it for a minute, gave him a price, and he said okay right there on the showroom floor. He wrote me a check for $35,000 - one half of the total purchase price so that I would install each of these home theaters in his married children's homes before Christmas. The Humbling part of this story is that he knew I was closing my doors in just a few days and still trusted me enough to write the check. He ended up being a production builder in Salt Lake City and was the cause for me getting into real estate.

My early days in real estate were phenomenal. I learned so much and I sold a lot of houses. I earned more money than I ever made in retail and was taking great care of my family. One day I had an old friend walk in the model home and asked me if I wanted to help him do seminars to real estate agents teaching them that they could actually make more money if they use technology programs like a CRM, a paperless listing presentation, and a digital camera. I was reluctant and said, "No, not really interested", but it was good to catch up with him. He then came back to me two months later and said he'd hired a broker out of Utah County that had done a couple events with them and they ended up selling zero of their solution and asked me one more time if I'd be willing to help him.

His name was Brent Gray. Brent and I decided we were going to put on 50-people, half day seminars, bring a half dozen laptops to the back of the room, and sell a $4,000 to $7,000 package to real estate agents to teach them how to make money with technology. While the complete details were a little bit sketchy and we really didn't know what we were doing, we were off to the races; the company was called Automation Quest.

Every time we would do an event Brent would sit at the computer and run my slides pointing to what I was supposed to talk about next. He also took pages of notes of all the things that I did well and all the areas where I needed to improve - things like using filler words such as "and", "um", or "okay" and calling the audience guys. He also questioned things like stories I told and whether or not they tied in to a closing or if they had a real meaningful part of the class. Each time we offered the class we did a little bit better and a little bit better selling more and more technology. I would have to say that Brent Gray is one of the major forces of my success, and the reason I've been able to build a career as a professional speaker is because he cared about me improving. We have continued to be business partners for more than 15 years now, and he still works with me today at WSS.

The first time we signed up to do the RE/MAX convention it was in Orlando, Florida. Brent and I signed up to play in a golf tournament so we could get to know a few people and see if we could make the event profitable. We were both nervous and spent money out of our own pockets to be there. Brent teamed up with a great foursome and played with a gentleman by the name of Chuck Lemire, who was the number two leader of RE/MAX of New England. They got along well and had fun playing golf and as I got on the bus to go back to the hotel, Brent introduced me to Chuck. We had a fun discussion about who we are and what we do and Chuck felt like it was a perfect fit, so he invited us to do a tech tour in RE/MAX of New England.

This was the launching pad for what became a multi-million dollar company. We went through New England putting on seminars and offering technology to agents. They all were excited about it and they ended up buying lots of products and when we got done, I simply asked Chuck if there were other regional directors like him who might be able to benefit from a tech tour like this. While the energy was high and the enthusiasm was off the chart, Chuck started making calls. He introduced me to RE/MAX of Florida and RE/MAX Mountain States. Each of these regions booked events and we became known as the top technology company for Real Estate.

When we got to RE/MAX of Florida we sold over a million dollars worth of computers and software in just 7 days. It was mind-blowing the energy and enthusiasm that happened as a result of one single referral from Chuck Lemire. RE/MAX of California had a similar result and we developed unbelievable relationships with regions like RE/MAX of Texas, Mid States, Dixie regions, Canada, and many more. The energy and excitement was so high around Automation Quest that when Homes.com, in their early days, started to raise capital, they looked at Automation Quest as a partner whose revenue could help them in their early stages of capital. Our several million dollars in revenue generated tens of millions of dollars in venture capital through the acquisition. I can honestly say that a single referral from a golf tournament turned into millions of dollars and launched the careers of many people in this industry. Almost 20 years later we continue to have a great relationship with RE/MAX and the RE/MAX regions, as well as many other brands. And by doing the right thing it allowed us to be able to continue to go back with different products and services over the years.

Raving Referrals in Action: Ryan Young, CEO of Fello, on Viewing Team Members as Business Partners

In real estate, as in most industries, the power of referrals can transform not just businesses, but lives. As I (Verl) sat down with Ryan Young, CEO at Fello and a seasoned real estate professional with The Young Team, in Cleveland, Ohio, his stories of impactful referrals resonated with everything we teach in Raving Referrals.

Ryan shared a remarkable tale of how a seemingly small referral blossomed into a substantial opportunity. He recounted referring Jen, a dedicated team member, to a new construction builder. Initially, the referral was for a non-monetizable task, simply to assist the builder with an existing project. However, Jen's exceptional service and dedication turned this small opportunity into something significant and remarkable.

"Jen did such an amazing job in that relationship that he ended up listing a 42-home site community with her. It started with one, which led to the second one, and ultimately, to an exclusive on everything."

This referral not only led to substantial business, but also strengthened the relationship with the builder, showcasing the ripple effect of a well-placed referral.

The key to Ryan's success lies in his approach to referrals. He views his team members as business partners, introducing them as such to clients.

"Everyone is my business partner. I'd like to introduce you to my business partner, Jen. The reason why I'm doing so is because she actually specializes in (exactly whatever you're looking for)."

This approach builds trust and ensures that clients receive the best service possible.

"I have such great team members, and I've invested so much into them that if any challenges arise, it rarely comes back to me. And if it does come back to me, I realize I have the wrong team member, and they're not getting any more referrals. What usually happens with these referral handoffs to my business partners is that I get a call six months later and I'm told, 'I can't thank you enough for introducing me', because there is trust built into my relationships which is why we get the results we do."

For those looking to harness the power of referrals, Ryan's story offers valuable insights. Here are some action items to consider:

1. **Empower Your Team**: Treat your team members as business partners. Empower them to take ownership of client relationships and trust them to deliver exceptional service.

2. **Focus on Contribution**: Approach referrals with a mindset of contribution. Seek to understand clients' needs deeply and provide value beyond immediate transactions.

3. **Build a Culture of Trust**: Cultivate a team culture where trust is paramount. Ensure that referrals are handled with care and that clients receive consistent, high-quality service.

4. **Leverage Relationships**: Use referrals as a tool to build and strengthen relationships. A well-placed referral can open doors to new opportunities and long-term partnerships.

By adopting these principles, real estate professionals can create a referral network that not only drives business growth but also enriches the lives of clients and team members alike.

Chapter 11:
Wealth Through Workshops

After meeting and being mentored by Mark Victor Hansen, one of the most important lessons he taught me was the power of producing events. There's simply no faster or more effective way to boost your expert status than educating audiences in person or online.

Hosting educational workshops is one of the most powerful ways for you to build wealth by strengthening relationships, increasing referrals, and establishing yourself as the go-to real estate expert in your community. When you take the time to teach and share your expertise, you position yourself as a trusted resource who genuinely cares about educating and empowering your clients and prospects.

Workshops are more than just events—they're opportunities to connect with your community on a deeper level, attract quality leads, and turn attendees into loyal clients who see you as their top real estate advisor. By hosting workshops, you'll set yourself apart in a competitive market. Teaching relevant and engaging topics allows you to build trust, showcase your professionalism, and demonstrate your value beyond transactions.

People do business with those they trust, and workshops are an excellent way to establish that trust while expanding your network. You can even invite local partners, like lenders or home service providers, to co-host and add extra value to your events. Whether in person or online, workshops amplify your visibility, enhance your reputation, and create a steady flow of referrals and opportunities.

The key is to fill your workshops with as many of your Perfect Prospects as possible so that you maximize the revenue you generate for your business. When it comes to holding educational events, quality trumps quantity every time. It is better to teach a class to 10 investors or business owners who match your Perfect Prospect Profile than to have 100 unqualified people in your audience. Be sure your event invitations and promotions are targeted to appeal to your ideal clients and Perfect Prospects.

Workshops Can Create Referral Relationships

As a real estate professional, creating and maintaining relationships is essential for the growth and success of your business. One effective way to establish these relationships is through workshops. There are several forms of workshops to explore, such as online sessions or in-person partner workshops. Let's take a closer look at the benefits of these opportunities and how you can get started.

10 Workshop Topics You Can Teach to Attract Clients and Grow Referrals:

1. **First-Time Homebuyer Guide**: Help buyers navigate the home-buying process step-by-step.
2. **Selling Your Home for Top Dollar**: Share proven strategies to increase a home's value and sell faster.
3. **Investing in Real Estate**: Teach the basics of building wealth through property investment.
4. **Navigating the HOA Process**: Explain CC&Rs, fees, and what buyers and sellers need to know.
5. **Preparing Your Home for Sale**: Give staging and repair tips to help sellers maximize profits.
6. **Down Payment Assistance Programs**: Educate buyers on resources that make homeownership more accessible.
7. **Understanding Market Trends**: Keep your audience informed on current real estate trends.
8. **Renovations That Add Value**: Show homeowners how to remodel with ROI in mind.

9. **Short-Term Rentals 101**: Teach buyers how to turn properties into income-generating assets.
10. **The Home Buying Process Explained**: Simplify the buying journey for prospective clients.

Partnering with Industry Professionals If you are a REALTOR looking to expand your network but are hesitant about hosting a workshop on your own, consider partnering with a title representative also seeking to grow their business. Collaborating with a mortgage lender, financial advisor, CPA, real estate attorney, or property manager who is interested in teaching workshops to attract new clients is another option. These partnerships provide support in the planning and execution of the workshop while also helping you reach a broader audience.

Hosting Lunch and Learn Sessions

A popular format for hosting workshops is the "lunch and learn" or "brown bag lunch" session. These casual events encourage a relaxed atmosphere and facilitate easy networking among attendees. Be sure to develop engaging topics like Top 50 and invite experts in your field to present at your workshops. The costs of these sessions can be shared with your industry partner, making it a win-win situation for both parties.

Expanding Your Network Through Workshops

By hosting workshops, you not only introduce your network to your industry partner but also have the opportunity to meet their connections. These events promote mutually beneficial networking opportunities and create lasting relationships within the real estate industry.

Whether taught online or in-person, webinars and workshops provide opportunities for real estate professionals to build valuable relationships while expanding their knowledge. Embrace these opportunities and leverage the support of your industry partners to grow your business and network.

7 Super Strategies to Fill Your Events with Perfect Prospects

The following seven time-tested and proven strategies will help you fill your next event with quality candidates for your services:

1. Invite Your Social Sphere

The best way to fill your events is with your own clients. They are the most likely to use your services again! In addition to your clients, you should also promote your upcoming events to both your personal and professional databases. Since these people already know, like, and trust you, they are likely to recommend your event once you have asked for their help and identified who the event will be most helpful for. If you charge for your events, you may want to offer a few gift guest passes people can give to their friends, clients, and colleagues. Just be sure to identify your Perfect Prospect Profile, so they invite the right type of people to your event.

Here are a few ways you can invite hundreds of prospects in a matter of minutes:

- Email flyers and invitations to family, friends, and people in your clubs, churches, or charities

- Post events in your social network through Facebook, X (Twitter), Instagram, and LinkedIn

- Email links to your training videos and post the links on your website, blog, and social sites

- Send LinkedIn messages to each of your current contacts inviting them to attend your event

- You can also print up and mail or hand out tickets to your next event, so people have something physical in hand which increases the perceived value of the event. The key is to spread the word far and wide with people who are most likely to attend and invite others.

2. Develop Promotional Partnerships

Another great strategy that helps leverage the recommendations of others is to partner with businesses, charities, and associations that already serve your ideal clients. By offering to teach a class or give guest passes to your workshop as a gift to their clients, customers, members, and social media followers, you give them a high-perceived value item they can provide at no or low cost. Simply ask about the biggest challenges their stakeholders face and offer training that solves those challenges. The more you help them win customer loyalty, the more passionately they will promote your events.

We will cover this in detail in Chapter 17 on cross-promoting with your partners.

3. Invite Your Clients to Invite Their Clients

There's no disputing the power of a personal recommendation. That's why one of the best ways to fill your seminars and workshops is to have your current or past clients invite their customers, clients, employees, and strategic alliances to attend your event. After all, as they share their personal story of the impact you and your training have had on their business, their contacts will be much more inclined to attend your events and to use your services afterward. This is especially powerful if you serve businesses or business owners since they will likely have a large database of your ideal clients. Just call up your best clients and let them know you've been thinking about their business. You can go on to explain that you have an idea you think will help them better serve their current clients and attract more clients at no cost to them. At that point, you've captured their attention and interest. Then you can walk them through your idea of providing exclusive training for their clients and prospects. You can even have them participate as a partner/sponsor for your upcoming workshop.

4. Co-Produce Events with Others

One of the most effective ways to promote your event to a larger audience is to co-produce seminars or workshops with other businesses or professionals who are looking to attract the same ideal client profile.

For example, suppose you are holding a real estate investing workshop for business owners. In that case, you might consider partnering with business coaches, CPAs, attorneys, financial advisors, banks, or commercial insurance brokers who serve the B2B market.

By partnering and sharing the costs of promoting and producing your seminar or workshop, you help other businesses gain access to new prospects at a reduced marketing expense for everyone. Plus, as your partners get new clients from the event, they will refer them back to you since you are the reason they won the business to begin with. This strategy also allows you to highly target your marketing while positioning you as the trusted expert and increasing your perceived credibility and expertise to a wider audience.

5. Speak at Other Events

There are numerous organizations that serve your ideal clients and are constantly looking for interesting speakers for their meetings and events. You gain tremendous credibility and visibility by volunteering to speak at events held by local Chambers of Commerce, banks, universities, the SBA, networking groups, and trade shows. Nonprofit organizations and associations that support and serve your target market are also great opportunities to reach prospective clients.

Once you have established your expertise throughout your training, the audience will be much more interested in attending your future workshops. Just be sure to include a closing slide that promotes your services and upcoming events. In addition, consider handing out worksheets that include details on your future workshops and offer your training services to those in need of a speaker. After all, sometimes, you need to do some shameless self-promotion to grow your business.

Be sure you have a call to action at the end of your presentation, letting your audience know the next steps you want them to take to move forward with you. Consider offering a free market analysis report, personalized staging, home decor assessment or seller's starter kit. Doing this each time you speak or teach will help fill your calendar with speaking engagements and bring more attendees to your events and clients to your business.

6. Offer To Reciprocate Referrals

As a REALTOR, offering to reciprocate referrals with partners who promote your workshop creates a win-win relationship that amplifies your reach and strengthens your network. When you collaborate with lenders, title companies, interior designers, contractors, or other service providers in your market, you gain access to their client base and establish yourself as a trusted professional in their network. By agreeing to refer your clients to these partners in return, you build goodwill, encourage mutual trust, and create a partnership that benefits everyone involved. This approach not only fills your workshop with highly engaged attendees but also positions you as a connector who delivers value to both clients and industry peers.

Reciprocal referrals also showcase your commitment to fostering long-term partnerships, which can lead to more consistent leads and opportunities over time. Partners who feel valued and supported are more likely to advocate for your services and recommend you to their clients. For example, a contractor who promotes your workshop may send you buyers who later become sellers, creating a full circle of opportunities. Additionally, these partnerships strengthen your brand as a community-focused REALTOR, increasing your credibility and influence in the market. By leveraging reciprocal referrals, you create a powerful network of advocates that expands your business while helping your clients connect with the trusted resources they need.

7. Outsource to Assistants or Interns

As a busy professional, one of your biggest challenges is most likely time management. That's why you should consider delegating your promotional activities to an assistant or intern. This will help you maximize higher profit activities that you enjoy more. By training an assistant to manage your promotional activities, you focus your valuable time meeting with profitable prospects and clients.

Just use the list we've given you and create a plan for them to execute for you. If you don't already have staff who can help promote your events, just reach out to a local employment agency to hire a temp who can make the calls for you.

You can also contact a university or business school in your area and let them know you'd like to offer an internship for their students. You can usually find some great talent in the school of marketing with young adults eager to build their resumes and hungry for their first real job. While many will agree to do an unpaid internship with you, you may want to pay them a minimal hourly rate or a set amount for the quarter, so they are amply motivated. You can also make the internship unpaid but give them a bonus based on the number of attendees they help attract or actual clients that you close from the event.

Verlism: Events Drive Revenue. This is more true now than ever before. Events really do drive revenue whether you're doing a business planning event for local business owners or you're teaching a first time home buyer seminar on how people who are currently renting could, even in today's circumstances, purchase a home showing the tax advantages, interest benefits, and cost of home ownership. A well thought out event can literally bring dozens of clients and their friends into the world of home ownership. Events Drive Revenue!

These seven powerful strategies can help you fill your events with profitable prospects for your business. These strategies will also help you attract top, trusted pros which we will cover in the next chapter.

If you are loving this book and would like to teach this content to other real estate agents and professionals who serve homeowners, consider becoming a Raving Referrals Certified Trainer. Our online certification process gives you a fast, easy, and fun way to elevate your expert authority while being on stages speaking to audiences of your perfect partners.

We will not only provide you the slides and training materials, we'll also teach you our proven process of partnering with real estate schools, title insurance companies and real estate associations who will be grateful to have you teach and train their agents and home service Pros. That is the absolute best way to stand out from your competition and draw in other real estate agents and home service pros who will be asking to partner with you because of your elevated authority.

Check out RavingReferrals.com/trainer for more information on how you can become a Raving Referrals Certified Trainer.

RavingReferrals.com/trainer

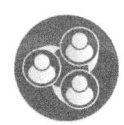

Chapter 12:
Partner with Top Trusted Pros

When it comes to building a steady stream of Raving Referrals, one of the most underutilized and most effective strategies is to partner with other professionals who already serve homeowners. That's because businesses and professionals who are serving homeowners consistently hear opportunities from people who are thinking of buying, selling or investing in real estate. Plus, when a respected professional or business owner recommends you to their clients, customers, and contractors, it increases trust and accelerates revenue.

While a happy client may know three or four ideal clients for you, a property manager, divorce or estate planning attorney may have three or four referrals for you each week or even each day. As you build your relationship and help them understand how you can help the people they serve, they will refer a steady source of profitable prospects.

Your job is to help them see you and your service as the solution their clients and customers are looking for. Once they view you as a trusted solution helping them solve problems for their clients, they will refer you more often because you add value to both them and their customers. The key is for you to be the solution to their client's problems.

Over the past decade, we have surveyed thousands of business owners and professionals, asking them to identify how many referral partners they have who refer at least one new prospect every 90 days. What has been surprising is that 32% of the professionals we surveyed said they had zero referral partners who sent them at least one referral in the past 90 days. These people reported having to constantly scramble and hunt for new business because they had no one sending them profitable prospects. As a result, only half of the people in this group reported achieving an annual income of $50,000 or more.

The second group, which comprised 47% of total respondents, reported having one or two referral partners. Although these people were getting a few referrals, they still found themselves in the bottom half of income earners in their companies or industries, with only 10% claiming to have achieved an annual income of $100,000 or more.

What was interesting was that the first two groups combined totaled 79% of everyone surveyed. Once again, the Pareto Principle (or 80/20 rule) proved to hold true.

The third group was made up of professionals who had three to nine referral partners, which equated to 19% of everyone surveyed. Over 70% of these people reported earning $100,000 or more per year, while under 20% of the first two groups achieved that income level.

Finally, the fourth group consisted of professionals claiming to have ten or more referral partners. What was shocking to our team was that only 2% of everyone who completed our survey was in this top group. Not surprisingly, this group reported much higher incomes, with respondents claiming annual earnings of more than $250,000 per year.

The key is to systematize the process, follow a personal touch system in reaching out, and remember that we give to receive, and you should track and make a practice out of giving a referral to each of your partners just as you ask them to do for you.

The Key to Success

I (Brandon) learned this strategy firsthand back in 1997 after starting as a mortgage loan officer. As I interviewed top producers in my firm and industry, I asked about their greatest source of business, and a common theme emerged. All of the top producers I interviewed revealed that the bulk of their business came from a handful of professionals they had built referral partnerships with. Without exception, their referral partners were all professionals who also served homeowners including REALTORs, insurance agents, financial planners, accountants, and attorneys along with home services providers like contractors, home inspectors, and appraisers.

Makes sense, doesn't it? After all, every one of these people shared the same ideal clients. Plus, they often had customers asking about interest rates and for recommendations and introductions to a trusted mortgage lender. My mission then became to add as much value to these people as possible, and generating referrals and opportunities for them was what they wanted most. Once I learned how to generate consistent leads to home buyers and sellers and was able to refer these people to my partner REALTORs, I locked up their loyalty which led to more business for us all.

Often, clients would share horror stories about their previous or current real estate agent. I would use these opportunities to introduce my partner agents sharing stories of how my agents went above and beyond for our mutual clients. People were thrilled to be referred to an agent they could trust and happily called my trusted agents rather than working with the agent they bumped into at an open house over the weekend. .

Best of all, since I had won the trust of these buyers and sellers, when I referred them to my top trusted REALTORs, I was able to transfer the trust I had built with the client onto my partner agents which led to higher client conversion rates, higher profitability, and a better overall service experience for everyone involved.

Assemble Your Power Team

To create your Power Team of trusted professionals committed to doing business with you, start by identifying the top industries that already serve your ideal clients.

At HOA.com, we serve homeowners and are building the #1 Referral Network for Professionals Who Serve Homeowners. Our company is literally in the business of helping people build their own trusted network of vetted and certified professionals who also serve homeowners. By helping these professionals connect, collaborate, and cross-promote each other, we help them generate more business by helping the people we serve together. Best of all, we've built the world's only community co-marketing engine that helps REALTORs like you turn your vendors into proactive partners who actually promote you to the homeowners they serve.

Power Partners

The list here outlines professions who serve homeowners. Write down names of the people you know in these industries:

Top 100 Home Service Categories

1. Accountants
2. Antiques
3. Appliance Sales/Repair
4. Appraisers
5. Artificial Turf
6. Awnings
7. Backflow Services
8. Barbeque Installation
9. Cabinetry
10. Carpenters
11. Carpet Cleaning
12. Carpet Installation
13. Chimney Repair
14. Contractors
15. Countertop Installation
16. Damage Restoration
17. Door Sales/Installation
18. Drywall Installation & Repair
19. Dumpster Rental
20. Electricians
21. Estate Planning Attorney
22. Excavation Services
23. Fences & Gates
24. Financial Advising
25. Fireplace Services
26. Flooring
27. Foundation Repair
28. Framing
29. Furniture Sales & Repair
30. Garage Door Services
31. General Contracting
32. Glass & Mirrors
33. Grout Services
34. Gutter Services
35. Handymen
36. Hardware Stores
37. Heating & Air Conditioning/HVAC
38. Home & Garden
39. Home Automation
40. Home Cleaning
41. Home Decor
42. Home Developers
43. Home Inspectors
44. Home Network Installation
45. Home Organization
46. Home Staging
47. Home Theatre Installation
48. Home Window Tinting
49. Homeowner Associations
50. Hot Tub Sales & Service
51. Insulation
52. Insurance
53. Interior Design
54. Irrigation
55. Junk Removal & Hauling
56. Kitchens & Baths
57. Kitchen Supplies
58. Landscape Architects
59. Landscaping
60. Lawn Maintenance
61. Life Insurance
62. Lighting
63. Locksmiths
64. Masonry/Concrete
65. Misting System Services
66. Mortgage Lenders
67. Movers
68. Nurseries & Gardening
69. Outdoor Furniture Stores
70. Packing Services
71. Painters
72. Pest Control
73. Pet Waste Removal
74. Plumbing
75. Pool Cleaners
76. Pool Construction
77. Pressure Washing
78. Property Management
79. Real Estate Agents
80. Real Estate Services
81. Recycling Center
82. Roofing
83. Rugs
84. Security Systems
85. Self Storage
86. Shades & Blinds
87. Sheds & Storage
88. Shutters
89. Siding
90. Snow Removal
91. Solar Installation
92. Stucco Services
93. Tiling
94. Tree Services
95. TV Mounting
96. Water Heater Installation/Repair
97. Water Purification Services
98. Waterproofing
99. Window Washing
100. Windows Installation

PARTNER WITH TOP TRUSTED PROS

Envision your power team with your Perfect Prospect in the center of the hub surrounded by all of the other service providers they entrust their business to. If you serve consumers or homeowners, your Power Team might look like this:

REALTOR
INSURANCE
MORTGAGE
FINANCIAL ADVISOR
HOMEOWNER
HVAC
PLUMBER
PAINTER
CONTRACTOR

While service workers, such as plumbers, electricians, and contractors were my primary source of real estate clients, I also received Raving Referrals from accountants, attorneys, and financial advisors whose clients indicated they were looking to buy or sell a home.

Once I won their trust and wowed their clients, it was easy to keep the referrals flowing. The key is to focus on building partnerships with business owners and professionals who serve homeowners or real estate investors.

This may be a great time to ask this simple question: "How can I make this work for me?" We have learned in training and coaching thousands of professionals that the systems work, but sometimes the student won't. You have to decide if you are willing to put in the work and make the effort. The results are shared in story after story. We can't wait to hear and share your success as a doer and a raving referral partner!

As you build your trusted team of referral partners, everyone will win more business together. In my case, I targeted remodelers because their clients usually needed financing. I helped the client refinance or get a home equity line of credit, which helped the remodeler get paid. A total win–win–win.

So, the question is, who do you want on your trusted team?

Identify Your Ideal Partners

What industries do you want to build referral partnerships with? Review the proceeding list and write down the professions that can bring you the most business.

1. _____
2. _____
3. _____
4. _____
5. _____
6. _____
7. _____
8. _____
9. _____
10. _____
11. _____
12. _____

Your network should include all the people you currently refer clients to including home inspectors, appraisers, insurance agents, painters, plumbers, landscapers, pest control, and so many more. As I promoted each of these trusted pros on my website, blog, newsletters, and events, I won their loyalty and became their go-to mortgage lender and the raving referrals flowed like a river.

To maximize your networking potential, think about how and where you engage with prospective partners. Focus on putting yourself in the path of opportunity, attending industry events, and actively participating in relevant community gatherings. By nurturing relationships with professionals across various sectors, you can create a robust referral network that will help drive business growth for all parties involved.

Remember, real estate professionals should not underestimate the power of networking with service providers beyond the traditional realm of finance and real estate. By engaging with a diverse group of professionals and being strategic in your conversations, you can create strong referral partnerships and set yourself apart in the competitive real estate industry.

Profitable Partnerships

Most likely, you know several people in these professions you just listed earlier in this chapter. Perhaps you've known them for years or even decades and have never bothered to ask about doing business together. You may have family, friends, or other connections you've never pursued professionally. If that's true for you, I'm happy to tell you that you are sitting on an absolute goldmine.

What if you show them a win–win–win system where everyone prospers by working together?

As you help them understand who and how you help, many will gladly offer to promote you, especially when you approach professionals strategically, which we will cover shortly.

For each of the industries you've identified, start by asking yourself...

1. Who do I already know, like, and trust in that industry?

2. Who do I already refer business to?

3. Who in each industry already refers business to me?

Asking these three questions will help you create a targeted list of complementary professionals who already know, like, and trust you. Since trust accelerates relationships, starting with people you know will dramatically speed up your referrals and revenue.

The Proven Referral Partner Script

Once you've identified your prospective partners, it's time to approach these professionals strategically. After 20-plus years of testing, here's what we've found works best for creating profitable partnerships. If you follow this proven script below, you'll have people lining up to meet with you.

Just say...

"Hi (name), the reason I'm calling is that I'm creating a team of professionals I'll be recommending to all my clients. I was thinking about you because I have a lot of clients who can benefit from your services. I'd love to sit down with you to discuss the possibility of adding you to my team and promoting you. When's a good time to get together and strategize?"

Imagine receiving that call from someone you've known for years who serves your ideal clients all day long. Wouldn't you be excited about the possibility of having them consistently referring clients to you? Of course you would! As long as they are someone you know, like, and trust.

When you follow this proven process, you can quickly create new referral partnerships with ease. But how do you create partnerships with target professions when you don't know anyone in that field?

Great question. Glad you asked.

Filling Gaps

As you start creating strategic alliances and profitable partnerships, there will undoubtedly be some gaps. You may find a few industries or professions where you don't know anyone in that field. That's when asking clients to introduce you to top professionals they know, like, and trust is a powerful way to expand your team and your referral business.

Asking your VIP clients to introduce you to their top professional service providers gives you quick and easy access to high-quality professionals with whom it otherwise might be challenging to develop a relationship.

The good news is that asking clients for introductions is extremely easy when you know how to do it. It also quickens your velocity to create profitable partnerships.

First, identify the profession to which you want to be introduced. Let's say you want to get connected with a quality CPA, for example. Just call up your client, or while sitting with them, simply say:

"Thanks so much for your time today. I'd like to ask for your help. As you may know, I am in the process of expanding my business, and I'm looking for a great CPA I can refer my clients to. I'm wondering if you know of any good CPAs you think I should meet. I'm planning to meet and interview two or three, and your CPA will be one of those I would like to meet with, not just for my personal business but also for the

opportunity to refer clients to them. Is there anyone you'd recommend I meet with?"

Once you ask, shut up and let them talk. It's normal to want to fill the space if they don't speak immediately but hold back and give them a few moments to think about who they can introduce you to. You will find most clients will be happy to help and introduce you to other professionals they use. Plus, since the introduction is coming from a mutual client, you already have something in common to start building rapport and trust with the other pro.

You can also post your request on social media. Not only will you increase the number of introductions you receive, but you will also let your clients and Social Sphere know they can turn to you and your team whenever they need help. You will be amazed to see top, trusted professionals reaching out to you proactively.

This strategy works extremely well because people love to help others. By giving them an opportunity to make an introduction, they are helping both you and the other professional they are introducing.

Ask for an Intro

Once your contact recommends someone for you to connect with, it's best to set the stage for the conversation. Just ask your contact to make an introduction and share the person's phone number so you can follow up proactively.

Simply say,

"Thanks so much for the introduction. Would you be willing to make a quick call or send them a text to tell them how we know each other and that I will be calling them (date and time of scheduled call)? Is there anything you think I should know before I call them?"

Using this approach, the person to whom you are being introduced will be expecting and even looking forward to your call... all before you even dial their digits.

Once you've been introduced, simply call the professional at the appointed time, mention your client's name, and share that they come highly recommended by your mutual client. This creates instant connection and is the common ground that opens the door and fast-tracks a mutually prosperous partnership.

By reaching out to professionals you already know, like, and trust – and then filling the gaps with quality introductions from key clients and colleagues – you can quickly gain access to great professionals and build a powerfully profitable referral team.

Raving Referrals in Action: Michelle Terry's Proven Path to Success

Introduction: From Humble Beginnings to Transformative Results

Michelle Terry's journey in real estate is nothing short of extraordinary. Starting at the age of 23 with nothing more than a phone book and a desktop phone, Michelle carved her path through sheer determination and hard work. Over the years, she transformed from a struggling agent to a referral-based powerhouse, thanks in large part to her partnership with WSS.

This chapter not only highlights Michelle's inspiring story but also breaks down her step-by-step system, offering actionable insights for agents and partners to replicate her success.

Building a Foundation of Hard Work

Michelle, a Broker/Franchisee of EXIT Real Estate Executives in Spencer, Massachusetts, and a Senior Coach with WSS, began her career in 1997, earning $45,000 in her first year despite having no formal training or tools. She credits her initial success to hard work, resilience, and a relentless focus on serving clients. By her third year, she had surpassed six figures, all while maintaining a second job in the food service industry.

Her early challenges taught her the value of connections, though she lacked a formal system to manage them. Reflecting on her growth, Michelle says, "Had I had my Top 50 back then, my business would have looked completely different."

Discovering Workman Success Systems

In 2017, Michelle attended an Exit Realty Conference, where Verl Workman's presentation on high-performance systems struck a chord. At the time, she was running a brokerage, coaching agents, and earning $336,000 annually in commissions—all while feeling burnt out and overextended.

PARTNER WITH TOP TRUSTED PROS

A lunch meeting with Verl that day changed everything. Michelle joined WSS and began implementing structured systems like database management and the Top 50 program. These tools revolutionized her business and allowed her to triple her income without the massive ad spend she had relied on before.

The Power of the Top 50 Program

Michelle credits much of her success to the Top 50 Program, a system focused on identifying and nurturing relationships with the top 50 people in her sphere of influence. These individuals became her biggest advocates, providing referrals that fueled her business growth.

Key Elements of the Top 50 Program:

1. **Database Management**: Michelle built and maintained a meaningful database of thousands of contacts, ensuring regular communication and personal touches.
2. **Personalized Care**: She prioritized loving on her top 50 by remembering their birthdays, offering meaningful gifts, and checking in regularly.
3. **Consistent Engagement**: From hosting events like baseball games and charity drives to casual Cape house gatherings, Michelle found ways to deepen relationships with her top 50.
4. **Going the Extra Mile**: Michelle frequently helped clients beyond the transaction, from assisting with home cleanouts to driving cancer patients to medical appointments.

Stories That Inspire: Referrals in Action

One of Michelle's most impactful referral stories involves her mortgage broker partner. Over 22 years, they have referred over 1,000 transactions to each other, creating a mutually beneficial partnership. This relationship exemplifies the power of trust and collaboration in a referral-based business.

Another example is Michelle's dedication to an elderly widow. After the woman's husband passed away, Michelle and her family helped clean out the home, provided emotional support, and ensured a smooth transition. A local senior living facility took notice and has sent Michelle dozens of referrals every year since then. These acts of kindness build lifelong loyalty and naturally lead to referrals.

Michelle's Step-by-Step System for Predictable Referrals

1. Build and Organize Your Database:
   - Collect and store detailed information about every contact
   - Segment the database to identify your top 50 key advocates
2. Show Gratitude Consistently:
   - Send handwritten thank-you notes for every referral
   - Offer personalized gifts based on the level of support (e.g., Tiffany or Louis Vuitton for top referrers)
3. Engage Regularly:
   - Host six to eight client appreciation events annually
   - Schedule regular pop-bys to check in and maintain relationships
4. Go Above and Beyond:
   - Help clients with non-transactional needs, like moving, vendor coordination, or personal challenges
   - Build a trusted vendor list, ensuring quality services for clients
5. Track and Measure Results:
   - Monitor referrals and contributions from your top 50
   - Share updates with referrers to keep them engaged and informed
6. Celebrate and Deepen Relationships:
   - Include your top 50 in fun, exclusive activities like group trips or local outings
   - Treat your top referrers as valued partners and friends

The Results: A Business and Life Transformed

Since implementing WSS, Michelle has stopped spending on Zillow and REALTOR.com, instead relying entirely on referrals. Her business has tripled in volume, and she now enjoys meaningful relationships with clients who also become lifelong friends.

Michelle's parting advice for agents is simple: "Love on your people, do a good job, and operate from the heart. The business will take care of itself."

Michelle's story demonstrates that a referral-based business is not only profitable but deeply fulfilling. By following this proven system, any agent can create a thriving business built on trust, care, and meaningful relationships that drive raving referrals.

Raving Referral in Action:
Tony Dixon and Delivering Value First

In real estate, as in most industries where relationships are the cornerstone of success, the power of referrals cannot be overstated. Tony Dixon, a founding partner of Advanced Tax Group, embodies this principle. His journey highlights the impact of referrals, not just on business growth, but on personal development as well.

Tony's story begins with one single referral that completely changed the trajectory of his career. Twelve years ago, a seemingly random introduction led him to set up an LLC for a client. Little did he know, this client would evolve into his biggest referral partner, integrating their systems and generating literally millions of dollars annually. "You just never know what comes from one single referral," Tony reflects. This experience underscores the importance of treating every client with the utmost respect and care, regardless of the immediate financial outcome.

Tony's approach offers valuable lessons. REALTORs, often independent contractors, face unique challenges in managing their finances and taxes. Tony emphasizes the importance of having a tax strategist as part of a REALTOR's team, akin to an assistant or buyer's agent. "Every REALTOR should have a tax strategist," he asserts, highlighting the potential pitfalls of poor financial planning. Many REALTORs, despite earning substantial incomes, find themselves unable to invest or grow due to tax liabilities. Tony's advice is clear: "Start thinking like a business from the outset, and engage with a tax professional early to structure finances correctly."

Tony's philosophy aligns seamlessly with WSS' approach to building communities of trusted advisors. By delivering value first, without the expectation of immediate exchange, professionals can cultivate relationships that yield long-term benefits. This principle is echoed throughout this book - advocating for creating networks of trusted professionals who refer clients to one another, enhancing service delivery and client satisfaction.

For real estate professionals, the action items are straightforward: integrate a tax strategist into your team, focus on delivering exceptional value, and nurture every client relationship as if it could be your next big referral. By doing so, you not only enhance your service offering, but also position yourself for sustainable growth in your market.

Tapping into the CPA Partner Opportunity

To add more value to your past clients, consider sending them a copy of their Closing Disclosure (CD) along with a cover letter at the end of the year. Congratulate them once again on their home purchase and encourage them to share their CD with their CPA when filing taxes. In the cover letter, offer your contact information for any questions their CPA may have and ask for the CPA's details in return.

After the tax season, reach out to the CPA to discuss potential client opportunities, as they have valuable insight into tax trends and know which clients are in the process of buying or selling homes. Establishing a professional relationship with CPAs can lead to a significant number of new client referrals.

Every professional network should start with a FIRM foundation consisting of a Financial Advisor, Insurance Agent, REALTOR, and Mortgage Lender. By partnering with financial professionals who have a steady stream of clients needing help with real estate transactions, you become an invaluable member of their team. That's important because these professionals tend to have significant trust and influence with their clients.

However, blue collar service providers including contractors, handymen, roofers, plumbers, electricians, and other technicians can also be valuable referral partners as they often get hired by homeowners who are doing renovations prior to listing their homes for sale. Since you have regular referrals to give out, you can win their loyalty as you teach them how they can grow their business through a strategic partnership where you work together and generate more opportunities for everyone involved.

Raving Referrals in Action: Stephanie Verderose's Journey to Community-Centered Success

Introduction: Coaching as the Catalyst

Stephanie Verderose of Vineland and Pittsgrove, NJ, a Team Leader, WSS Senior Coach, and Broker/Owner at EXIT Homestead Realty Professionals, epitomizes how adopting a structured coaching approach can transform a real estate business. Initially overwhelmed by the demands of maintaining connections with her network, Stephanie's journey with WSS' coaching helped her hone her approach, focus her efforts, and see exponential results. From refining her Top 50 relationships to leveraging community-driven events, Stephanie's story is one of growth, resilience, and creativity.

A Personal Touch: Harnessing the Power of the Top 50

Stephanie's transformation began with an important coaching principle: the Top 50. Her coach, Sara, emphasized that Stephanie's wide-reaching network needed structure and focus. Together, they identified the most impactful individuals in her sphere who consistently generated referrals and opportunities. By maintaining a dynamic list and nurturing these relationships, Stephanie laid the foundation for success.

During the COVID-19 pandemic, when traditional client interactions were limited, Stephanie's Top 50 became even more critical. This focus allowed her to adapt and maintain a consistent referral pipeline.

Innovation During a Crisis: The Drive-In Movie Event

One standout strategy Stephanie embraced was hosting a community-focused drive-in movie event. Initially a response to pandemic restrictions, it evolved into a cornerstone of her marketing and community engagement. The event wasn't just about hosting a movie—it became a branding powerhouse:

- **Building a Database**: Registration for the event was managed through Eventbrite, growing her client database with every iteration

- **Client Touchpoints**: Guests received branded trick-or-treat bags filled with logo merchandise and contributions from vendor partners

- **Community Recognition**: The drive-in marquee prominently displayed her brokerage's name, solidifying her brand's association with the event

- **Referrals**: The event not only brought her closer to her existing clients but also introduced her to new prospects, some of whom have since become clients

The event expanded beyond its original purpose, leading to additional initiatives like "Cookies with Santa," toy drives, and cornhole tournaments. Each event not only furthered her community ties and generated more business opportunities, but greatly benefitted local charities and non profit organizations.

Quantifiable Success: Results from the Drive-In Event

Stephanie measured the success of her drive-in movie events in several ways:

- **Database Growth**: Each event added new contacts to her list
- **Referrals**: Referrals from attendees and even the movie theater owners themselves
- **Agent Engagement**: Encouraging her agents to invite their clients fostered deeper relationships within her brokerage
- **Brand Recognition**: The consistent visibility and community goodwill translated into increased trust and market share

Delegation and Leadership: Stepping Out of the Day-to-Day

Coaching also empowered Stephanie to delegate effectively and build a team capable of supporting her vision. With a well-structured team in place, she then focused on strategic leadership, allowing her to scale her operations.

Her EEC Leadership Group meetings—designed to keep her in tune with her team's challenges and opportunities—highlight her commitment to staying connected while empowering her team to excel.

Key Lessons and Takeaways for Agents

Stephanie's journey illustrates that growth stems from a combination of structured coaching, creative outreach, and strategic delegation. For agents looking to replicate her success, the following steps offer a clear path forward:

1. Leverage the Top 50 Strategy:
    - Identify your most impactful relationships
    - Regularly review and update this list based on engagement and referrals
    - Maintain consistent, meaningful touchpoints

2. Engage Through Events:
   - Host creative, community-focused events that align with your brand
   - Use these events to collect contact information and grow your database
   - Partner with local businesses and vendors for cross-marketing opportunities

3. Measure Success:
   - Track referrals, database growth, and brand impressions after every event
   - Use these metrics to refine and improve future initiatives

4. Delegate Strategically:
   - Build a capable team to handle day-to-day operations, freeing you to focus on leadership and growth
   - Establish regular check-ins with your team to stay informed and provide guidance

5. Adapt and Innovate:
   - Embrace changes in the market and use coaching as a tool to pivot effectively
   - Create scalable systems that allow for consistent community engagement

Conclusion: From Coaching to Community Impact

Stephanie Verderose's success is a testament to the power of structured coaching and a willingness to think outside the box. By focusing on her Top 50, building strong community ties, and leveraging coaching insights, Stephanie transformed her business into a trusted, community-centered brand. Her story reminds us that real estate success is built on relationships—and with the right strategies, those relationships can create endless opportunities.

Now it's time for you to put the power of partnerships to work for your business.

I

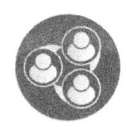

Chapter 13: Network Strategically

Another way to meet prospective referral partners is by attending networking events. In every city, there are dozens of monthly opportunities to meet other professionals. Typically hosted and led by local chambers of commerce or professional networking companies, these groups exist to help professionals and business owners connect and collaborate. That means everyone in attendance is there for the same reason. You are there to meet new people in hopes of doing business together.

Have a Plan

Before investing any time going to a networking event, be sure you have a plan for who, where, and how.

- Who do you want to meet?
- Where do they usually meet?
- How will you meet them?

First, get crystal clear on the type of people you want to meet. Maybe you only want to meet CPAs, financial advisors, divorce attorneys, estate planning attorneys, property managers, or real estate investors. Just be clear who you want to connect with so you can ask for an introduction when the time is right.

Second, find out where these people connect and congregate. Research local groups or events where your ideal referral partners meet and get together. The best way to do this is to call your top referral partners and ask what groups they belong to or recommend. If they belong to a chamber of commerce or networking group, you'll find them eager to invite you as their guest. These organizations typically track how many guests each member introduces to the group, so inviting guests is encouraged and celebrated.

Third, have a plan for how you will meet your ideal connections. There may only be one or two great contacts for you in the room. Rather than walking around randomly introducing yourself to strangers, ask the people running the event to introduce you to the people you want to meet.

Since the event leaders check everyone in as they arrive, they meet each and every person who walks through the door. That means they are perfectly positioned to help you. You just need to ask for your ideal introduction, which is super easy when you use the following script. Once you've checked into the event, simply smile and say, "I'm wondering if you can help me. The primary reason I'm here is to find a top (Estate Planning Attorney) that I can refer clients to and build a referral partnership with. Can you tell me if there are any quality (Estate Planning Attorneys) here I can connect with?"

The beauty of this question is that you are actually helping them be successful in their job. After all, the reason they are at the event is to help members and attendees connect, collaborate, and cross-refer each other. By asking for an introduction to the precise professionals you are looking to connect with, you make it easy for them to help you.

Top 10 Tips for Networking Strategically

After attending and leading networking events from coast to coast, we've learned there are ten top tips for networking success:

1. **Visualize Success** – Success starts long before you walk into any meeting or event. Remember, just one referral partner can double your business in a year or even less. As you think about the event, visualize exactly who you want to meet. Get clear on the industry they are in and have a plan for how you would like to work together. Then, before the event, take a few moments and envision yourself having a great time meeting an incredible referral partner in that industry who has been looking for someone just like you to help their clients. As you visualize the future you want to create, you activate the law of attraction, which is always good to have working for you.

2. **Bring A Buddy** – Invite one of your referral partners to join you and work the room together. Before the event, get clear on who each

person is looking to meet. Then, as you meet a potential match for your referral partner, make an enthusiastic introduction to the person you just met. This helps you add value to both parties and elevate your status in their eyes. Be sure to praise and edify your networking buddy to help them feel good and raise their perceived status. As you help your referral partners succeed, they will naturally return the favor and go out of their way to help you in return. WIN–WIN–WIN.

3. **Meet The Leaders** – Introduce yourself to the people hosting the event. They are often servant leaders dedicated to helping people succeed. Since they have the respect of the members, when they make an introduction, people take the meeting. Befriend these folks, and you will win faster.

4. **Ask For Introductions** – Ask the event leaders for introductions to the top pros they know in your target profession. Simply say, "The main reason I am here is that I'm looking for a quality (CPA) to whom I can refer my clients. Do you happen to know any good (CPA)s you would recommend I connect with?"

If they know trustworthy people in that industry, they will be happy to help and make an introduction.

5. **Be Confident** – First impressions matter. As you meet new people, smile, look them in the eye, and introduce yourself confidently with a firm handshake. When you exude confidence, people feel it. Especially if they have a high nurturing personality style. The truth is that while you are interviewing potential partners, they are evaluating you as well. Show them you are comfortable in your own skin and confident in your ability to get the job done right. Your confidence will give them confidence in you.

6. **Ask Quality Questions** – Show you are interested by asking great questions to learn about the people you're meeting. If you aren't a natural networker, just ask: **Who? What? When? Where? Why?**

    - Who is your ideal client?
    - What is the primary problem you solve?
    - When do people most need your services?
    - Where do you get most of your clients currently?
    - Why did you choose this industry?

The answers to these questions will give you quick clarity as to how well you trust this person and how well they match your perfect partner profile.

7. **Listen And Learn** – You're here to meet good people to partner with, not to sell. After asking each question, really listen to what the person is telling you. Study what they say both verbally and non-verbally. You'll learn a lot about them in a very short time. As you listen, ask yourself if you like this person and can see yourself eventually feeling comfortable referring your clients to them.

8. **Schedule A 1-on-1 / Discovery Call** – Your primary goal for attending any networking event should be to schedule one-on-one discovery calls with Perfect Prospects or referral partners. Rather than trying to have a meaningful conversation in a busy, crowded, noisy environment, ask to schedule a one-on-one call at a later date. When you find someone who may be a fit, simply say, "From what you've shared, I have a number of clients who might benefit from what you do. Can we get together another time so I can ask you a few questions? Maybe next Tuesday afternoon or Wednesday morning? What works best for you?" Scheduling your next meeting right then and there fills your calendar and avoids you having to play phone tag later on to schedule a time to meet up.

9. **Be Brief, Be Brilliant, Be Gone** – Once you have synced calendars and scheduled a discovery call, thank them for their time and excuse yourself from the conversation. Don't overstay your welcome. Always leave them wanting more.

10. **Follow-Up and Follow-Through** – As you know, the fortune is in the follow-up. After the event, think about each person you met and send an email, text, or direct message to those with whom you want to explore relationships. If you scheduled a discovery call, send a calendar invite with the date, time, and location or description of how you will connect. You may also want to send a friend or connection request on social media to accelerate the trust-building process.

When you follow these top ten networking tips, you will build your referral team quickly and easily.

Networking With Intention

Consider this scenario. Let's say you encounter a contractor who has likely never used or referred a real estate agent before. But after interacting with you, observing your work ethic, and professionalism, he becomes familiar with your team. Now, when someone in his network expresses an interest in buying or selling a home, there's a high probability that he would recommend your team; not because he was asked to, but because he observed firsthand the quality of service you provide.

This is the power of intentionality in action. It's about creating an impression that lasts, one that convinces people to refer you, even if they've never done it before. It's about being proactive, making people feel valued, and leaving a positive impact that prompts them to advocate for you.

Networking groups are an excellent example of this dynamic. These groups provide a structured environment for passing referrals, allowing members to build trust and familiarity over time. However, the same principle can apply outside of these formal settings. By demonstrating your commitment to service and relationship-building, you can inspire others to become referral sources, even those who aren't typically accustomed to doing so. In essence, building referral relationships is about more than mere networking. It's about intentionality, about making every interaction count. It's about demonstrating your value to those around you, so much so that they become willing advocates for your service. Remember, every relationship holds the potential for referrals. It's up to you to cultivate these opportunities with purpose and intention.

Real Estate Investment Associations

As a REALTOR, joining a real estate investment association can be one of the smartest moves you make for your career. These associations are hubs of opportunity, filled with seasoned investors, industry professionals, and people who are actively involved in your local market. By being part of this network, you'll gain insights into the investment side of real estate, which can expand your expertise and give you a competitive edge. When you understand what investors are looking for—whether it's properties with cash flow potential, undervalued homes, or development opportunities—you position yourself as a valuable partner who can help them achieve their goals. Plus, you'll learn strategies to identify investment opportunities, evaluate deals, and create new income streams for yourself.

One of the biggest benefits of joining a real estate investment association is the relationships you'll build. These groups connect you with not only investors but also contractors, lenders, property managers, and other professionals who can support your business. Imagine the power of having an investor client base that buys and sells multiple properties every year or a trusted contractor who you can recommend to your clients. By building these relationships, you can open the door to referrals, repeat business, and opportunities to co-invest or partner on projects. Associations are also a great place to learn about off-market deals and creative financing strategies, giving you insider knowledge that can make you stand out in your market.

Finally, being part of a real estate investment association will elevate your professional growth. These groups often host workshops, guest speakers, and educational events that teach you skills to increase your income and serve your clients better. You'll learn how to speak the language of investors, analyze market trends, and even explore opportunities to invest in real estate yourself. By aligning yourself with like-minded professionals, you'll not only grow your knowledge but also expand your network and create more opportunities for success. If you want to stand out as a REALTOR and grow your business, joining a real estate investment association is an essential step.

Networking Groups

In addition to referral mixers and events, you may also want to join a chamber of commerce, MeetUp, or a structured referral group like LeTip or BNI. While chambers allow unlimited members per industry, referral groups often only allow one member per profession, which is great if they have an opening in the real estate industry. When I (Brandon) was starting out in the mortgage business, I joined a chapter of LeTip International in Beaverton, Oregon. The 15 members of this chapter met for breakfast every Thursday at 7:00 am sharp. Breaking bread together each week was a great way to get to know each other and build long-term relationships and referral partnerships. It was awesome to have a team of people committed to helping each other win and constantly scouting for opportunities for each other.

In 2013, I was referred to LeTip CEO Kim Marie Branch-Pettid, a wonderful woman committed to helping businesses grow faster together. Having visited her international headquarters many times and spending time with her, her husband, and her executive teams over the years, I can tell you her organization goes above and beyond to help their members grow their businesses, with chapters nationwide from coast-to-coast.

Each chapter hosts a weekly online or in-person meeting, along with evening mixer events and large-scale conferences. The entire LeTip referral machine has been built to ensure every member receives massive value. Each chapter has officers who lead the meetings following a regimented agenda set by LeTip headquarters. Guests are welcomed warmly and thrilled to find so many opportunities to build relationships with quality professionals. After announcements are made, each attendee is asked to quickly stand and share their message of who and how they help. Then they report new referrals and business opportunities they have given or received from members of the group. Referrals are tracked on their proprietary Wired platform which helps each club track and measure the business passed and the return on investment (ROI) each member has received from the group. Those who refer most are celebrated and sought after. To search for a LeTip chapter in your area, visit LeTip.com.

After thoroughly studying and researching the professional networking industry, Dr. Ivan Misner saw a gap and created BNi (Business Network International) back in January of 1985. Over the past four decades, this organization has grown to be the single largest global face-to-face networking organization with over 330,000 members worldwide.

I (Brandon) have never been an official BNI member, but I have attended countless chapter meetings and conferences over the decades. I've also had the great honor and pleasure of meeting and interviewing BNI founder Dr. Ivan Misner, who is largely considered the godfather of networking. He is a humble servant eager to educate and empower as many people as possible. That's just one of the reasons BNI members are so passionate and loyal to the BNI company and community. With over 11,000 chapters, you can find a group near you at BNI.com.

Every group needs a great REALTOR so if there's an opening in the group, visit the group and see if these are people you can see yourself enjoying doing business with. Openings for real estate agents don't come along very often so you may even consider starting your own networking group which we will walk you through in the next chapter - Create Your Referral Alliance.

We've also compiled a list of great networking organizations and referral groups at the end of this book. There's no substitute for meeting people in the real world, so go find a local group and start networking strategically.

The Fortune Is In The Follow-Up

As you start networking, you will be meeting some awesome people that can send you a lot of business. Your goal should be to get into the know, like, and trust zone as quickly as possible.

Connect with them on social media and be sure to like, comment, share, retweet, and invite them often and you can accelerate the trust building process. A tactic we learned from Casey Eberhart in his awesome Networking Riches course is his ATM social strategy:

1. **ADD** people to your FB group
2. **TAG** them in the post
3. **MESSAGE** them personally

Do this consistently and you'll start attracting great referral partners who send you a steady stream of Perfect Prospects.

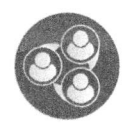

Chapter 14:
Create a Referral Alliance

After 43 years of living in the rainforest of Oregon, my wife and I (Brandon) decided to move our family down to the sunny blue skies of Phoenix, Arizona in 2014.

That meant leaving behind the hundreds of professionals with whom I had spent decades creating relationships and building an entirely new tribe down in the desert.

Connect With Connectors

I started my Phoenix networking tour at a Network After Work event because they always draw a great crowd. When I arrived, I met Danielle, the leader of the event who I quickly connected with, shared who I was looking to meet, and asked for introductions to top trusted pros. This led to some great conversations, for which I thanked Danielle at the end of the night.

The next day, I connected with her and started building a long-term relationship over the months that followed. From that connection came a referral to James Miller, the CEO of Network After Work, who I've since built a relationship and profitable partnership with. Remember, the leaders of these events know everyone and are happy to make introductions.

Next, I found NetworkingPhoenix which combined all the daily networking events throughout the Valley into one centralized site and calendar. With over 40,000 members with searchable profiles on their platform, this group helps you stay connected long after you've met. Brilliant!

While the website helped me locate the various events taking place locally, I was really drawn to meet the leader behind it all – a woman named Gelie Ahkenblit. I attended one of her signature events and followed these same steps I've just shared with you. Meet the leader, ask for introductions to the people you want to meet, report back to the leader thanking them for the introductions. Rinse and repeat.

Over the following months of building a relationship with Gelie, I learned she is passionate about speaking and coaching, so when producing my Profit Partners Summit, I was thrilled when Gelie agreed to share her wisdom with our audience.

This gave me an opportunity to give back and support her in fulfilling her mission.

Over the months that followed, I attended the Phoenix Metro Chamber of Commerce, led by Jason Bressler, Network Together led by Robert and Shawn Jones, and Networking360 led by Thomas and Melina Evans. Each of these people are passionate local leaders committed to helping business people connect and collaborate. They go above and beyond to help people succeed and will do everything they can to connect you to people that bring value to your life.

It was fascinating seeing the differences in the type of people each group attracted. Each organization had their own culture, which varied based on the leader. Some emphasized education and impact, while others focused on cocktails and connections.

As you explore your local networking options, look for leaders you admire and respect. When you attend, introduce yourself to the leaders, ask for introductions, and report your results back to the leader thanking them for the connection. Then, make it your mission to build relationships with these influencers. You will find they will eagerly connect you with your Perfect Prospects and potential referral partners.

The reason we're sharing these stories with you is to illustrate what is possible when you apply the Raving Referrals system.

Create a vision and plan for using these events to connect with your Perfect Prospects and referral partners, and both your network and net worth will grow. Be strategic and you can meet powerful people and build profitable partnerships quickly and consistently.

Invite Your Trusted Team

If you are serious about taking your business to new heights, consider starting your own personal referral group or what we call a Referral Alliance. For best results, bring together your best referral partners and ask them to join you in launching your own group. As you unite your team, you elevate your status and establish yourself as a leader and influential connector.

The best way to accomplish this quickly and easily is to schedule a meeting at your office, a restaurant, or even via zoom. Simply choose a time and location then send a quick message to each person inviting them to attend.

Say something like:

"Hi (name), as you may know, I am in the process of expanding my business, and I'm creating an alliance of vetted and trusted professionals I can refer my clients to. I truly value our relationship and would like to invite you to be a core member of my referral team. I will be gathering my most important referral partners (date/time) at (location) and hope you can attend.

Please let me know if you can join us."

For best results, send a calendar invite to each person you want to attend so they have the date, time, and location already in their calendar. That makes it super easy for them to accept your invite with one quick click. This also helps you see who is interested, available, and committed to attending. You may also want to create an event on Facebook, LinkedIn or another social network if you are connected to these people on those platforms.

Your Alliance Meeting

As your group gathers, you may have a few early arrivals. Welcome them warmly and let them know when your meeting will begin. If you are not an extrovert or natural nurturer, you may want to have an assistant greet your guests, so they feel the love from the get-go.

Start your meeting by greeting the group and thanking them for attending. Ask each person to introduce themselves and describe who they help and how they help. Once everyone has introduced themselves, simply review some of the co-marketing campaigns outlined in the Referral Partner Blueprint outlined in Chapter 16.

Here's a script you can use as a guideline:

Greeting

"Thank you for coming today. The reason I asked you all to join me is that I am expanding my business and creating an alliance of vetted and trusted professionals I'll be referring my clients to.

I truly value each and every one of you and view you as one of the best in your respective industries. Not only am I hoping to do more business with you personally, but I also want to connect each of you so you can do more business together.

After all, everyone in this room serves (consumers/homeowners/business owners), so we share the same ideal client and can grow our businesses faster and further by cross-referring and cross-promoting each other."

Introductions

What I'd like to do now is go around the room and give everyone a chance to introduce themselves and share who you help and how you help. That will help everyone here understand the services you provide and who your perfect prospects and ideal clients are.

Before you leave, I'd like to ask you each to fill out a Referral Partner Optimization Form so I can train my team on what type of clients we should refer to you.

I'll go first. As you all know, my name is _____ and I help _____ (share your Service Statement).

To give you an example of what I do, I recently had a client who_____. (share a story of a problem you solved and the difference it made for them).

I'm passionate about helping people _____, and a great referral for me is a (share your Perfect Prospect Profile). Before we move on, does anyone have any questions about the services I provide?

Answer any questions that come up and remember to tell success stories so people can visualize who and how you help. Telling a memorable story of someone you've helped turns people into referral scouts because when they hear someone facing the challenge you solve, they will immediately think of you.

"Hopefully, that gives you more clarity on how I can help your clients and customers. Now let's go around the room starting to my left."

After each person shares who and how they help, be sure to compliment and edify them to boost their confidence and status among your guests. Your job is to help everyone feel honored and special.

Share stories of how these people have helped you or your clients in the past. Describe what you appreciate most about each person, and you will instantly expand your value in their eyes. This process ensures people view you as the connector and influencer you are. It also locks in their loyalty and commitment to doing business with you going forward.

Instructions

Once all attendees have shared who and how they help, share your plan for doing more business together. Using the Referral Partner Blueprint in Chapter 16 as a guide, mention some of the strategies you plan to use to introduce your trusted referral partners to your clients and colleagues. This will give them a vision for how they will win more business through your Referral Alliance.

We recommend your strategy include interviews with your referral partners to add value to them and build their credibility in the eyes of your clients. Simply record a quick zoom interview and post the video recording on Facebook, YouTube, and/or LinkedIn. Alternatively, you can broadcast your conversation live on these platforms as well.

Wrap-Up

As you conclude your Alliance meeting, thank each person for attending and let them know you'd like to schedule a one-on-one conversation with them to plan out how you can grow your businesses together. Be sure each person leaves with your Referral Kit, business cards, referral cards, brochures, and any other marketing materials you'd like them to give to their clients when they recommend your services. That way, each Referral Partner leaves empowered to refer you quickly and consistently.

Hang-Out

If your schedule allows, recommend they hang out and connect with the people in the room who would be the best fit for their business. You will add additional value by connecting them with other business owners and professionals with whom they can build relationships. Plus, the more time you spend with each person, the more likely they are to send profitable prospects your way.

Consider printing a form each Partner fills out so you have a written record of who they help, how they help, how they want to be referred, and a success story you can share with your clients.

Raving Referrals Partner Profile

Name: _____

Company: _____

Profession: _____

Phone: _____

Who are your Perfect Prospects?

How would you describe your perfect prospects and ideal clients?

_____

_____

_____

How do you help?

What is most important for me to share about your product or service? What makes you unique?

_____

_____

_____

CREATE A REFERRAL ALLIANCE

How would you like me to refer people to you?

Do you offer free consultations or any special promotions you'd like me to share?

_____

_____

_____

What's your best success story?

Share your best client result or testimonial so I can retell the story to my clients.

_____

_____

_____

Following these steps will help you create a highly productive and profitable referral alliance you can build your business with for years to come. The best part is that a client for one of you can be a client for all of you. Once you attract a new client for your business, think about which of your referral partners you can introduce them to. There are likely other services this client would benefit from. As you refer them to your partners, and they refer their clients to you, everyone wins together.

Raving Referrals in Action: Brooke Sines' Journey

Building Success Through Community and Connection

Brooke Sines' story is a testament to the power of community engagement and strategic networking in real estate. Her journey began in Michigan, where she quickly made a name for herself selling 30 homes in her first year. Recognizing the need for systems and processes, she joined WSS, which transformed her approach from a chaotic hustle to a life built with intention. "I went from running like a chicken with my head cut off to living a life by design". With Workman's guidance, Brooke learned to balance her professional ambitions with her personal life, ensuring she was present for her family while growing her business.

Next, Brooke moved to North Carolina - a bold step, yet she seamlessly transitioned her success by leveraging the tools and strategies she had honed. Despite the challenges of starting anew during the pandemic, Brooke's commitment to community involvement paid off. She joined local groups, initiated a working moms' group, and even started a Zoom book club, fostering connections that would later translate into business opportunities.

One of Brooke's standout stories involves a couple she met through Orangetheory Fitness, a fitness community she joined upon moving to town. Despite the disruption of COVID-19, Brooke maintained her relationship with them, adding them to her top 50 list. When the couple decided to sell their home, Brooke was their first and only call, leading to multiple referrals and transactions in their neighborhood, highlighting the trust she had built.

Brooke's stories don't stop there. With her dedication to community shining through in her working women's group, her genuine effort to help a neighbor find a babysitter led to a referral for a high-value property, underscoring the impact of authentic relationships. "If you work that hard to find a babysitter, I know how hard you'll work in real estate," a group member told her, resulting in a significant transaction.

Brooke's success is not just in the numbers but in the systems she built around referrals. She meticulously tracks and nurtures these relationships, ensuring that every referral is acknowledged and appreciated through personalized touches, like send-out cards and gifts. This approach not only strengthens her network but also creates a ripple effect of goodwill and trust.

Brooke's journey illustrates that with the right systems and a focus on community, real estate success is not just achievable - but sustainable.

Consistency Is The Key

A common challenge many real estate agents and other professionals face is the desire for instant gratification, a quick return on their networking efforts. They might meet a potential client who already has a real estate agent with established relationships in the industry. However, it's crucial to understand that building trust and establishing meaningful relationships take time.

Maryann Farlino, my (Verl's) youngest sister, is what I would call a master networker. Her consistent presence and enthusiasm in calling on real estate agents as a marketing rep for Old Republic Title is nothing short of legendary. Maryann is met every day with agents telling her that they already have a title partner and that they would never switch. Her consistency in follow up and serve before sell attitude has earned her hundreds of transactions. She has maintained great relationships through good and tough markets that have carried her to success in every environment. Maryann runs Workman Top 50 classes for agents who want to grow, teaching them how to sell more by being consistent with their Top 50. One of my favorite calls from Maryann is when she calls to let me know one of the agents she trained is having their best year ever because of the Top 50 system. She also hosts and participates in pickleball events, golf tournaments, lunch and learns, and rewards referrals every time a new deal is sent. I am so proud of her and love that she has become so well liked and respected in the industry. She is a great example of how No, never really means never in business. She is now the referral partner that agents say they would never leave.

Action Items:

1. **Engage with Your Community**: Actively participate in local groups and events to build genuine relationships.

2. **Leverage the Top 50 Strategy**: Identify and nurture key relationships that can lead to referrals.

3. **Show Gratitude**: Implement a system to acknowledge and thank referral sources throughout the process.

4. **Customize Your Approach**: Adapt systems and processes to fit your unique style and market needs.

Go to your toolkit to find The Referral Alliance Agenda.

ReferralChampion.com/toolkit

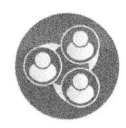

Chapter 15: Leverage LinkedIn

Another way to attract and enroll great referral partners is to activate your LinkedIn connections, converting these people from casual connections to active referrers for your business. Everyone knows LinkedIn can be a powerful source of new business. However, most people have a ton of LinkedIn connections that just sit there idle, doing nothing for their business. The good news is that you can mine the acres of diamonds you are sitting on by activating your LinkedIn connections, so they introduce you to your perfect partners and prospects.

This strategy requires some research and preparation, but the results are definitely worth the effort. Especially if you serve business owners or provide services to businesses.

The LinkedIn Activation strategy consists of six steps:

1. Research your contact's LinkedIn connections and identify five people to ask them about.
2. Invite your contact to talk on the phone or over lunch about their LinkedIn connections.
3. Ask about their connections with a goal of getting two to three introductions or referrals.
4. Thank your contact for the introductions and referrals.
5. Reach Out to each referred person.
6. Follow-Up with your contact and let them know how things went.

Step 1: Research

Once you have identified the desired professions for your Power Team of referral partners, LinkedIn is a great way to research the connections of people who already know, like, and trust you, so you can effectively ask for introductions to those you want to meet.

Even if you've done a great job connecting with your contacts on a personal level and they want to refer people to you, it can be difficult for them to effectively think through all of their contacts to identify who they should refer to you. To make the process easier for them, take a few minutes to research the LinkedIn connections of your strongest relationships and identify the people you'd like to get introduced to. After all, no one knows your Perfect Prospects and ideal referral partners better than you.

Strive to pick just five LinkedIn connections to ask about. Ultimately, your goal should be to receive two or three referrals and introductions from each of your contacts. If you ask about more than five people, it can feel a bit burdensome and overwhelming for them.

When you choose less than five, you decrease your chance of receiving referrals/introductions since they may not have very deep relationships with each of the people you've chosen and will not be able to make many introductions for you. Plus, you can always circle back to them and ask for additional introductions once you've connected with their initial contacts.

In order to begin the process, you must be connected with your contacts on LinkedIn, and they must allow their connections to be able to search their contacts (which most people do). So, if you are not connected with them, send them a connection request.

Search Strategically

Searching your contacts' connections can seem overwhelming and extremely time consuming. Many of your contacts may have 500 or more connections. Fortunately, there is a very effective and time-saving approach you can use to filter your contacts' connections and view only their most relevant connections.

Step A: Log in to your LinkedIn account.

Step B: Enter the name of the contact you want to ask for referrals. Click the search button.

One of my favorite people on the planet is Gail Watson, President and founder of WSA, the Women Speakers Association. Gail empowers women everywhere to share their voice as a paid public speaker. Over the past decade, WSA has helped tens of thousands of women get seen, booked, and paid all over the world. Gail has an amazing global network of influencers, so if I were looking for an introduction, I would locate her LinkedIn profile and click the Connections link under her name, title, and location.

What you will see is a list of your contact's connections sorted by what LinkedIn believes is most relevant for you.

Step C: Enter a job title for your ideal prospects and/or connectors. For example, you might want to search the following job titles:

- REALTORs outside of your area
- Real Estate Attorney
- Business Attorney
- Family Law Attorney
- Estate Planning Attorney
- Insurance Agent
- Financial Advisor
- CEO
- Business Owner
- President

Step D: Click on "Locations" and enter your city if you want to narrow the results.

Step E: This will give you a targeted list of their contacts that most closely match the type of professionals you are looking to connect with. Just review the search results and pick up to five people to ask your contact about.

If more results are needed, simply repeat these steps using a different job title. Once you have found five people to ask your contact about, it is time to send your contact an invitation.

Step 2: Invite

Once you've identified people you'd like to be introduced to, it's time to reach out to your contact and invite them to connect so you can ask them about these five LinkedIn connections.

Sample Email Invitation:

"Hi Gail,

Hope all is well in your world. I'm reaching out because I am looking to expand my network of business contacts and noticed you are connected to a few people on LinkedIn that I'd like to meet. I have a few contacts I think you would benefit from meeting as well.

Do you have a few minutes to jump on a quick call so we can connect and collaborate? Let me know what day and time works best for your schedule.

All My Best, Brandon"

Messaging them before you call allows them to prepare for the conversation, so you don't catch them off guard. Identify a few people you can introduce your contact to. Then start by giving them an introduction to add value to them and their business.

Step 3: Ask

Prior to your call or meeting, print off the profiles of the five LinkedIn connections with whom you would like to be introduced. That will make it easy for you to share what interests you in that person.

During your conversation, remind your contact that you were viewing their LinkedIn profile and had a few questions about some of their connections. Then simply share the list of profiles you've printed.

Ask questions you have about each person, such as:

- How well do you know them?
- Have you done much business with them in the past?
- What can you tell me about them and their company?
- What types of clients do they serve?
- Do you recommend this person to others?
- Do you think this would be a good person for me to connect with?

After hearing about each person, if you decide you would like to meet this person, simply ask to be introduced by saying something like:

"Stephen really sounds like an interesting person I would love to meet. Would you mind introducing the two of us? Or, if you would prefer, I am happy to send an email and mention you had great things to say about him and I would like to get to know him myself."

This is an important statement because you are giving your contact the choice of how the introduction will take place. If your contact knows the person really well and consistently communicates with them, they will likely feel comfortable making the introduction personally.

However, if your contact is busy or hasn't had any recent contact with that person, they might prefer that you reach out, introduce yourself directly, and use their name and recommendation as a reason for connecting.

The goal is to get at least two to three introductions from each of your contacts. If you get two or three introductions before asking about all five of their LinkedIn connections, stop asking so you don't overwhelm them. You can always ask about others later.

Step 4: Give Thanks

After your calls, be sure to follow up with your contacts to:

(1) thank them for their time and introductions, (2) remind them of who each agreed to introduce you to, and (3) let them know you will be following up to let them know how things turned out.

Sample "Thank You" Email:

"It was great connecting with you today. Thanks for helping me learn about some of your LinkedIn Connections. I really appreciate your willingness to introduce me to these people.

To make it easy for you, I've written the introduction below so you can just copy and paste into an email or direct message to [referral #1] and [referral #2].

Thanks again. This really means a lot to me. I'll let you know how things turn out."

[Insert e-introduction here]

Step 5: Outreach

If you agreed to introduce yourself directly, be sure you start your call, message, or email by sharing the name of the person who referred you and why they thought the two of you should connect.

Sample LinkedIn Connection Request:

SUBJECT: Gail Watson suggested we connect

"Hi Nancy, I met with Gail Watson the other day and she had great things to say about you and suggested we connect. I would love to get to know you and find out more about your business. Would you like to chat and collaborate?"

If your contact made the introduction on your behalf, follow up with the referred person as soon as possible after the introduction. This way, you are already on their radar and they will be more likely to take your call and agree to a meeting.

Sample Outreach Email:

SUBJECT: Gail Watson suggested we connect

Hello <name>, I was talking with Gail Watson, and she suggested you and I connect. Gail had some great things to say about you, so I'd love to connect on a quick call or zoom.

Sounds like we may have some great business possibilities together. What does your schedule look like next week? Do you have a few minutes to talk on the phone? Let me know what works best for you. You can reply to this email or give me a call back at (xxx) xxx-xxx

Step 6: Follow Up

After you've connected with the people your contact has introduced, be sure to let the person who made the introductions know what happened with each referral. Just send a quick email or direct message with a quick summary of each conversation you had.

Sample Follow-up Email:

"Hi Gail. Thanks again for the introductions you made last week. You know some great people, and I wanted to send you a quick update on our conversations:

Shelly Anderson – We had lunch together and have already started working together. Shelly is everything you said she was. Thanks again for the great referral.

James Smith – Briefly spoke and we're meeting next week.

Andrew Lewis – I sent an email but haven't heard back yet."

If you strike gold with one of their contacts and they end up becoming a client or referral partner, thank them immediately so they can celebrate your success. You may even want to send them a thank you card or gift card so they feel appreciated. Recognizing and thanking people for making referrals and introductions is an important step in the Raving Referrals system.

LEVERAGE LINKEDIN

This LinkedIn Activation strategy can help you grow your network quickly. Just two introductions from ten people will bring you twenty new potential clients and/or referral partners. That's one new conversation for each business day of the month.

Verlism: Anything you do 3 times you must create a system for it. First, you have to know the who, then you can do the what. One of the biggest challenges in building a referral framework and alliance is deciding who belongs in your network and what you can add to the relationship.

I (Verl) have found that new technology and AI have put our LinkedIn prospecting on steroids. With the ability to identify specific types of connections, AI tech such as IntelNgin.com, a powerful tool that sits on top of your Linkedin, provides fast access to leaders, potential partners, and intel that will help you connect at a much higher level.

IntelNgin.com founder and friend Sam Richter explains it this way, "What the Heck is an Intel Engine? An Intel Engine (IntelNgin) is a distraction-free, online search resource that helps you find the business and sales information you care about faster than you might be able to locate on your own, and even helps you discover information that you probably didn't even know existed. An Intel Engine is not a proprietary database nor is it a list building tool. Rather, think of it as a search engine overlay."

Raving Referrals in Action: Sam Richter and the Art of Authentic Connection in the Age of AI

Well entrenched in the world of sales and communication is Sam Richter, CEO of SBR Worldwide, LLC and the founder and creator of the IntelNgin | Business and Sales Intel Engine program. He is a Hall of Fame speaker, a bestselling author, and is considered one of the world's leading authorities on sales intelligence and digital reputation management. There's no doubt he stands out as a beacon of authenticity. Sam has dedicated his career to teaching others how to leverage AI and technology to foster genuine connections. "Everyone's massively passionate about themselves," Sam often says, highlighting the fundamental human trait that drives meaningful interactions. By knowing something about the other person, you can ask better questions, leading to more authentic and engaging conversations.

Sam's journey into the world of referrals is a testament to the power of building relationships. Early in his career, he was introduced to Harvey Mackay, renowned author and businessman, through a series of referrals. This connection blossomed into a mentorship that profoundly influenced Sam's career. "I can pretty much trace everything I've ever done to that phone call," Sam reflects, underscoring the impact of a single introduction.

In his work, Sam has developed a suite of intelligence products designed to help professionals gather insights and build relationships. His IntelNgin, for example, allows users to conduct in-depth research on companies and individuals, uncovering valuable information that can be used to tailor interactions. "The more you know about another person, the more you can talk about what you know they care about". This approach not only enhances communication but also makes the process more enjoyable.

Sam's philosophy aligns perfectly with the principles of WSS, where the focus is on creating systems that facilitate meaningful connections. By systematizing follow-up processes and leveraging technology to gather insights, professionals can build lasting relationships that lead to referrals and business growth.

Make Your Meetings Matter

Before meeting with someone you've never met, spend a few minutes researching them online. Check out their website, LinkedIn profile, and social media accounts to see what common interests you have. Nothing builds rapport faster than sharing your love for the same university, charity, or football team.

I (Verl) call this BRT, or Building Relationships with Trust. That means finding common interests, values, recreations, and more. I have learned that when you are genuinely interested in someone it's easy to find common interests. I'm a square guy from Salt Lake City, Utah, with six kids and 12 grandchildren, who loves his family, boating, pickleball, Utah football, and any sport my kids or grandkids are currently involved in. I have had challenges with teenagers. I have a wife that is amazing and is a professional shopper, and we recently purchased emountain bikes because we want to be more active. My business is focused on helping people, and I wanted to build a company my children would want to be part of. As I lay all of this out, my question to you is, "Can we find something in common? Is it possible you have children, or love sports, or pickleball or mountain biking? Do you have a business you want to grow?" It is rare, if ever, that I have met someone from anywhere in the world that I don't find interesting, even fascinating, as I get to know them. Being interested instead of interesting is where BRT becomes most valuable.

When you're meeting with your prospective partner, you always want to give value first before asking for anything from them. Focus on helping them achieve their goals. The faster and more effectively you do that, the faster they will feel like they know, like, and trust you enough to refer their valuable clients to you. When you first connect, consider starting the conversation by saying,

"Thanks for meeting with me today. I've heard a lot of great things about you. You come highly recommended. The reason I wanted to meet with you is that I serve a lot of homeowners who may be able to use your services. I'm hoping to learn more about you and your business so I'm referring you the right types of clients."

5 Power Questions for Prospective Partners

Now your job is to ask questions and listen closely to learn all you can about this person. The following questions are designed to help you build rapport, uncover opportunities, and create lasting partnerships. Plus, these questions will get your conversations going naturally and comfortably:

1. **"How long have you been in this line of work?"**
   Start with this easy-going question. It's a natural icebreaker that helps you gauge their expertise. Think about whether you'd feel confident recommending them to your clients. Once they've shared their journey, hit them with the next power question:

2. **"What do you like best about what you do?"**
   This question digs into their WHY—the passion and purpose driving their work. You're looking for motivation beyond the paycheck. Ideally, they'll share a client success story you can later use when referring them. You're assessing if their values align with yours and if they're someone you'd trust with your clients. After they reveal their WHY, move to power question #3:

3. **"How would you describe your ideal client?"**
   This helps you see if your Perfect Prospect Profiles align. If their ideal client matches yours, you've found a potential partner. If not, you can still be valuable referral sources for each other. Follow up with the fourth power question:

4. **"What would you say is your biggest business challenge?"**
   Most professionals will say they need more prospects, clients, or business. If they do, you've found an opportunity to discuss strategic alliances and mutual growth. But first, dig deeper into their business development with the final power question:

5. **"Where do most of your clients come from?"**
   Often, the answer is referrals. That's your cue to say something like:

   "It's great to hear referrals are key for you. I work almost exclusively by referral, which is why I'm here today. I'm seeking quality partners to grow our businesses together. Based on what you've shared, you're exactly the type of professional I want on my trusted team. Let me tell you a bit more about myself..."

Now share some information about yourself and the services you provide that are most in alignment with what they shared that their clients need. Then, share your Perfect Prospect Profile and Service Statement so they are clear on who you are looking to serve and how you help those clients live better lives.

We sincerely believe that referrals come in all shapes and sizes and they show up when you least expect it. Activity breeds productivity, when you are anxiously engaged in serving and giving referrals, opportunities will present themselves, not always as a result of an exact activity, rather you will be blessed by doing the right thing.

Action Items:

1. **Leverage Technology for Insights**: Use tools like Sam's IntelNgine to gather information about clients and prospects, allowing for more personalized and meaningful interactions.
2. **Focus on Authentic Connections:** Prioritize understanding the needs and interests of others to foster genuine relationships.
3. **Systematize Follow-Up**: Implement a structured follow-up system to maintain and nurture relationships over time.
4. **Embrace Mentorship**: Seek out mentors and be open to learning from others, as these relationships can have a profound impact on your career.
5. **Give More Than You Receive**: Adopt a mindset of generosity, offering referrals and support without expecting anything in return.

Chapter 16:
The Referral Partner Blueprint

The fastest and easiest way to build referral partnerships is by using the Referral Partner Blueprint. This easy-to-use system gives you a paint-by-numbers approach to guide people through a collaboration conversation.

Once you've identified someone you would like to form a referral partnership with, simply pull out the Referral Partner Blueprint to guide your conversation. Discuss the cross-promotion strategies you think will work best for this particular referral partnership. Check off what each person is willing to do for the other so both parties have a clear agreement in place.

As you follow the format and fill in the blanks, you will find it makes the process of creating referral partnerships with complementary professionals virtually dummy proof. We will cover each of these cross-promotion campaigns in the next chapter. First, you need to understand how to educate and empower your referral partners to send you new client opportunities quickly and consistently.

Train Your Team

As you start using the Referral Partner Blueprint, you will find people are eager to partner with you. That's why it's important to train your referral partners on the specific clients you are looking for, and how best to refer you.

To ensure you attract a steady stream of profitable prospects coming to your business, follow these five proven steps:

1. Discuss your Perfect Prospect Profile and Service Statement so they understand how you help and what challenges you solve.

2. Share stories of clients you've helped so they will remember and refer you when a client mentions facing a similar challenge.

3. Supply them with your Referral Kit, including brochures and business cards, social media contact information, that they can set out in their lobby and give to their clients. Tap and go QR codes with all your contact information work great.

4. Create customized gift certificates or referral cards so your referral partner feels special, and their clients know you are a trusted professional.

5. Print a list of your top ten Frequently Asked Questions (FAQs) so your referral partners are informed and can educate their clients about the services you provide.

These are the top five ways you can empower your partners. The key is to help them understand how you help so you become their go-to, number one trusted resource for each and every client who faces the problems you solve. The more you educate your referral partners on the value you provide, the more clients they will send your way. So long as you follow up consistently.

Follow-Up and Follow Through

After you've met with each prospective referral partner, be sure to follow-up and follow through on any commitments you made. Take action immediately, and you will impress them with your professionalism. Once you have committed to making introductions, make them quickly and effectively. Go above and beyond to gain your new referral partner's respect and reciprocity.

Be sure to update and thank the person who made the introduction. Give them an overview of how well the conversation went and whether you believe this person will be a fit for your clients. Following up honors the introducer and shows them you take good care of the introductions they give you. Often, this alone leads to more referrals because you are demonstrating your professionalism in communication.

If you're really serious about building a solid referral base, you may want to send whoever introduced you a thank you card or small gift as a token of appreciation. This will lead them one step closer to singing your praises to everyone they know. The more people feel you care, the more they will care about you.

Play the Long Game

One thing you need to understand is that building referral partnerships takes time. Although you will likely receive referrals from some partners quickly, others will need to know, like, and trust you over time. The more relational equity you build with people, the more referrals you will receive.

Rather than expecting instant results, make a goal for how many referral partnerships you plan to create over the coming year. Keeping your eye on the prize will help you build a solid business that will generate profitable prospects for years to come.

Connect with the people you want to do business with regularly. Calendar consistent communications to them every two weeks at a minimum. Seeing them in person always creates the deepest connections but isn't the most time efficient. That's why you want to mix in regular phone calls, text messages, video messages, emails, and social media messages to stay top-of-mind and continually add value.

I (Verl) have always maintained that your Top 50 should be clear. They should know they are a part of it and they should receive a minimum of one personal touch per month on top of all the other touches and value ads. Remember to get face to face with as many on your Top 50 as you can each month.

Before reaching out, think of a way you can add value to them and their clients. Never call saying you are just "checking in" or "following up". Those are two of the worst statements you can make because you are telling them you have no other reason to call other than to ask them for business. Instead, you can:

- Give them a referral
- Provide an update on a client they referred
- Offer to connect them with a professional or business owner
- Share an idea you think will help their business
- Ask a question about their industry or the services they provide
- Offer to promote them using one of the co-marketing campaigns in the next chapter

- Invite them to join you at an industry or networking event
- Let them know about new events you are hosting or services you are offering
- Share industry insights you think they should know about
- Stop by to drop off gifts, books, brochures, or branded swag

It's A Numbers Game

Using these strategies and scripts can make a profound impact on your business over the months and years to come. Just imagine what your business will look like 12 months from now if you take the time to meet just one new prospective partner each week for the next year.

Of those 50 people, if only 20% are a fit and become your referral partners, you will have ten new professionals referring you profitable clients consistently for years to come. Then, for the rest of your career, you will be on easy street never having to wonder where your next client is coming from. In reality, most professionals experience much better results than partnering 20% of the time, so you can truly accelerate the process and your revenue by following the Referral Partner Blueprint.

Give More

When building referral partnerships, you should always be on the lookout for ways to add value to your partners. Truth is that the more you give in life, the more will be given to you. I (Brandon) am such a passionate proponent of this strategy that I had customized license plates for my BMW back in Oregon that said, GIV MOR.

For me, it's much more than just a slogan. It's a life philosophy. I'm always looking to add value to everyone I meet and to give as much as humanly possible. When you adopt the GIVE MORE attitude and look for ways to practice random acts of kindness, you'll find life becomes easier in ways you would never have imagined. This might sound a little "woo-woo" to you right now, but in my experience, karma and the law of attraction are very real. The more you give, the more serendipity shows up in your life.

Back in 1998, my wife and I took a two-week trip to Italy and Greece. While it was tough to leave my mortgage business for two weeks, I made sure to bring back some exotic gifts for the REALTORs I was building referral partnerships with. In addition to some of the standard tourist trinkets, I also brought back metal bottles filled with Greek Ouzo, as well as the most delicious baklava I've ever tasted.

THE REFERRAL PARTNER BLUEPRINT

When I returned home and dropped off these sweet treats and exotic liqueurs to my top referral partners, they were blown away that I was thoughtful enough to think of them while on my European vacation. Especially since I had transported these gifts over 6,000 miles to bring them back something special.

Next, I traveled to Hawaii and brought back cases of chocolate-covered macadamia nuts. While my referral partners enjoyed the gift, what they really appreciated is that they were important enough to me that I was thinking of them while away with my family. The truth is that those tasty treats helped solidify relationships and win referrals worth thousands of times the cost of the gifts. While I'm sure they enjoyed what I gave them, what won them over was my generosity and thoughtfulness.

As you start building your referral partnerships, be on the lookout for ways you can make a difference in their lives. Do everything you can to give more to your partners, and you will activate the law of reciprocity and watch your business grow. Especially when you start cross-promoting with your partners, which is the final key to profitable partnerships.

Ready to create more profitable partnerships? The Referral Partner Blueprint makes it easy to guide your conversations and create a powerful plan where you and your referral partners get into action and win together.

In your toolkit, you'll find a PDF copy of our Referral Partner Blueprint.

RavingReferrals.com/toolkit

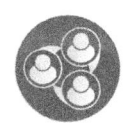

Chapter 17:
Top 21 Cross-Promotion Campaigns

Marketing is the lifeblood of your business. Marketing is what spreads your message and brings in profitable prospects that become lifetime clients. That's why partnering and cross-promoting with others who already serve your market can be the fastest and most powerful way to grow your business.

When it comes to promoting yourself and your services, there's nothing like the credibility and visibility you gain when someone else raves about you. People don't care what you say about yourself as much as they care what others say about you. Your goal is to get seen, get hired, and get paid.

When people see your name or brand being recommended by someone they respect, they automatically trust you more and are more likely to hire you; especially when people endorse you authentically and passionately. Whether your goal is to attract a few ideal clients, or gain millions of fans and followers, cross-promoting with influencers, experts, businesses, and professionals who serve your ideal clients can produce real results rapidly.

You've Seen This Before

Often called co-op marketing or simply co-marketing, this is a strategic marketing and advertising partnership between two or more companies or referral partners who promote each other to their respective audiences.

Collaborating on a marketing campaign can help both parties generate twice the results with half the effort. What's great about co-marketing is that both partners leverage their Social Sphere to generate more buzz, awareness, fans, followers, and profitable prospects together. These campaigns can quickly provide the extra boost that attracts more leads and revenues. Even if you have never co-marketed yourself, you've seen the biggest brands on the planet doing it for years.

One of the best examples is the shoe brand Nike partnering with Michael Jordan to create the Air Jordan brand. According to Forbes magazine, their partnership has generated over $1.3 billion for Michael Jordan since 1984. This alliance not only made Jordan richer than any contract from playing basketball, but it also simultaneously solidified Nike as the dominant leader in the shoe game. In Nike's 2019 fiscal year, the Jordan Brand generated $3.1 billion in sales accounting for 8% of total Nike revenue for the year.

Back in Portland, one of the fathers whose boys I (Brandon) coached in youth sports was the son of Reggie Saunders, Nike's Senior Director of Entertainment Marketing for Air Jordan. He was one cool cat. His stock really rose with the boys on our basketball team when he gave each player a free pair of the latest and greatest brand spanking new Air Jordans. Reggie told me story after story of the athletes the company was able to attract as partners because these players grew up wearing Air Jordans and always wanted to "Be like Mike." The value Jordan brought Nike went far beyond shoe sales and solidified the brand as the king of the shoe game. As Nike would say, when it comes to co-marketing, JUST DO IT.

Another great example of creating profitable partnerships and co-marketing campaigns comes from the larger-than-life Shaquille O'Neal. After having a hall-of-fame career on the court, Shaq cashed in on his notoriety by creating strategic alliances with a number of companies and brands, including:

- 24 Hour Fitness
- Arizona Beverage Company
- Auntie Anne's Pretzels
- Avalanche Brands
- Boys & Girls Club of America
- Buca De Beppo
- Buick
- Carnival Cruise
- Comcast
- Dove
- Dunkman Shoes
- Epson Printers
- Five Guys Burgers & Fries

TOP 21 CROSS-PROMOTION CAMPAIGNS

- Frosted Flakes
- Gold Bond
- Home Depot
- IcyHot
- JC Penney
- Jimmy John's
- Krispy Kreme
- Lining Shoes
- Macy's
- Monster Headphones
- Muscle Milk
- NBA 2k
- Nestle Crunch
- Papa John's Pizza
- Pepsi
- Reebok
- Ring Doorbell
- Skechers
- Sleep Apnea Mask
- SportsCastr
- Steiner Sports
- Susta Sugar Substitute
- Taco Bell
- The General Insurance
- The Original Soupman
- Vitamin Water
- Walmart
- Zales Jewelry

While you may never collaborate with a major corporation like those listed above, the strategy is the same when promoting your personal services.

Now that you are aware of co-marketing campaigns, you are going to start seeing these campaigns over and over. The power and influence you can unlock through partnerships are unmatched. In fact, teenagers are now making millions as instant influencers on Instagram and TikTok partnering with companies as brand ambassadors to promote their energy drinks, clothing, makeup, and jewelry products.

The Ultimate Trust Transfer

Co-marketing gives you the ultimate marketing leverage because as you cross promote your referral partners, they transfer the trust they've built with their clients and prospects onto you.

By collaborating and cross promoting each other, both you and your partner:

- Increase awareness for each other's businesses and services
- Attract more prospects, fans, and followers
- Generate leads, referrals, and business opportunities
- Reduce marketing costs while increasing closing rates

Creating cross promotions and co-marketing campaigns with just ten other professionals or businesses over the next year can increase your marketing reach by 1,000% or more. The way this works is simple. Let's say your ideal clients are homeowners and that you have 1,000 homeowners on your email list. If you partner with ten other professionals who also serve homeowners with similar size databases, you are now being promoted, endorsed, and recommended to 10,000 prospective clients in addition to your own 1,000 contacts. Plus, by helping your partners gain more visibility and grow their books of business, you dramatically increase the likelihood they will return the favor by promoting and referring you to their clients and colleagues.

So how can you leverage the power of co-marketing to promote your products and services in your local market? Glad you asked!

21 Top Cross-Promotion Campaigns

As you meet with prospective Referral Partners to create a strategic alliance, just pull out your Referral Partner Blueprint to guide your conversation. This powerful tool will help you steer your discussions through the various ways you and your partners can cross-promote each other to win more business together. The basic strategy for each of these campaigns is for you and your partners to promote and recommend each other to your respective databases and Social Spheres.

The top 21 ways you and your partners can proactively promote or recommend each other are:

1. Introductions
2. Client Referrals
3. Ratings and Reviews
4. Special Offers
5. Gift Certificates
6. Consultations
7. Referral Cards
8. Websites

9. Social Posts
10. Newsletters
11. Team Brochures
12. Bundled Offers
13. Direct Mail
14. Client Events
15. Sponsorships
16. Workshops
17. Podcasts
18. Video Interviews
19. Webinars
20. Referral Mixers
21. Charity Champion Campaigns

1 – Introductions

When meeting with a new Referral Partner, an easy YES to get things moving is making introductions to other professionals you each know. After all, your new referral partner likely knows some great prospective partners for you.

Can you imagine what life will be like when people start referring you to their best clients who are a pleasure to work with? Think about the difference you will be able to make in other people's businesses. As we work together and cross-refer through our Referral Alliances, WE ALL WIN TOGETHER.

The reason to start with making introductions is that it is an easy ask you both should be very comfortable moving forward with. Starting the conversation by getting them to agree to something small will increase the likelihood they will agree on other campaigns later on.

Remember to give first. Start by suggesting a few people you know might be a good prospective partner for them. Tell them about each person and offer to introduce them. You might even want to set up a Zoom or face-to-face meeting with the three of you so you can meet socially.

The beauty is that every time these people talk to each other in the future, they will inevitably talk about you. After all, you are the one thing they always have in common. Naturally, one of them will ask the other if they have talked to you lately and how you are doing. That means the more introductions you make, the more often you are coming up in other people's conversations, which keeps you and your business top of mind.

Once you've suggested a few introductions, the other person will likely offer some people they can introduce you to. This is where you want to make sure you communicate exactly what types of professionals you want to be introduced to. The clearer you are, the more likely they are to connect you with quality professionals who have the ability to refer a lot of Perfect Prospects your way.

2 – Client Referrals

Next, we suggest you discuss referring each other to your respective clients. As you start sending each other new client opportunities, both partners win more business together. Again, start by giving first and mention that you have quite a few clients you can refer their way. If you have a referral you can give them there and then, even better. The more you refer them, the more they will reciprocate.

Explain that as you build referral partnerships, you are always scouting and looking out for new clients you can introduce to your partners. If that sounds like something they are interested in, you would be happy to proactively refer them clients and hope they will do the same for you. Then simply ask them how that sounds. Their response will tell you a lot. If they sound hesitant, they either may not be the right partner you are looking for, or they need time to get to know, like, and trust you more before committing to that level of alliance.

3 – Ratings and Reviews

Another way to help your referral partners boost their credibility and visibility is to give each other ratings or reviews on Google, Yelp, Angi, HOA.com, or any other sites and services where you each promote yourselves.

Just ask your partner if they use ratings and reviews in their marketing and if they'd like you to give them a rating or review. You should also let them know which sites you are using and see if they'd be willing to give you a rating or review. You can even get it done right then before you end your meeting.

The importance of reviews cannot be overstated. Recently, I (Brandon) was in New York City for a C-Suite Network event led by its charismatic CEO Jeffrey Hayzlett. During the conference, I was talking with Helena, the SVP of Global Strategic Partnerships and Business Development for the Amazon company Audible. Helena shared that Audible now uses reviews as their top marketing strategy to drive revenue. Their testing shows member reviews are far more effective in attracting and retaining new subscribers. In the online world, reviews rule. If a tech giant like Audible who has done extensive marketing research believes in the power of reviews, so should you.

We humans trust the collective power of reviews because we feel like the research has been done for us. Again, people care far more what other people say about you than what you say about yourself. Especially when those people are high Blueprint or Knowledge personality types.

4 – Special Offers

Everyone loves to save money and get a deal. That's why offering special discounts is another great way to help your partners promote your products or services. This helps your partners give their clients something special and gives your partners an easy way to introduce your services. You can even combine this with a closing gift to introduce your partner's services right when your client needs them most.

You may want to offer referred clients to reimburse them for the cost of their home inspection, appraisal or offer to pay for their moving truck rental. Just be sure to quantify the value they are receiving so they understand they are saving $250 or even $500 as a result of your referral partner's introduction.

5 – Gift Certificates

There's no better price than free. That's why gift certificates are the ultimate way to package your special offer. Gift certificates allow your partners to recommend your services by giving their clients and customers something with high perceived value. While you may not want to give away your products and services for free, you can package a discount as a gift certificate to boost the perceived value.

Examples of gift certificates that you and your referral partners may want to offer include:

- REALTORs providing a free home cleaning or moving truck rental after closing
- Pool installation companies offering free lights with a new pool or spa
- HVAC companies offering a free HVAC system check
- Accountants offering a free tax return review
- Landscape maintenance companies offering one free month of service or a free landscape design as move in gift
- Interior designers offering a complimentary interior design consultation

- Home Security companies offering a free security analysis
- Solar companies offering a free home energy audit
- Home automation companies providing a complimentary home automation design package

Simply have your partners print their gift certificates and include a brochure or flyer on their services that you can give to your clients. You may even want to print a special gift certificate envelope or new home welcome kit featuring your referral partners to create a special impression for your new clients.

6 – Consultations

Since you likely provide market analysis consultations as part of your listing process, encourage your referral partner to include your service as part of theirs. Giving their clients a free market analysis from you makes your referral partner look good and provides value to everyone involved.

You might also offer a consultation on turning a home into a short-term-rental which gives you a unique service that will draw homeowners looking at becoming real estate investors. After all, once they decide to give up their primary residence, they are going to need to buy a new home. Plus, many who consider turning their primary home into a short-term-rental will choose simply to sell their home once they understand all the variables involved.

Consider creating a special landing page on your website or printing gift certificates or brochures that describe the service you provide to your partner's clients. Place a value on the assessment so the client understands they are getting something special thanks to your referral partner.

7 – Referral Cards

If you want to attract more Raving Referrals, it is imperative you make it easy for people to refer you. The fastest way to accomplish that is by giving people printed referral cards they can quickly hand to anyone who may need your products or services. This also helps you track where your business is coming from so you can recognize and reward your referrers.

You have probably received a referral card from your dentist, chiropractor, or home services professional. They are an inexpensive and effective way to help people help you. By including all the essential referral program information, these cards provide a simple way for people to refer others to your business.

One of the simplest ways to add a referral card into your business is by adding your referral offer to the back of your existing business card. You can also print a special postcard size promotional piece that gives people details about your product or service along with a special offer. Be sure to include a catchy headline or slogan like:

- **Your Referrals Mean the World to Me!**
  Know someone looking to buy or sell? Hand them this card, and I'll ensure they receive top-notch service. Your trust is my greatest compliment!

- **Helping Your Friends & Family Find Their Dream Home!**
  Give this card to someone you care about, and I'll treat them like family while helping them achieve their real estate goals.

- **Let's Work Together to Help Others Move Forward!**
  Pass along this card to anyone thinking about buying or selling a home. I'll guide them every step of the way!

- **Your Trusted REALTOR, Always Ready to Help!**
  Referrals are the heart of my business—send this card to someone who needs real estate assistance, and I'll make sure they feel supported and informed.

- **Turn Your Referrals into Results!**
  When you refer someone to me, I'll help them navigate the real estate process with care and expertise. Call or text today!

- **Refer a Friend, Help Build a Dream!**
  Know someone ready to make a move? Hand them this card, and I'll make their home-buying or selling experience seamless and stress-free.

8 – Websites

Another great way to cross promote with your partners is by adding and recommending them on your respective websites. Simply add them to a page that lists your resources, trusted partners, or preferred providers with links to their website or social media pages. Create a page on your site where your clients and customers can explore and connect with your trusted team of referral partners.

When creating a referral partner page on your website, list each partner with a sentence or two about the services they offer. Display their contact information, including phone number and website URL. Include their logo or banner ad linked to their website. If your partner offers special pricing or promotions, position that prominently so people know you are helping them unlock special pricing or treatment.

You may also want to add a testimonial or success story from one of your clients or customers. Years ago, my company was a Preferred Supplier for Prudential Real Estate Affiliates, which was later purchased and rebranded as Berkshire Hathaway Home Services. Being listed on their website brought instant credibility to our company and led to hundreds of their REALTORs joining our online referral program.

While many of their agents found us through the listing on their global Prudential corporate website, we also used the endorsement as a strategic partner when marketing to their agents directly. The credibility and visibility you gain when partners promote you on their website can be significant. Especially when you partner with influential brands and people.

This is built into the Pro Profiles on HOA.com. In fact, we've created the ability for you to feature your entire Trusted Team of referral partners directly on your HOA.com Certified Pro profile. Your Trusted Team will also be featured and promoted on the HomeSafe Reports you can send to your homeowner database each month. Similar to HomeBot, the HOA.com Homesafe Reports provide homeowners with a monthly valuation of their home while simultaneously featuring local events as well as a list of professionals they can trust and hire to maintain, upgrade, or even sell their home.

This is the only automated co-marketing system we've ever seen, so check out HOA.com/realty now to set up your Certified Pro profile and feature all your best referral partners automatically. The beauty is that the HOA.com HomeSafe reports help convert your vendors into proactive partners who automatically promote you to all the homeowners in their database every single month. You just set it and forget it and let the referrals come to you automagically.

9 – Social Posts

Social media is a powerful way to cross-promote with your partners. It's fast, easy, and free. When you combine forces and collaborate on Facebook, Instagram, X (Twitter), or LinkedIn, you reach new audiences creating instant credibility through the exposure and endorsement from your partner. The key to this strategy is to coordinate a conversation by posting publicly. This creates an opportunity for your referral partners to answer, comment, and create a dialogue that others see and participate in. We recommend you pre-plan or at least coordinate what you and your partners are going to post so that both parties are promoted and provide value to your respective tribes of clients, fans, and followers. Some of the most effective ways to co-market with your partners include:

- Success Stories – Thank your partner publicly for helping clients get great results. Share the thanks you received from your clients for introducing your referral partners.
- Testimonials – Share your personal story of how impressed you've been by their knowledge, professionalism, and expertise. If you've personally used their product or service, share that as well to build social proof and trust.
- Expert Content – Provide special reports or whitepapers that educate people on the real estate industry, products, or services.
- Giveaways – Get your referral partners to send free samples of their products or services.
- Special Offers – Post discounts, promotions, or special offers for local businesses you support.
- Events – Invite people to attend online or in-person events with you and your partners.
- Questions and Quizzes – Post questions about your partner's industry or area of expertise, tagging them to respond.
- Photos and Videos – Show happy homeowners along with before and after photos or videos of fix and flips or remodels you've helped make happen to give visual examples of the impact you make.
- Go Live – Have a social conversation for the world to watch about anything from the list above.

10 – Newsletters

If you send out printed or email newsletters to your clients and prospect database, consider adding a section for your Referral Partners or top trusted pros. This adds value to your referral partners and shows you are committed to helping them win more clients. As you lead the partnership, they will feel indebted and want to return the favor either by giving you referrals directly or by cross-promoting you to their networks and Social Sphere. Just be sure to ask if they send out newsletters to their client list or database. If so, you can use any of the strategies above to cross-promote with your partners.

I've been using this strategy for over 20 years, and it is still as powerful today as it was back in the 1990s. Back then, my newsletter would feature mortgage loan programs and interest rates, as well as a segment thanking the REALTORs, financial advisors, and other professionals who referred clients my way. I made sure each of my referral partners received my newsletter, so they felt appreciated for the business they sent.

The real secret of this strategy was the social proof I manufactured by including the names of the people who trusted me enough to refer their clients and co-workers. As people saw the list of referral partners who trusted me, they gained confidence in my ability to deliver results which led them to refer their best clients too.

11 – Team Brochures

As you start creating your trusted team of professionals, consider printing brochures featuring you and each of your referral partners. This gives both you and your partners a physical marketing tool you can share with your clients and display at your office or place of business. If you use this strategy, be sure all of the partners make a habit of giving these out to each new client you all have so everyone in your referral team is continuously promoting each other.

Team brochures work extremely well when you have a core group of professionals serving a specific target market or life event. Simply write an introduction as to the joint services and solution your team provides. Then list each partner including their name, company, logo, phone number, and website address. You may also want to include a brief statement or bulleted list of the specific services each partner provides. Call it your Dream Team so everyone feels special and they will share it with all the homeowners they serve promoting you as the top trusted REALTOR on their Dream Team.

12 – Bundled Offers

Another way to cross-promote your partners is to actually bundle their services with your own. The way this strategy works is that you and your referral partner combine your services into one integrated solution or offer at a bundled price.

As a REALTOR, bundling the services of your trusted referral partners into your listing package can significantly enhance the value you provide to clients while setting you apart from the competition. By including services such as professional home staging, pre-listing inspections, landscaping touch-ups, or handyman repairs, you demonstrate your commitment to maximizing your client's home value and ensuring a smooth sale process. Collaborating with referral partners also allows you to offer a seamless, stress-free experience for sellers, as they can rely on your curated network of reliable professionals to handle every aspect of preparing their home for market.

This bundled approach not only adds tangible value to your listing package, but also strengthens your relationships with your referral partners. As you showcase their services to your clients, your partners benefit from increased visibility and potential business, creating a mutually beneficial ecosystem. Additionally, by integrating these services, you position yourself as a full-service REALTOR who goes above and beyond to deliver results. Whether it's offering a complimentary cleaning session, discounted photography, or access to movers, bundling referral partner services elevates your reputation, attracts more clients, and helps you close deals faster and more efficiently.

13 – Direct Mail

Once you are in agreement with your referral partners on a special offer, bundled service, or joint promotion you want to offer, sending your campaign through direct mail is a great way to get the word out. It gives your respective clients something tangible they can touch and feel forcing them to view your message and offer.

This allows you and your partners to target people in transitory life events. There are several top life events that cause people to search out new service professionals which you can target through direct mail campaigns including:

- Renters
- Engaged Or Just Married
- Expecting Or New Parents
- Retiring Or Recently Retired
- Divorcing Or Recently Divorced

When you utilize referred introductions and bundled offers into your direct mail campaign, you can leverage and maximize the results for both you and your referral partners. While you may choose to mail your joint campaign to your respective client lists, you can also purchase or rent a list of Perfect Prospects you share with your partners.

14 – Client Celebration Events

Events are a great way to bring people together and create new opportunities to connect. Consider hosting a quarterly or annual client celebration event with your referral partners. This can be as simple as hosting a happy hour at your office, or a local restaurant, bar, or hotel.

What's great about hosting these types of events with your referral partners is you can expand your audience while having fun celebrating great people. The key is to communicate to your referral partners the type of clients or professionals you would like them to invite so they fill the room with your Perfect Prospects.

As a reminder, some of the client appreciation events you can produce with your referral partners include:

- Art Showings
- Awards Parties: Oscars, Grammys, Golden Globes
- Bowling Parties
- Casino Nights
- Charity Fundraising Events
- Cigar Nights
- Concerts
- Cornhole Tournaments
- Golf Tournaments
- Holiday Parties: Valentine's Day, Independence Day, Halloween, Thanksgiving, Christmas, New Year's Eve
- Private Movie Showings
- Sporting Events
- Top Golf Tournaments
- Wine Tours and Tasting

Be sure to capture everyone's contact information so you can follow up with them after the event to explore a relationship together.

15 – Sponsorships

If your referral partners already produce or participate in their own training events or conferences, you may want to consider sponsoring or exhibiting at their events. This shows your partners you support them and are committed to helping them achieve success.

Sponsorship also creates opportunities for your referral partners to introduce or promote you and your services to their clients and strategic partners. You'll be amazed how many other partnership opportunities present themselves when you support your partners. The more you help

TOP 21 CROSS-PROMOTION CAMPAIGNS

your partners in their passions and pursuits, the more they will recommend you and the services you provide. In addition to sponsoring existing referral partners, you may want to sponsor:

- Association Events
- Bridal Expos
- Business Expos
- Chamber Of Commerce Events
- Charity Events
- Community Impact Events
- Concerts
- Conferences
- Golf Tournaments
- Home And Garden Expos
- Little Leagues
- Networking Events
- Podcasts
- Races
- School Carnivals
- Sporting Events
- Trade Shows
- Webinars
- Websites

When considering a sponsorship opportunity, look to maximize exposure to your Perfect Prospects. If the event sponsor is gathering your ideal clients, the return on investment may justify the opportunity, especially since many event promoters will provide you the database of attendees as part of your sponsorship package.

Sponsorship benefits you should ask for include:

- Award Presentations
- Banner Ads on The Event Website and Mobile App
- Brochures Or Samples included in Attendee Gift Bags
- Direct Mail Campaigns
- Email Promotions before and after the Event
- Exhibitor Booth Space

- Logo Placement in Attendee Gift Bags
- Press Release
- Product Placement throughout the Event
- Signage throughout the Event
- Social Media Promotion
- Speaking Opportunities
- Tabletop Promotion
- VIP Sessions

16 – Workshops

As we discussed in Chapter 11, workshops are a great way to educate people about the services you provide and the value you deliver. That's why you should talk to your partners about putting on a seminar, workshop, or lunch-and-learn training for your combined clients with each of you delivering a portion of the content. Just identify the top tips people need to know about the challenges you solve and how you help.

Training events help you attract qualified clients and boost your status as experts in your field. Once people have attended your class, they will understand why they need your service, and how you can help them solve their challenges and overcome their obstacles.

By establishing your expertise, you instantly elevate your status, especially to those guests invited by your partners. There's simply no better way to gain the credibility and trust that gets transferred from the introduction of your referral partners. Plus, by mutually promoting the event to your respective clients, customers, fans, and followers, you leverage your combined audience to attract more profitable prospects. If you produce the event and get your referral partners to promote it to their lists, you can expand your prospect database by capturing the contact information for all the people who register for the event. Then you can follow up with a variety of offers using your CRM or follow up system.

17 – Podcasts

Podcasts have grown in popularity and are now one of the best ways to establish yourself as an expert. Similar to a live workshop, podcasts give you an opportunity to interview your referral partners on their area of expertise. The strategy works just like a workshop, except rather than producing an in-person event, you simply record and broadcast your conversation much like a radio interview. Then you can post the audio file for people to listen to on their mobile device or computer. This allows them to download and listen to your conversation when it's most convenient for them.

Podcasts give you valuable content that both you and your referral partners can give away to prospects. You can also transcribe the recording and produce a special report your clients and Social Sphere can benefit from. The beauty of this strategy is that your referral partners will be happy to share the recording with their network because you are helping them boost their status and showcase their expertise. Just imagine how many referrals and leads you will attract when you get the right partners to promote your podcast to their audience because you have made them the star of the show.

Be sure to ask for a bio or some background on your referral partner so you can introduce them effectively. You may also want to research them on LinkedIn, their website, or social media to identify some interesting information to include in your conversation.

Here are some great questions you can ask during your podcast:

- How did you get started in the real estate industry?
- What are the biggest challenges people come to you with?
- What is the most important thing you hope people learn from our conversation today?
- What would you say are the most common myths people have about the real estate industry?
- What are some specific warning signs people should watch out for in the real estate industry?
- What are you most proud of in your business?
- What are you most passionate about?
- Outside of work, what do you spend your time doing?
- What charities or social causes are you most passionate about?
- How has social media changed the way you do business?
- In your opinion, what is the future of…?
- How is technology impacting the real estate industry?
- Tell me something that's true that almost nobody agrees with you on.
- How can people learn more about you and the solutions ou provide?
- What's the best way for our listeners to connect with you?

We always recommend you give first and offer to interview your referral partners on your own podcast. This activates the law of reciprocity and will often lead them to return the favor. This strategy works powerfully when you interview people who already have significant social followings. Once the interview is over, offer to help them further by allowing them to interview you.

Just say, "By the way, if it would be helpful, I would be happy to have you interview me so you have some content you can share with your audience." You will find they will be happy to return the favor, especially because they now feel indebted to you.

Checkout Podmatch.com and Matchmaker.fm to see podcast hosts you can reach out to and offer to be a guest on their show.

18 – Video Interviews

While audio podcasts are quick and easy to produce, video interviews via Zoom and going live on social media are great ways to educate audiences about who and how you help. Before your interview, ask your partner what topics they want to cover and if they have any specific questions they would like you to ask. Then you can talk about the problems they solve and the solutions they provide.

Again, make sure they give you some background information so you can introduce them properly and establish their credibility. To prepare your partner, ask them to identify top tips people should know about their subject. This will give them confidence going into the interview and help you guide the conversation. Then, ask the questions you've agreed to beforehand and invite any live viewers to ask any questions they have.

The video itself doesn't have to be a major Hollywood production. It can be a simple video shot on your mobile phone. Just do some testing and make sure the camera is steady, the lighting is good, and the audio is loud enough for your audience to hear clearly. You can shoot the video at one of your offices or out at a jobsite. If you can show visual examples of the work your referral partner does, even better.

Your goal is to give great content that helps your audience solve their challenges. Include a call to action at the end that makes it clear how to contact you and your referral partners should the person have questions or want to move forward.

19 – Webinars

Another way to present your expertise and attract clients for both you and your referral partners is by offering combined online webinars. The beauty of webinars is you can educate your audience and present your solutions far and wide. You can give presentations, perform product demonstrations, and deliver worldwide messages to thousands of people at a time. And if you create content that is informative and inspirational, you'll get great results and build a large list of prospects for your respective follow-up funnels.

Plus, because webinars are virtual, they save people from having to travel to attend your training in person and help you avoid the considerable costs of paying for meals or conference rooms to host live physical events.

To maximize the success of your webinar, follow these 10 Steps:

1. Choose a Topic – Identify a topic that points out the pain points of your Perfect Prospects to inspire them to register for your training.

2. Choose a Date and Time – Select a time that works well for people locally and nationally if appropriate.

3. Choose a Webinar Platform – Zoom, GoToWebinar, and Webinar Jam are the platforms we've personally used and recommend.

4. Invite Your Audience – Both partners should text and email their databases and promote the event on your websites, blogs, and social media accounts.

5. Build Your Content – Create slides that identify the challenges you solve and spotlight the solutions and expertise each partner delivers.

6. Practice – Be sure to do a quick test run to ensure you're comfortable with the technology and that both speakers know which slides or sections each will be presenting.

7. Host and Record Your Webinar – Present your webinar as a masterclass, panel discussion, interview, case study, or product demo. Be sure to record it so you can post and share afterwards.

8. Ask For Action – Have a compelling call-to-action asking attendees to buy, try, or schedule a consultation to learn more.

9. Follow-Up – After your event, be sure to email, text, message, or call everyone who attended as well as those who registered but did not attend.

10. Share Your Webinar Recording – Post your webinar recording on your social media channels and email to your prospect and client database. You can even add the video to your website to provide ongoing education for your audience.

Some people choose to charge for their webinars, but if you're looking to attract a larger audience and build your prospect database, you should offer your class for free. This will give you the largest prospect list to follow up with after the webinar.

Landing the right promotional partner for your webinars can lead to hundreds or even thousands of Perfect Prospects being added to your sales funnel. One of our recent webinar campaigns attracted over 5,000 webinar registrants over a two-week period with over 2,000 people joining our live class. Rather than having to rent a conference center and incur the costs of producing an event of that size, we were able to host our event virtually which made it easy for everyone to attend.

As you join our Raving Referrals, Workman Success, and HOA.com families, you will see this principle in action as we often host combined webinars with trusted advisors such as CINC, REDX, SISU, INMAN, RIS Media, NAR, HAR, ATG, FLOW, FELLO and more. Combining marketing to each other's databases and offering real value helps all our businesses grow.

20 – Referral Mixers

Hosting Referral Mixers is a fun and effective way to meet high quality professionals and prospects. When you host mixers, you become the central connector elevating your status as the leader of the group. Asking your top referral partners to co-host mixers helps you add value to your referral partners while you create a community of high-quality professionals.

Mixers provide the opportunity for people to meet in a festive and friendly atmosphere. Your role is simply to meet and introduce the people in your tribe. The more you help other people make new connections, the more your own network will grow.

This can easily be coordinated either at your office or a nearby restaurant, hotel, bar, or golf course. Once you know the location, date, and time, start promoting the event using email, Eventbrite, Evite, a Facebook event, or other event invitation system. Then, enlist your referral partners to help get the word out by inviting their clients along with top professionals they know, like, and trust.

You can even target the event for a certain industry or group of professionals. Just be specific with your referral partners, letting them know the types of people you are looking to attract so they fill the event with your Perfect Prospects.

Then, when your mixer starts, you get to meet every single person who walks in the door as they check in at the registration table.

Best of all, you are meeting them from a position of prominence. You'll find them grateful for the invitation and impressed to meet the event producer bringing together so many fabulous people. The more you position yourself as a connector and catalyst, the more people will seek you out, asking how they can earn your trust and win your business.

21 – Charity Champion Campaigns

We love to partner with charities and causes. You don't need to create your own charity to tap into the power of cause-related marketing. You can simply raise awareness, funds, and support for great causes and charities already doing good work.

Ask your referral partner if they have any charities or causes they are passionate about. If so, discuss how you might join forces and create more awareness and support for the causes that are near and dear to them. If you have a favorite charity or cause, suggest they join forces with you to create more impact together.

Some of the most fun and inspiring cause related marketing campaigns Brandon has produced over the years include:

- Christmas Kindness – We produced a Christmas drive collecting toys, clothing, and canned food culminating with a concert and community celebration in Pioneer Square, the community courtyard in the center of downtown Portland. We gave points for each donation and awarded the top donation raiser a one-week trip to Cabo San Lucas, Mexico.

- Virtual Veteran Salute – We created VirtualSalute.com to honor U.S. veterans helping people nationwide post photos and share stories honoring the veterans in their lives.

- We've Been Booed – A fun and festive community-based campaign to spread joy before Halloween.

- Donate Profit or Revenue – One of my training companies donated 40% of our gross sales to charity partners who provided food, water, education and microloans in developing nations.

- Empowerment Trainings – We sent a volunteer team to lead the single largest private teacher training in the African nation of Liberia with the nation's President commencing over the day's event.

- Voluntour Trips – We led volunteer teams overseas in Mexico and Africa as well as to South Dakota to build infrastructure for a Native American reservation.

- Water Wells – We helped drill water wells in Kenya.

- Food Drives – We helped produce the largest single food donation distribution day in the city of Los Angeles in partnership with Feed The Children led by Larry Jones and NBA legend Shaquille O'Neal.

- Candle Wishes – We supported a charity that provides birthday parties and gifts for underprivileged kids.

- Toys For Tots – We collected and donated toys for kids at Christmas.

- Super V Pumpkin Shoot – We created a 2-day competition hurling pumpkins hundreds of yards using canons and roman catapults with all proceeds donated to Northwest Medical Teams.

- Dog Rescues – We regularly shelter, transport, and help dogs get rescued and adopted in the U.S. and Mexico.

These are some of my favorite give-back campaigns that have brought immense joy to me, my family, my employees, and my referral partners. While the business benefits are great, the personal satisfaction you get when you make a difference in the lives of others is immeasurable. There's simply nothing better than being a Charity Champion.

As my company and I (Verl) deliver on our promise to provide service regardless of opportunity, our communities that create so many opportunities for us are a great place to start. Whether it's a pie day for first responders, a pink pumpkin decorating contest for breast cancer awareness month, or stepping up as a company, group, or team when a catastrophic event occurs, I have witnessed first hand, the greatness and power of networks coming together to make a difference in their own communities and around the world.

As a young boy, living in a 1500 sq.ft. home with seven children, when my dad was sent to a nursing home, our family had outgrown the house. It was the generosity of neighbors, and our community, that included Charlie Teams, a real estate agent who put together a group of people who added an addition to our home. This selfless act of kindness allowed us to stay close to friends, church groups, and a support system that buoyed us up as a family struggling to make ends meet for the next many years. One neighbor, one agent, and a network of specialists made a difference for my family. It is their example that drives my serving and prompts me to lead others to give and serve.

Each event creates an opportunity to invite your referral partners to participate and collaborate. Plus, when they see you as a leader committed to improving your community, they will want to do business with you for years to come. Whether you donate your time, talent, money, or promotion, everyone wins. Do more and give more for others and your life will be richly rewarded.

It Works When You Work It

These are the top 21 cross promotion campaigns you should consider implementing in your business. Hopefully you now see how using the Referral Partner Blueprint in your meetings with prospective and existing referral partners will help you have highly productive meetings that lead to profitable partnerships.

As you review each of the strategies, you will quickly gain clarity and agreement on what each person is willing to do for the other. Then, as you put these 21 proven co-marketing campaigns to work in your businesses, you and your referral partners will be thrilled as you attract more client opportunities together.

Keep it simple. Start with the easiest campaigns you both feel most comfortable with and confident in. Then, as you start seeing results and attracting more profitable prospects, you can implement additional co-marketing campaigns down the road at a later date.

In your toolkit, you will find copies of our Referral Partner Blueprint, the Top 21 Cross-Promotion Campaign Worksheet, The My Perfect Week Scheduler, and the Daily Success Habits Tracker.

ReferralChampion.com/toolkit

That Is My Excuse (TIME)

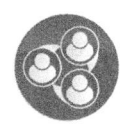

That Is My Excuse - TIME: the number one excuse for why we don't execute on the basic fundamentals at a high level. I (Verl) am here to say that we all have the same amount of time in a day, and running out of time is nothing more than a lack of planning or overscheduling. When you are intentional about how you will spend each day and you create non negotiables that include prospecting and lead follow up you will always have a good and productive day. It all begins with a WSS system called My Perfect Week.

Mastering Your Perfect Week

The Power of Planning

In the midst of a hectic schedule - or even just your average day, the key to success often lies in how well we plan our days. Imagine waking up each morning with a clear vision of what you want to achieve. This is the essence of using a system to plan your day, and it can have a profound impact on your ability to follow through on your goals. Enter the My Perfect Week Scheduler—a simple yet powerful method to organize your life and business activities.

Crafting Your Perfect Week

At the start of each week, take a moment to sit down and map out your schedule. The My Perfect Week Scheduler encourages you to time block each activity that holds significance in your life. Begin with personal commitments—those non-negotiable activities that are essential to your well-being and relationships. Whether it's attending your child's ball game or enjoying a date night with your partner, these moments take precedence in your schedule.

Building Your Business Blocks

Once personal commitments are in place, turn your attention to business activities. This is where you focus on prospecting for new opportunities. Consider this your hunting ground for new business. Following this, allocate time for lead follow-up and nurturing your top clients or referrals. The goal is to have a clear plan for both your day and your future, ensuring that every moment is accounted for.

Tracking Your Success

To truly maximize your productivity, introduce the Daily Success Habits Tracker into your routine. This tool allows you to compare your planned activities with what you actually accomplish. By measuring the right metrics and being intentional about your day, you'll discover how much more you can achieve. You'll also gain insight into how little time is often spent on dollar-productive activities.

Becoming Intentional

The journey to success is paved with intentionality. By using the My Perfect Week Scheduler, you take control of your time and your future. Plan in advance, track your progress, and watch as your productivity soars. It's time to embrace the power of planning and transform your life, one perfect week at a time.

Conclusion: Your Path to Success

As you embark on planning and intentional living, remember that the key to success lies in your hands. With the My Perfect Week Scheduler and the Daily Success Habits Tracker, you have the resources to create a life of purpose and achievement. Start today, and watch as your dreams become reality.

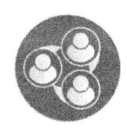

Time For ACTION

You are now empowered with the strategies, scripts, tips, and tricks you need to succeed. Everything you hope to accomplish can be achieved using the knowledge and wisdom you have in your hands. My question to you is, will you take the ACTION you need to win big?

The key to activating the Law of Attraction is taking MASSIVE ACTION. The more ACTION you take, the faster your business will grow. The good news is you can easily integrate what you've learned into your daily activities. With a few tweaks to what you already do, you can easily and effortlessly attract more Perfect Prospects and ideal clients.

As you start receiving Raving Referrals, we want to hear from you. Please take a moment and share your success story on our social channels. We'll reward you with a super-secret gift you'll be thrilled to receive.

These are some of my (Verl's) favorite Og Mandino quotes: "Only action determines our value in the marketplace", followed by: "I will act now." Opportunities are everywhere if you open your ears and open your mouth but none of these opportunities will be yours unless you act now!

Raving Referrals in Action:
The Power of Acting Without Hesitation:
Christy Buck's Story in Her Own Words

One of my favorite stories from Christy Buck, a powerhouse coaching client, perfectly illustrates the importance of acting boldly when opportunity knocks—or, in her case, when opportunity sits just one table over.

"I was at a Mexican restaurant, and I couldn't help but overhear a family at a nearby table discussing real estate. It was clear they were trying to figure out their next steps—buying, selling, who knows what else. My heart started racing. I thought to myself, 'What's the worst that can happen? They tell me no? That's already a guaranteed no if I don't do something.' So, I walked over, introduced myself, and handed them my card. I didn't pitch them, just casually mentioned I was a real estate professional and happy to help with any questions they might have."

What happened next? That small act of boldness turned into something incredible.

"The entire family turned around and started asking questions right there. By the time we finished that first conversation, I had leads spanning three generations. Over the next year, I closed a $1.5 million deal with one family member, which led to another referral and another. That one family from the restaurant is now a multi-transaction client—and all because I didn't hesitate."

Lessons from the Mexican Restaurant Encounter

Christy's story underscores a vital lesson: **Opportunities are everywhere, but they don't wait for you.** Acting in the moment, even when it feels uncomfortable or bold, can lead to life-changing outcomes.

"I didn't just earn commissions from those deals; I built relationships. That family now refers me to everyone they know. It all started with hearing them talk about real estate and deciding I wasn't going to let that opportunity walk out the door."

The Ripple Effect of Bold Referrals

This philosophy—being proactive and intentional about asking for business—extends into every facet of Christy's career. Whether it's engaging vendors, networking at events, or setting up her infamous client gatherings,

Christy has mastered the art of creating referral opportunities.

Her secret? **Always ask.**

"What's the worst that can happen? They say no? No doesn't hurt; inaction does. Every time I've chosen to act, it's paid off in some way. From selling a million-dollar house to building connections that come back years later, it's about creating the space for referrals to happen."

As Christy puts it, every opportunity—whether it's at a restaurant, a neighborhood event, or a client check-in—is a chance to grow your business and build connections that last a lifetime.

Start now by sharing your AHA moments and breakthroughs - right now.

You are now equipped with a powerful arsenal of strategies, scripts, and insights designed to guide your success. The tools are now yours, and the potential to achieve your goals is within your reach. The only question that remains is whether you'll seize the moment and take the bold ACTION required to turn your aspirations into reality. The choice is yours—commit to the path and make it happen!

Takeaways for Real Estate Professionals

From chasing a lead in a restaurant to structuring events that bring her sphere of influence together, Christy's approach is a masterclass in leveraging relationships for referrals. Here's what we can all learn from her:

1. **Listen and Act Quickly**: If you hear someone talking about real estate, engage. The window of opportunity is fleeting.
2. **Be Relational, Not Transactional**: Focus on the relationship, not the immediate sale. Trust builds referrals.
3. **Be Persistent, But Kind**: Not everyone will need your services right away, but staying in touch keeps you top of mind.
4. **Create Events that Connect**: Hosting events is more than just marketing; it's about fostering meaningful relationships within your community.

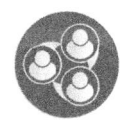

Success Scripts

Scripts for Generating Raving Referrals

The following call and conversation scripts have been refined over decades of testing. Our goal is to give your clarity and confidence to help you generate Raving Referrals and profitable partnerships. Customize your conversations based on each person's BANKCODE and you will accelerate your results even faster.

Scripts for Building Referral Partnerships:

Hi (name), the reason I'm calling is that I'm creating a team of professionals I'll be recommending to all my clients. I was thinking about you because I have a lot of clients who could benefit from your services. I'd love to sit down with you to discuss the possibility of adding you to my team and promoting you. When's a good time to get together and strategize?

Thanks so much for your time today. I'd like to ask for your help. As you may know, I am in the process of expanding my business and I'm looking for a great CPA to refer my clients to, so I'm wondering if you know of any good CPAs you think I should meet. I'm planning to meet and interview 2-3 and your CPA will be one of those I would like to meet with. Not just for my personal business, but also for the opportunity to refer clients to them. Is there anyone you'd recommend I meet with?

Stephen really sounds like an interesting person I would love to meet. Would you mind introducing the two of us? Or, if you would prefer, I am happy to send an email and mention you had great things to say about them and I would like to get to know them myself.

Thanks so much for the introduction. Would you be willing to make a quick call or send them a text to tell them how we know each other and that I will be calling them (date & time of scheduled call)? Is there anything you think I should know before I call them?

Thanks for meeting with me today. I've heard a lot of great things about you. You come highly recommended. The reason I wanted to meet with you is that I serve a lot of (type of client – homeowners/ business owners) who may be able to use your services. I'm hoping to learn more about you and your business so I'm referring you the right type of clients."

I'm glad to hear referrals are important to you. I work almost exclusively by referral which is exactly why I am here today. As I mentioned earlier, I'm looking for quality people I can partner with to grow our businesses together. Based on what you shared about your business, you are the type of person I'm looking to add to my trusted team of professionals that I promote and refer clients to.

Just to give you a little more background on me....From what you've shared, I have a number of clients who might benefit from what you do. Can we get together another time so I can ask you a few questions? Maybe next Tuesday afternoon or Wednesday morning? What works best for you?

Hope all is well in your world. I'm reaching out because I am looking to expand my professional network and noticed you are connected to a few people on LinkedIn that I'd like to meet. I have a few contacts I think you would benefit from meeting as well. Do you have a few minutes to jump on a quick call so we can connect and collaborate? What day and time works best for your schedule?

Hi (name), As you may know, I am in the process of expanding my business and I'm creating an alliance of vetted and trusted professionals to refer my clients to. I truly value our relationship and would like to invite you to be a core member of my Top 50. I will be gathering my most important referral partners (date/time) at (location) and hope you can attend. Please let me know if you can join us.

Referral Partner Alliance Meeting Script:

Thank you for coming today. The reason I asked you all to join me today is that I am expanding my business and I'm creating an alliance of vetted and trusted professionals to refer my clients to.

I truly value each and every one of you and view you as one of the best in your respective industries. Not only am I hoping to do more business with you personally, I also want to connect each of you so you can do more business together. After all, everyone in this room serves (consumers /homeowners / business owners), so we share the same ideal client and can grow our businesses faster and further by cross-referring and cross-promoting each other.

What I'd like to do now is go around the room and give everyone a chance to introduce themselves and share who you help and how you help. That will help us all understand the services you provide and who your perfect prospects and ideal clients are.

I'll go first. As you all know, my name is _____ and I help _____ (share your Service Statement).

To give you an example of what I do, I recently had a client who _____. (share a story of a problem you solved and the difference it made for them).

I'm passionate about helping people _____ and a great referral for me is a (share your Perfect Prospect Profile).

Before we move on, does anyone have any questions about the services I provide?

By the way, if it would be helpful, I would be happy to have you interview me so you have some content you can share with your clients/network/audience.

Scripts for Networking Events

The main reason I am here is that I'm looking for a quality (CPA) I can refer my clients to. Do you happen to know any good (CPA)s here you would recommend I connect with?

I'm wondering if you can help me. The primary reason I'm here is to find a top (CPA) that I can refer clients to and build a referral partnership with. Can you tell me if there are any quality (CPA)'s here I can connect with?

By the way, if you ever have a friend or family member you think might benefit from my services, I would be happy to meet with them at no charge to see how I might be able to help them.

Scripts to activate the Referral Triggers

I hope you're pleased with the service I've provided so far. Is there anything I can do to make you even happier?

Now that we've been working together for a while, I'm wondering if you can tell me what you have found most valuable about working with me?

I'm committed to growing my business through exceptional service. On a scale of 1-10, how happy would you say you are with my services?

Do you mind if I ask what you have liked best about working with me?

Thanks for sharing your feedback. Before you go, I'd like to ask you, if someone you know was asking about me or the services I provide, what would you tell them?

If you don't mind me asking, if you knew someone who was looking for a {insert your profession} how likely would you be to recommend me? What would you say?

Scripts to use when you hear the Referral Triggers

I'm so glad to hear that. I hope you'll recommend me any time you hear any {describe your Perfect Prospect} mention that they are looking for a good {insert your profession} or need help {share your Service Statement}. Is there anyone who comes to mind who might need my help?

I'm so glad you feel that way. I love helping clients like you {share your Service Statement}. By the way, I may have mentioned before that I am expanding my business so if you know any {describe your Perfect Prospect} who might need help {share your Service Statement}, I'd love to connect with them and see if I can help them the way I helped you?

Do you know anyone who is looking to {share your Service Statement}?

Scripts for Asking Clients for Referrals

Thanks for meeting with me today. Before you leave, I'd like to ask for your help. As you may know, I am in the process of expanding my business

SUCCESS SCRIPTS

and I work primarily by referral. Once I've taken care of you and hopefully have exceeded your expectations, I'd like to ask your permission to ask you for referrals. Would that be all right?

As you may know, I prefer working with people who are referred to me/us. And of course, I'll take extra special care of them since they're coming from you. Is there anyone you can think of who might like to take advantage of this?

As you know, nearly all of my business comes from referrals. A good referral for me is {describe your Perfect Prospect} who might need help {share your Service Statement}. Of everyone you know, who would be the best referral for me? Why do you say that?

As you know, nearly all of my business comes from referrals. I'm hoping we can brainstorm for a few minutes to see if we can identify some people you care about who should at least know about the work we do and the process we use to help people. Would that be alright? Great. Please let me know if there's anyone you know I can help. I'm always here for you and your clients.

Congratulations on completing the Raving Referrals book and proving your commitment to growing your business. You now have the proven strategies, scripts, tips and tricks you need to succeed. Scan this QR code or visit the link below to access your Certificate of Completion

ReferralChampion.com/completion

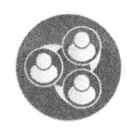

Experts & Influencers

When it comes to expanding the social reach of your business or brand, nothing matches the credibility and visibility you can gain from partnering and cross-promoting with experts and influencers. If you are looking for a podcast guest, joint venture partner, industry expert, best-selling author, keynote speaker, advisor, or board member, these are the people we highly recommend as some of the best in business:

Alex Saenz
@alexsaenz

Alex embarked on his real estate journey at just 18 years old, starting with no capital. Now in his twenties, he has successfully closed over 750 deals. With a strong presence on YouTube, Twitter, and Instagram, Alex is dedicated to helping both beginners and seasoned professionals close more deals by sharing the strategies and lessons that propelled his success.

https://alexsaenz.com

Andy Dane Carter
@andydanecarter

Andy, one of the top real estate influencers on Instagram, is an expert in all things relating to the realty business. Whether it's buying, selling, flipping, developing, or investing, if it's related to real estate, Andy is the guy for you. He ensures the best value for money for his clients and maximum profit for his investors.

https://www.andydanecarter.com

Barbara Corcoran
@barbaracorcoran

Barbara Corcoran, renowned for her role on ABC's Shark Tank, is a successful REALTOR, author, investor, and entrepreneur. She founded The Corcoran Group, sold for $66M in 2001, and boasts a net worth in the hundreds of millions. Barbara shares business insights, family moments on Instagram, and writes for major publications like The New York Daily News.

https://www.barbaracorcoran.com

Ben Wegmann
@benwegmann

Dallas REALTOR Ben Wegmann has a star-studded clientele that includes sports stars and entertainment bigwigs. Ben's motto is to keep the client's interest above everything else. His social media following makes him one of the most successful real estate influencers on our list.

https://www.rogershealy.com/agents/72872-ben-wegmann

Brendan Fitzpatrick
@brendanfitzp

Brendan is a luxury real estate expert that deals with high-value property from all over the world. Brendan enjoys every bit of his lavish lifestyle and makes sure to share some of his best moments with his Instagram fan club.

https://getfitzy.ca

EXPERTS & INFLUENCERS

Brian Iregbu
@housebuyingbrian

Soon after investing in real estate as a part-time gig, Brian struck gold and was financially independent enough to leave the job that many lust for. Today, this real estate influencer runs the Creative REI Academy where he encourages others to follow in his footsteps and achieve beyond their goals.

https://www.creativereiacademy.com/new-sp-20211629818345072

Bryan Casella
@bryancasella

Bryan Casella, #1 Real Estate Educator by INMAN Los Angeles, is a bestselling author and founder/CEO of Team BC, a leading coaching and training company. With over 30,000 coaching hours, Bryan helps agents and brokers build thriving businesses, master accountability, and balance personal fulfillment with professional success.

https://bryancasellacoaching.com

Cami Lincowski
@cami_li

One of the top real estate influencers on social media, Cami built her empire from scratch in Las Vegas. She believes in giving each client her undivided attention. Due to her preference for quality over quantity, Cami keeps her list of active clients small and her impact large.

https://camilincowski.com

Carito Betancourt
@caritobetancourt

Colombian actress and model Carito Betancourt transitioned from the showbiz industry to a successful career as a real estate agent. Her unique background allows her to connect deeply with Miami's large Hispanic community. Carito is dedicated to making the home-buying process seamless and enjoyable for her clients.

https://www.facebook.com/caritoREALTOR

Carlos Reyes
@carlosreyes

Reyes, a successful real estate agent and life coach, overcame a challenging childhood raised by a single immigrant mother to become an 8-figure earner. Now, he dedicates himself to sharing his journey and empowering others with the strategies that helped him achieve success in real estate and life.

https://allinnation.com/carlos

Chad Carroll
@chadcarroll

Chad, a Miami real estate mogul, has built a remarkable career selling ultra-luxurious properties to high-profile clients. Known for his commitment to constant reinvention, he has consistently ranked among the top 100 real estate agents for the past ten years.

https://thechadcarrollgroup.com/

Charles Curry
@smartagents

Charles Curry, Head of Marketing for Smart Agents & Authorify, has been shaping real estate marketing strategies since 2008. He developed the "Listing Funnel," a proven system that guides clients from lead to closed deal. His tailored funnels address niches like expired listings, inherited properties, divorces, vacant homes, and FSBOs.

https://www.smartagents.com/

Chelsea Roy
@chelsea_roy

As a Maine real estate agent, Chelsea is passionate about her city and enjoys travel, beauty, fashion, and fitness. She combines her love for community with her expertise in real estate, showcasing her favorite properties and providing valuable guides about local businesses to help clients feel at home in the area.

https://www.instagram.com/chelsea_roy

EXPERTS & INFLUENCERS

Chris Choi
@chrischoi

Chris has achieved remarkable success as a real estate investor, managing over 100 Airbnb properties nationwide. Specializing in the legal sublease of rental properties, he has built a thriving career and credits his mentors for guiding his journey. Now, he's dedicated to helping others achieve success through short-term rental investments.

https://www.instagram.com/chrischoi

Christy Buck
@christy_buck_REALTOR

With over 25 years in the business, Christy Buck, broker and founder of Infinity Real Estate Group, leads a top-performing team in Houston's real estate market. With over 3,500 transactions and $1.7 billion in sales under her belt, Christy emphasizes client relationships, education, and community involvement. A Master Business Coach and industry leader, she prioritizes exceptional service and lifelong connections.

https://www.christybuckteam.com

Clayton Morris
@claytonmorris

A celebrated REALTOR, investor, and host, Clayton Morris is dedicated to helping others achieve financial freedom through his Morris Invest project. He shares his extensive knowledge of real estate and investment strategies on his podcast, Investing in Real Estate, inspiring listeners to take control of their financial futures.

https://www.claytonmorris.com

Cleve Gaddis
@clevegaddis

Cleve Gaddis, managing partner and broker of Modern Traditions Realty Group at RE/MAX Center, is deeply passionate about coaching and empowering others in real estate. With 23 years of sales and management experience, Cleve leverages his expertise to mentor agents, develop systems for success, and help teams achieve exceptional results in the industry.

https://www.moderntraditionsrealty.com

Cody Sperber
@officialcodysperber

Cody Sperber is a renowned real estate investor, entrepreneur, and direct response marketer with a proven track record of success. Over the past 20 years, he has built and scaled six 8-figure businesses, generating over $250 million in sales. Cody mentors others, empowering them to achieve their full potential.

https://codysperber.com

Craig Sewing
@craigsewingmedia

Craig Sewing is best known as the creator and TV host of 'The American Dream.' The motto of his talk show is "Educate, Empower and Engage with his viewers on topics related to the American dream" and he does so by going against the grain of the negative media, and instead offering concrete and constructive advice to his viewers on issues that matter most to them.

CraigSewing.com

David Dodge
@davidalandodge

With over two decades of experience, David has flipped more than 600 houses and offers expert coaching to aspiring agents and property dealers. As an accomplished author and podcast host, he shares valuable insights and actionable tips, helping others excel in the real estate industry.

https://www.davidadodge.com

David Horsager
@davidhorsager

Wall Street Journal bestselling author of The Trust Edge, David Horsager has advised leaders and delivered life-changing presentations on six continents, with audiences ranging from FedEx, Toyota, MIT, and global governments to the New York Yankees and the Department of Homeland Security.

https://trustedge.com

EXPERTS & INFLUENCERS

Deb Cohen
@thefrontdoorproject

Deb is a real estate agent with an aesthetic eye for houses. Her Instagram features stunning images of exteriors and interiors of beautiful homes. Buyers and followers looking for ideas and inspiration can go through hundreds of photos on her feed.

https://lnk.bio/thefrontdoorproject

Dennis Chernov
@dennischernov

Dennis helms the Chernov Team with his wife Yana at his right hand. Together, the couple runs a successful real estate business that has received several accolades and earned millions in profit. Dennis's Instagram is all about his family and his love for beautiful houses.

https://chernovteam.com

Dina Goldentayer
@goldendina

A verified Top 10 Agent with over $2 billion in sales since 2021, Dina Goldentayer is Douglas Elliman's #1 agent and an ultra-luxury specialist. Known for record-breaking transactions in Miami Beach, including a $79 million sale in Indian Creek Village, her expertise spans from Golden Beach to Coral Gables.

https://dinagoldentayer.elliman.com

Dottie Herman
@dottieherman

Dottie embodies the American success story as a visionary leader and trailblazer in real estate. Starting her career in 1978, she purchased Prudential Long Island Realty in 1990, transforming it into a powerhouse. In 2003, she and Howard Lorber acquired and now serves as CEO of Douglas Elliman, making it New York's largest residential brokerage.

https://dottieherman.com

Egypt Sherrod
@egyptsherrod

Renowned REALTOR, author, and public speaker, Egypt Sherrod's clientele ranges from executives and celebrities to first-time homebuyers. Best known as the host and executive producer of HGTV's Married to Real Estate, now in its fourth season, the show remains a top-rated hit worldwide. She has also hosted popular shows like Flipping Virgins and Property Virgins, solidifying her reputation as a leading figure in real estate entertainment.

https://egyptsherrod.com

Eric Goldie
@ericgoldie

The real estate landscape of New York is ever-changing. With Eric Goldie on the case, finding the best property is a breeze. Eric caters to each of his clients with a tailor-made method and makes sure they always find the best value.

https://www.compass.com/agents/eric-goldie

Farrah Brittany
@farrahbritt

Farrah is a founding member and dynamic agent at The Agency, known for her expertise in working with affluent buyers and sellers. As an accomplished real estate professional, she has also appeared as a main cast member on Netflix's reality series Buying Beverly Hills since 2022, showcasing her skills in the luxury property market.

https://farrahbrittany.com

Freddy M. Delgadillo
@judahrealty

With 20 years and an impressive track record, Freddy is a seasoned and skilled REALTOR in the Seattle WA luxury market. His network spans the globe. Freddy's goal is to make sure his clients get only the best, no matter where it is.

https://www.sothebysrealty.com/eng/associate/180-a-df200821211610853181/freddy-delgadillo

EXPERTS & INFLUENCERS

Gabriella Michin
@gabriellamichin

Gabriella Michin is an award-winning real estate professional with over a decade of experience in Manhattan's competitive market. A skilled negotiator and financial analyst, she offers expert guidance to clients buying, selling, or investing. A Brooklyn and Manhattan native, Gabriella brings a nuanced local perspective and has earned The Agency's prestigious Chairman Award for top-tier performance.

https://brokersnbags.com

Gogo Bethke
@gogosrealestate

Gogo Bethke is an immigrant from Transylvania, Hungary, who came to the U.S. in 2003 at 21 years old. She built her career from the ground up, closed over $80M in production and founded #teamgogo, an international real estate organization of 1,400+ agents that has sold over $2.7 billion in sales in 2024 alone. Now, she's on a mission to help entrepreneurs reach 7 figure success through the GoGet'Em Community and The Circle ⭕ Mastermind. She has been featured in Success Magazine (March/April 2025 edition) in the "Women of Influence: 50 Women Who Shape Our World" article and is a TEDx speaker and host of the Gogopreneur podcast.

https://gogobethke.com

Graham Stephan
@gpstephan

Graham is a successful real estate investor and REALTOR with over 4 million YouTube followers. He began his career at 18 after earning his real estate license. By focusing on overlooked strategies, such as enhancing property advertising, he quickly outpaced his peers. Stephan has worked with celebrity clients like Orlando Bloom and Chloe Grace Moretz and appeared on shows like Selling Sunset and Million Dollar Listing LA.

https://www.grahamstephan.com

Grant Cardone
@grantcardone

Renowned as the top sales and marketing trainer worldwide, Grant Cardone has built a vast fortune through real estate and business ventures. He owns successful firms like Cardone Acquisitions and Cardone Enterprises and authored bestsellers, including The 10X Rule. This dynamic entrepreneur has over 10 million followers online.

https://grantcardone.com

Jade Mills
@jademillsestates

Known as the $9 Billion woman, Jane is the #1 agent worldwide for Coldwell Banker. Respected for her expertise, integrity, and professionalism, she is highly sought after by A-list celebrities, tech founders, and business leaders. Jade frequently shares her insights as a keynote speaker and luxury real estate expert at global conferences.

https://jademillsestates.com

Jake Leicht
@jakeleicht

Jake has a proven talent for turning distressed properties into profitable investments. Through his "Flip Secrets" system, he shares strategies and insights with new homeowners and inexperienced sellers, helping them navigate the market and achieve success. His expertise has made him a trusted resource for those seeking guidance in property investments and flipping.

https://theflipsecrets.com

Jemal King
@9to5millionaire

Jemal King is a Chicago-based real estate investor who transformed his dream of financial success into reality through strategic property investments. While serving as a full-time Chicago Police Officer, he built a thriving real estate portfolio, reinvested profits into successful ventures like childcare centers, and now operates multiple multi-million-dollar businesses, inspiring others to achieve generational wealth.

https://www.jemalking.com

EXPERTS & INFLUENCERS

Jerry Norton
@flippingmastery

Jerry is a real estate expert specializing in buying, renovating, and flipping distressed properties, a craft he has mastered since 2004. As the owner of Flipping Mastery, an education company, he has helped students flip over $100 million in real estate. Jerry's journey from construction worker to self-made millionaire showcases his commitment to success.

https://flippingmastery.com

John Turley
@remax

Former #1 top-selling RE/MAX agent in the world, John Turley serves as CEO and co-owner of RE/MAX Caribbean and Central America. John oversees nearly 100 offices with nearly 1,000 agents across 35 countries and territories. A true icon in the industry and recipient of the prestigious Circle of Legends Award, John champions real estate licensing and education throughout Belize and has closed over 1,850 transactions in Ambergris Caye, Belize.

https://turleyco.com

John Yunis
@johnyunis

John Yunis' passion for real estate and design has defined his career. Beginning at 18 in his family's commercial real estate firm, he transitioned to residential sales at Corcoran, leveraging his deep knowledge of New York City's finest buildings. With an exceptional eye for potential, John helps buyers envision dream homes and optimizes properties for sellers, achieving exceptional results.

https://www.corcoran.com/real-estate-agents/detail/john-yunis/5180/regionId/1

Jordan Cohen
@jordancohen1

Jordan is the six-time #1 RE/MAX Agent Worldwide, with over 30 years of experience in luxury real estate, specializing in high-end estates. With more than $314 million in annual sales, he works directly with clients, offering personalized service. Jordan's clientele includes celebrities, athletes, and executives, with his work featured in publications like Unique Homes and DuPont Registry.

https://jordancohen.com

Josh Altman
@thejoshaltman

Josh Altman is a renowned real estate agent and broker, specializes in ultra-luxury properties in California, catering to celebrities and high-profile athletes. Co-starring in Million Dollar Listing LA, he has become a prominent figure in the industry. A bestselling author of It's Your Move, Altman shares insights on success and real estate with over 1 million followers.

https://www.thealtmanbrothers.com

Josh Kilby
@thejoshkilby

Josh, a Nashville real estate agent with Village, transformed early setbacks into remarkable success as CEO of his own real estate company. Dedicated to providing exceptional service, Josh focuses on creating lasting relationships while guiding clients through buying or selling homes. His passion for real estate and commitment to serving others define his approach to the business.

https://benchmarkrealtytn.com

Joyce Rey
@joycereyrealestate

Joyce Rey is a renowned real estate agent specializing in ultra-luxury properties and serving an elite clientele. With numerous sales records, she is recognized as one of the most influential figures in the industry. Honored by Haute Living and Unique Homes, Joyce is celebrated for her expertise in high-end and entertainment industry real estate.

https://joycerey.com

EXPERTS & INFLUENCERS

Julia Wang
@juliawang_htx

Houston-based REALTOR and real estate influencer Julia Wang specializes in high-value properties across the Texan metropolis. With a background in Marketing and Business, she leads Houston's fastest-growing brokerage, managing over 230 agents. Julia's innovative approach and dedication to client relationships have earned her numerous accolades and industry recognition.

https://juliawanghtx.me

Kelly Killoren Bensimon
@kellybensimon

American Lifestyle Icon Kelly Killoren Bensimon has been touted by The New York Times as one of the "most fabulous tastemakers," but millions know her as a noted author, model, tv personality, influential editor, and now, real estate phenom. Kelly takes her insights gathered from years in the fashion, entertainment, and real estate industry and translates trends & contemporary culture for the public with her unique take; one that is fresh, playful, and always accessible.

https://kellykillorenbensimon.elliman.com

Kelly Robinson
@kellyrobinsonnewyork

Kelly Robinson is a 20-year veteran of Manhattan's luxury real estate market and founder of Compass's One Global Advisory Team. Known for blending creative marketing with data-driven strategy, she consistently ranks in the top 1.5% of U.S. real estate professionals. Kelly's tailored approach drives record-breaking sales across New York City's premier neighborhoods.

https://kellyrobinsonnewyork.com

RAVING REFERRALS FOR REAL ESTATE AGENTS

Kevin Paffrath
@meetkevin

Meet Kevin, with over 2 million YouTube subscribers, Kevin's business IQ can't be denied. Kevin is a top-producing, energetic, no-pressure real estate broker & property manager who passes his knowledge about stocks, investment, property purchase, and wedge deals to his millions of fans. Family run since 1984, Kevin's firm raises the bar in real estate with a 2x award-winning TV commercial, sophisticated website, strong social-media presence, and the sincerest professionalism to help become his clients' REALTOR for Life.

https://www.youtube.com/@MeetKevin

Kim Stoegbauer
@tomkatstudio

Kim, a seasoned real estate agent and interior designer, brings over 25 years of expertise in real estate, remodeling, and home flipping. As founder of TomKat Real Estate and The TomKat Studio, she combines vision and attention to detail to deliver exceptional results for clients and lead her successful team.

https://thetomkatstudio.com

Kimberly Mason
@broker_kim_mason

One of Atlanta's premier real estate brokers is Kimberly Mason. In addition to being one of Atlanta's top producing brokers, Kimberly personally invests in Airbnb properties and prides herself on providing exceptional service to her clients. Kimberly expertly guides buyers and sellers through the ever-changing market, ensuring successful transactions and lasting relationships.

https://masonkimberl.georgiamls.com

Kris Krohn
@kriskrohn

Author of The Straight Path to Real Estate Wealth, Kris specializes in guiding clients to invest in undervalued single-family homes in high-growth markets, achieving 25%+ ROI. Over 3-7 years, he helps double portfolios, cash flow, and tax benefits. Supported by his expert team, Kris manages investments seamlessly, allowing clients to enjoy the rewards.

https://www.kriskrohn.com

EXPERTS & INFLUENCERS

Kristin Messerli
@kristinmesserli

As Executive Director of FirstHomeIQ, Kristin is dedicated to educating and empowering Millennial and Gen Z buyers to achieve homeownership. With a background in social work, homebuyer education, and program development, she authors the NextGen Homebuyer Reports and is spearheading the creation of a national network of FirstHomeIQ Ambassadors.

https://www.kristinmesserli.com

Lace Morris
@lacemorris3

After learning lessons from her time on The Bachelor, Lace prides herself on being available for her clients at all times. Her motto is to fulfill dreams, not to sell homes. Lace loves to travel, dine, and work out. Her Instagram shows her personal life with a focus on her hobbies.

https://hoo.be/lace

Loida Velazquez
@loidavelas

As a real estate agent serving both the California and Florida markets, Loida specializing in expired listings and FSBOs. She shares her expertise in cold calling and door knocking as a traveling speaker and coach, empowering agents to elevate their real estate game through sales, communication, and video strategies.

https://www.loidavelasquez.com

Madison Hildebrand
@madisonmalibu

Madison, an original star of Bravo's Million Dollar Listing LA for 10 seasons, has been directly involved in over a billion dollars in Los Angeles real estate sales since 2006. Known for his expertise in luxury properties, Madison has built a successful career representing high-profile clients across the city.

https://themalibulife.com

RAVING REFERRALS FOR REAL ESTATE AGENTS

Mahsheed Barghisavar
@mahsheedluxuryrealestate

Mahsheed Parsons, a top 1% Las Vegas REALTOR, is a leading luxury real estate broker serving affluent buyers and sellers in Las Vegas and Southern California. Specializing in luxury homes and high-rise condos, she owns brokerages in both states. Known for integrity, expertise, and exceptional negotiating skills, Mahsheed delivers outstanding results.

https://mahsheed.com

Mark Salerno
@salernorealestate

Mark Salerno, founder of Salerno Realty Inc., is a trusted real estate professional with over 17 years of experience and $1 billion in transactions. Serving Vaughan and the Greater Toronto Area, Mark's extensive market knowledge, fearless negotiation skills, and commitment to clients make him a top choice in the real estate market.

https://www.salernorealestate.ca/agents/mark-salerno

Matt Altman
@themattaltman

Matt Altman is another reputable name in the luxury property market. Aside from making millions from his nifty investments and profitable sales, Matt also co-stars with his brother Josh in the reality series Million Dollar Listing.

https://www.thealtmanbrothers.com/about/matthew-altman

Mauricio Umansky
@mumansky18

Mauricio, Founder and CEO of The Agency, leads a billion-dollar brokerage renowned for innovation and collaboration. With nearly $5 billion in sales, he has represented iconic properties like the Playboy Mansion. The Agency, boasting over 100 offices worldwide, is recognized as one of the top luxury real estate brokerages globally.

https://www.theagencyre.com/agent/mauricio-umansky

EXPERTS & INFLUENCERS

Max Maxwell
@maxmaxwell

Max is a self-taught real estate investor and a top real estate influencer who took just two years to become a multi-millionaire. Upon reaching that goal, Max expanded and founded his own real estate company. His story of self-made success makes him a must-follow real estate influencer.

https://www.therealmaxwell.com

Quiana Watson
@quianawatson

Quiana Watson, MBA, is a top Atlanta real estate broker, CEO of Watson Realty Co., and founder of Agents Tool For Success. Recognized among the top 1% by the National Association of REALTORs, she combines exceptional expertise, negotiation skills, and a marketing background to help clients achieve their dreams and agents build thriving businesses.

https://www.quianawatson.com

Raphael Vargas
@realraphaelvargas

Raphael's journey from a broke, jobless high school dropout to a millionaire at 23 is truly inspiring. Overcoming challenges, he became a powerhouse in real estate. Now a successful multi-millionaire, Raphael shares his expertise, empowering others to achieve success in the competitive world of real estate.

https://linktr.ee/raphaelvargas

Ricky Carruth
@rickycarruth

Based on Alabama's Gulf Coast, began selling real estate in 2002. Despite setbacks from hurricanes and the BP oil spill, he rebuilt his career, becoming Alabama's #1 RE/MAX agent in 2014. A resilient businessman, Ricky now sells over 100 properties annually and is also an acclaimed author and mentor.

https://carruthteam.com/about-ricky-carruth

RAVING REFERRALS FOR REAL ESTATE AGENTS

Ross Bernstein

Ross Bernstein, a best-selling author of nearly 50 sports books, is an award-winning business speaker who has keynoted on all seven continents. For over 25 years, his program, The Champion's Code, has explored championship teams' DNA, emphasizing integrity, accountability, and values in sports and their relevance to business success.

https://rossbernstein.com

Ryan Serhant
@ryanserhant

Founder and CEO of SERHANT, Ryan Serhant is a globally renowned real estate broker, entrepreneur, and innovator. Starting with humble beginnings, he rose to close nearly $10 billion in sales, including record-breaking deals like Florida's $140M home sale. SERHANT. is a groundbreaking brokerage integrating media, education, and technology, becoming one of the fastest-growing real estate firms in the U.S. Ryan's mission to revolutionize the industry includes bestselling books, educational platforms, and philanthropic initiatives.

https://serhant.com/agents/ryan-serhant

Sean Terry
@flip2freedom

CEO and founder of Flip2Freedom, Sean is a seasoned real estate investor and mentor dedicated to helping others achieve financial freedom. A former U.S. Marine recognized for leadership in Desert Storm, Sean transitioned into real estate, completing over $120 million in transactions. Through Flip2Freedom's Academy, he offers cutting-edge coaching programs designed to help individuals leave their 9-to-5 jobs in just 19 weeks, empowering them to build thriving real estate careers.

https://www.rbprofits.com

EXPERTS & INFLUENCERS

Shawn Elliott
@shawnelliottrealestate

Shawn Elliott, a renowned power broker, is synonymous with ultra-luxury real estate, boasting over $5 billion in sales. As head of Nest Seekers International's Ultra Luxury Division, he leads a team of 25 elite agents across major markets, offering unparalleled service to high-profile clients with utmost privacy and discretion.

https://shawnelliott.com

Sue "Pinky" Benson
@pinkyknowsnaples

Sue "Pinky" Benson is an accomplished Florida REALTOR & loyal RE/MAX agent for over 15 years. Serving as the team lead at Think Pink Properties in Naples (RE/MAX Affinity Plus), Pinky consistently sells millions in real estate throughout Southwest Florida. She is also a sought-after keynote speaker and has presented at many industry-leading conferences.

https://www.pinkladyofrealestate.com

Tirajeh Mazaheri
@tirajehm

Tirajeh Mazaheri is a highly regarded REALTOR in Vancouver, B.C., known for her exceptional real estate expertise and natural selling ability. Her deep market knowledge and dedication have earned her a place among the city's top real estate professionals, making her a trusted choice for buyers and sellers alike.

https://www.vancouverelites.ca

Tony Giordano
@tony_giordano

Based in Los Angeles, Tony Giordano is the Founder and President of Giordano Industries, a best-selling author of "The Social Agent", renowned speaker, and celebrity real estate agent featured on Bravo's Million Dollar Listing and HGTV. Known for his innovative techniques, Tony built a successful real estate business and now coaches professionals across industries to achieve excellence.

https://www.giordano.global

Tony Robinson
@tonythecloser

Tony Robinson, a former NFL player turned real estate mogul, entrepreneur, and philanthropist, champions financial freedom through real estate investing. Specializing in short-term rentals like Airbnbs, Tony provides resources to help others build successful Airbnb businesses, empowering individuals to achieve financial independence and create wealth through real estate opportunities.

https://therealestaterobinsons.com

Tracy Tutor
@tracytutor

With 25 years of experience, Tracy Tutor is a top agent at Douglas Elliman Beverly Hills and a key figure in their Sports & Entertainment division. Representing iconic architects and developments, she has led over $400 million in branded real estate sales, including projects like Amangiri, West Hollywood EDITION, and Royal Atlantis Dubai.

https://tracytutor.com

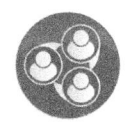

Industry Icons

The real estate industry is shaped by visionaries who redefine success, innovate new strategies, and elevate the profession. Here we highlight industry icons who have made a significant impact, transforming the way agents serve families, generate referrals, and grow their businesses. These servant leaders have not only achieved remarkable success but have also shared their insights to help others thrive. We can all gain valuable insights from their expertise, proven strategies, and innovative approaches to building a real estate business that not only thrives but also creates a lasting impact—helping families achieve the American dream of homeownership for generations to come.

Alvaro Erize
CEO of CINC

Alvaro Erize was born and raised in Argentina, where he graduated as a Civil Engineer before starting his entrepreneurial career in industries ranging from publishing to automotive. In 2009, Alvaro moved to the United States to complete his MBA at Stanford University before transitioning into management consulting and private equity. Since 2016, Alvaro has led CINC's passionate team in providing technology solutions for the best real estate professionals in North America.

https://www.cincpro.com

Andy Florance
Founder and CEO, CoStar Group

In 2023, Andrew Florance accelerated CoStar Group's growth in residential real estate through a revamped Homes.com. As founder and CEO since 1987, Florance has significantly increased Homes.com's traffic since its 2021 acquisition. With a "My Listing, My Lead" strategy, he is driving CoStar toward dominance in the real estate sales space.

https://www.costargroup.com/leadership/andy-florance

Anthony Hitt
President and CEO, Engel & Völkers Americas

As the leader of Engel & Völkers Americas, Hitt leads the U.S. operations for the German luxury real estate franchisor. The brand's more than 5,400 American agents do an estimated $17.2 billion in annual sales.

https://www.evrealestate.com

Art Carter
CEO, California Regional MLS

Carter leads CRMLS, the nation's largest MLS with over 108,000 members, and is a prominent MLS executive. An innovative leader, he has driven key initiatives like REdistribute for data monetization and a 2023 data-sharing agreement with Bright MLS and BeachesMLS, enhancing collaboration and advancing the MLS industry.

https://cmls2022.com/speakers/art-carter

Ben Kinney
Owner, Place

Kinney, a visionary real estate leader, co-founded Place in 2020, a platform supporting over 100 real estate teams nationwide with back-office solutions. In 2021, Place raised $100 million. Kinney also owns brokerages, technology platforms, and runs the Built How event series, showcasing top real estate leaders' success strategies.

https://place.com

INDUSTRY ICONS

Bess Freedman
CEO, Brown Harris Stevens

Freedman, CEO of Brown Harris Stevens (BHS), leads the nation's 20th largest brokerage with 2,700 agents and over $10.4 billion in annual sales. Celebrating 150 years in 2023, BHS operates under Terra Holdings. A former attorney, Freedman serves on the Real Estate Board of New York's Board of Governors.

http://www.bhsusa.com

Bill Scavone
President, Weichert REALTORs

Bill Scavone leads Weichert Real Estate Affiliates, Inc., the nation's eighth largest franchise brand. He's been part of the organization since 2005, serving as Senior Vice President of Franchise Development and Chief Operating Officer before being appointed President in 2016. He oversees a franchise footprint spanning more than 40 states, over 350 offices and close to 7,000 agents.

https://www.weichert.com

Brian Donnellan
CEO, Bright MLS

Donnellan leads the nation's second largest MLS in Bright MLS, which serves over 104,000 members in the Mid-Atlantic region, with a steady, clear focus on innovation and serving members. In 2022, he helped spearhead a new data-monetization strategy for MLSs through the creation of the REdistribute initiative and, in 2023, helped launch a new MLS-powered national portal in Nestfully.

https://www.brightmls.com

Budge Huskey
President and CEO, Premier Sotheby's International Realty
(a Peerage Realty company)

Huskey leads Premier Sotheby's International Realty, a top affiliate in the SIR global network with offices spanning Florida's Gulf Coast to North Carolina's High Country. Formerly CEO of Coldwell Banker Real Estate, he retired in 2016 and now serves as vice chairman of Premier SIR's parent company, Peerage Realty.

https://www.premiersothebysrealty.com/leadership

Robert "Bob" Hale III
President and CEO, Houston Association of REALTORs

In 2023, Hale marked 50 years at the Houston Association of REALTORs, where he became president in 1988. Under his leadership, HAR grew to over 45,000 members, becoming the nation's second-largest local REALTOR association. Its portal, HAR.com, attracts 8 million monthly visitors, ranking among the nation's most trafficked real estate sites.

https://www.har.com

Candace Adams
President and CEO, BHHS New England Properties (a HomeServices of America company)

Adams is president and CEO of Berkshire Hathaway HomeServices New England Properties, a HomeServices of America brokerage with 2,600 agents across 63 offices in Connecticut, Massachusetts, New York, and Rhode Island. With over 20 years at HomeServices, he expanded the brand into New York City and serves on key industry boards.

https://www.bhhsneproperties.com

INDUSTRY ICONS

Chad Ochsner
Broker-Owner, RE/MAX Alliance

Ochsner, a second-generation REALTOR, is the owner of Denver-based RE/MAX Alliance, with 650 agents generating $4.5 billion in annual sales. Ochsner is also a partner in RE/MAX Northwest, Equity Group and Integrity in the Pacific Northwest. He has served as a director of the Colorado Association of REALTORs, on the boards of Denver Metro Association of REALTORs and REColorado and volunteers time with Children's Hospital of Colorado.

https://www.homesincolorado.com/about-chad-ochsner

Christopher Alexander
President, RE/MAX Canada

Alexander, president of RE/MAX Canada since 2021, leads the country's largest real estate franchise, overseeing operations in all provinces except Quebec, while collaborating on national brand strategy. Starting as a RE/MAX sales associate in 2010, he continues his family's legacy as the grandson of Frank Polzler, a RE/MAX co-founder.

https://news.remax.com/bio/christopher-alexander

Christy Budnick
CEO, Berkshire Hathaway HomeServices

Budnick leads Berkshire Hathaway HomeServices, the flagship franchise of HomeServices of America, overseeing the nation's fifth-largest real estate brand with over 50,000 agents and $146 billion in annual sales. Previously CEO of Berkshire Hathaway HomeServices Florida Network Realty, she is renowned for her pragmatic and strategic approach to the industry.

https://www.bhhs.com

Craig Cheatham
President and CEO, The Realty Alliance

As president and CEO Cheatham supports a powerful network of large brokerages comprising more than 100,000 agents across North America. His close to 35 years in leadership in the industry also includes time as CEO for the international federation of real estate regulatory agencies and COO for a state association of REALTORs. In addition, he represents brokers on NAR's RES Advisory Board, on RESPRO's board of directors and on the Broker Public Portal's board of managers, among other posts.

https://www.therealtyalliance.com

Damian Eales
CEO, Move (a News Corp company)

Eales became CEO of Move, operator of REALTOR.com, in June 2023, succeeding David Doctorow. Previously EVP and global head of transformation at News Corp, he also contributed to REA Group's realestate.com.au achieving market leadership in Australia. Eales now focuses on strengthening REALTOR.com's position as a leading U.S. real estate portal.

https://www.move.com

Dan Duffy
CEO, United Real Estate

Duffy leads United Real Estate, a large network with residential, country, and auction divisions. Known for its fee-based model, the firm ranks as the 12th largest U.S. brokerage with 14,000 agents and $21 billion in annual sales. In 2023, it expanded with acquisitions and launched healthcare and wellness programs.

https://www.unitedrealestate.com

INDUSTRY ICONS

Erik Carlson
CEO, RE/MAX Holdings

Erik Carlson joined RE/MAX Holdings, Inc. as Chief Executive Officer in November 2023. He drives the strategy of RE/MAX Holdings, overseeing all operations for the Company and providing direction for its brands. Erik is an accomplished public company executive, who for six years served as President and CEO of a Fortune 200 company with over 14,000 employees and more than $15 billion in annual revenue.

https://www.remaxholdings.com

Gary Keller
Co-Founder and Executive Chairman, Keller Williams Realty

As the visionary founder of Keller Williams, Gary has led the company to grow to nearly 170,000 U.S. agents generating over $439 billion in annual sales. Gary still has ambitious goals including doubling its agent count. Under Keller's leadership, the company continues to drive growth and innovation. Recognized as one of the most influential figures in real estate, his impact on the industry is unmatched.

https://kwri.kw.com/leadership/gary-keller

Gavin Swartzman
CEO, Peerage Realty Partners

Swartzman leads Peerage Realty Partners, a network of luxury brokerages across North America. With over 4,700 U.S. agents generating $28 billion in annual sales, Peerage ranks as the eighth-largest brokerage. Since joining in 2014, Swartzman has driven rapid growth through acquisitions, including many Sotheby's International Realty affiliates.

https://www.linkedin.com/in/gavin-swartzman

Gino Blefari
President and CEO, HomeServices of America

As CEO of HomeServices of America, Blefari leads the nation's third-largest brokerage, with over 44,500 agents generating nearly $166 billion in annual sales. He also serves as chairman of Berkshire Hathaway HomeServices, guiding the company through significant milestones and challenges while maintaining its position as an industry leader.

https://www.homeservices.com

Glenn Kelman
President and CEO, Redfin

Kelman, Redfin's CEO since 2005, leads the nation's sixth-largest brokerage through a push for profitability. In 2023, Redfin integrated RentPath, generating $136 million in revenue, despite an overall net loss of $103 million. The company also introduced pilot agent compensation plans and began operating more as a marketplace.

https://www.redfin.com

Glenn Sanford
Founder and CEO, eXp World Holdings

Glenn Sanford, founder of eXp Realty and CEO of eXp World Holdings, launched the first cloud-based brokerage model in 2009, eliminating traditional brick-and-mortar offices. Starting with 25 agents, eXp Realty now boasts over 85,000 agents in 24 countries. The company pioneered agent equity distribution and revenue sharing to support its agent-focused model.

https://expworldholdings.com

Guy Gal
Co-Founder and CEO, Side

Guy Gal, co-founder and CEO of Side, champions a future of local, boutique, agent-owned real estate. A seasoned tech entrepreneur, he previously founded Kingmaker, Biz, and Kognitive. As an advisor to Vidyard and former entrepreneur-in-residence at Matrix Partners, Guy combines innovation with a passion for empowering real estate professionals.

https://www.side.com/team/guy-gal

INDUSTRY ICONS

Harold Crye
Owner and CEO, Crye-Leike REALTORs

Since co-founding Crye-Leike in Memphis over 40 years ago, Harold Crye has grown the firm into a Mid-South leader with nearly 2,900 agents generating over $7 billion in annual sales. Crye serves as secretary of LeadingRE's board and is a past chair of The Realty Alliance.

https://www.crye-leike.com

J. Lennox Scott
Chairman and CEO, John L. Scott Real Estate

As a third-generation leader of his family's brokerage, founded in 1931, Scott oversees 2,900 agents across 100 offices in Washington, Oregon, Idaho, and Northern California, generating over $17 billion in annual sales. He is active with NAR, serving as past chair of the Large Residential Firms Advisory Group and Research Committee.

https://www.johnlscott.com/home

James Huang
Managing Director of Commercial, RESaaS.com

James is a highly accomplished leader with over 25 years of experience in commercial real estate. As Managing Director of RESAAS Commercial, he brings extensive expertise in brokerage, investment, management, and scaling global businesses. RESAAS, a premier real estate technology platform, connects 700,000 agents across 160 countries, facilitating referrals, listing promotion, and real-time market insights. Drawing on his leadership background—including founding eXp Commercial and serving as president of AREAA and board of director of REALTORs Property Resource—James is dedicated to enhancing agent-to-agent referrals, fostering global collaboration, and driving innovation through business intelligence on the RESAAS platform.

https://corporate.resaas.com/management

RAVING REFERRALS FOR REAL ESTATE AGENTS

Jason Mitchell
CEO, The Jason Mitchell Group

Jason Mitchell leads America's #1 real estate team, renowned for partnerships with industry giants like Quicken Loans, Zillow, and Rocket Homes. Since 2010, JMG has achieved over $15 billion in sales and 30,000 transactions, with 80% of business driven by trusted referrals. Operating in 40 states and 150 metro areas, JMG is the nation's top referral team, delivering world-class service through innovative technology and talented professionals.

https://thejasonmitchellgroup.com

Jason Waugh
President, Coldwell Banker Affiliates

As president of Coldwell Banker Affiliates, Waugh oversees operations, growth, and service enhancements for over 100,000 agents affiliated with the brand. Previously president of BHHS Northwest Real Estate and BHHS Real Estate Professionals, he assumed his current role in October 2023, collaborating with leaders to drive the franchise's success.

https://www.coldwellbanker.com

Jeremy Crawford
CEO, First Multiple Listing Service

As CEO of First Multiple Listing Service (FMLS), Crawford leads the nation's fourth-largest MLS with over 57,000 subscribers. A champion of collaboration, he initiated data sharing with Stellar MLS, Gulf Coast MLS, and Miami Association of REALTORs in 2023. Crawford, in real estate since 2001, joined FMLS in 2019 from RESO.

https://firstmls.com

Jeremy Wacksman
CEO, Zillow

Wacksman, promoted to CEO in August 2024, has been with Zillow since 2009, holding roles such as chief marketing officer, president, and COO. A driving force behind Zillow's vision, he pioneered mobile real estate shopping and played a key role in establishing the company as a household brand.

https://www.zillow.com

INDUSTRY ICONS

John Berkowitz
Co-Founder and CEO, Ojo Labs

As founder of OJO Labs, John built the company to empower consumers with personalized technology, leveling the playing field for homeownership regardless of race or class. Under his leadership, OJO Labs has achieved rapid growth, earning recognition from Inc. and Deloitte for its mission to remove barriers and make homeownership accessible to all.

https://www.ojo.com

John G Stevens
Founder, Weekly Real Estate News

Stevens is a dynamic leader and influential voice in real estate. As the founder of Weekly Real Estate News, John created a powerful platform that delivers the latest industry insights, market trends, and critical updates to real estate professionals nationwide. John continues to influence the future of real estate, championing growth, professionalism, and innovation at every level. His goal is simple: to keep agents, brokers, and industry leaders informed, inspired, and ahead of the curve.

https://wrenews.com

Kamini Rangappan Lane
President and CEO, Coldwell Banker Realty

Lane became president and CEO of Anywhere Real Estate's Coldwell Banker company-owned offices in March 2023, overseeing 52,000 agents across 700 offices in 50+ U.S. markets. A Harvard Business School graduate, she previously held leadership roles at Sotheby's International Realty and Compass, with expertise in marketing, communications, and fashion.

https://www.coldwellbanker.com

RAVING REFERRALS FOR REAL ESTATE AGENTS

Kuba Jewgieniew
Founder and CEO, Realty One Group

Jewgieniew founded and leads Realty One Group, the nation's 10th largest real estate enterprise with over 19,000 agents in 49 states and 16 countries, generating over $40 billion in annual sales. Established in 2005, the fee-based brokerage has sold more than 400 franchises, including 70 in 2023.

https://www.kubajewgieniew.com

Lawrence "Larry" Flick, V
CEO, BHHS Fox & Roach REALTORs (a HomeServices of America company)

Flick V, CEO of BHHS Fox & Roach REALTORs, leads over 5,000 agents across 80+ offices in Delaware, Maryland, New Jersey, and Pennsylvania. CEO since 2018, he expanded the firm in 2023 with the acquisition of BHHS New Jersey Properties, adding 19 offices and 600 agents. He also oversees The Trident Group, the company's mortgage division.

https://www.foxroach.com

Liz Gehringer
President and CEO, Anywhere Franchise Brands

Liz Gehringer, President and CEO of Anywhere Franchise Brands, oversees strategic growth and operations for Coldwell Banker Affiliates, Better Homes and Gardens Real Estate, CENTURY 21, and ERA Real Estate. A Georgetown graduate, she joined Anywhere in 2006, leveraging her operational, franchise, and legal expertise to drive innovation and diversity initiatives in real estate.

https://anywhere.re

Margy Grant
CEO, Florida REALTORs

Grant leads Florida REALTORs, the largest state REALTOR association in the U.S., with over 223,000 members across 49 boards and associations. Before becoming CEO in 2019, she served as the association's chief operating officer and general counsel, bringing extensive expertise to her leadership role.

https://www.floridaREALTORs.org

INDUSTRY ICONS

Mark Willis
Former Chief Leadership Officer, Keller Williams Realty

Mark Willis, who led Keller Williams Realty's significant growth as CEO from 2005 to 2015, returned to the role in 2023. In January 2025, Willis took on a newly created role, Chief Leadership Officer, where he is focused on helping KW leaders grow and achieve their highest potential.

https://kwri.kw.com/leadership/mark-willis

Matt Widdows
Founder and CEO, HomeSmart

Widdows, founder and CEO of HomeSmart, leads the Scottsdale-based brokerage operating on a fee-based model where agents keep 100% of their commissions. With 24,000 agents across 38 states generating $37 billion in annual sales, HomeSmart continues to grow as a leader in the real estate industry.

https://homesmart.com

Matthew "Matt" Consalvo
CEO, Arizona Regional Multiple Listing Service

Consalvo leads Arizona Regional MLS (ARMLS), one of the nation's largest MLSs with nearly 41,000 members. A founding member of MLS Aligned, he collaborates with other major MLSs, including Beaches MLS and Metro MLS, collectively serving over 150,000 real estate professionals across multiple states in 2023.

https://armls.com

Merri Jo Cowen
CEO, Stellar MLS

Cowen leads Stellar MLS, one of the largest and most influential multiple listing services in the U.S., serving over 84,000 customers across Florida and Puerto Rico. In 2023, Stellar expanded its reach through data-sharing agreements with Gulf Coast MLS and First MLS, increasing inventory and referral opportunities for its customers. A two-time past president and current director of the Council of MLS, she also serves as the dean of the CMLX certification program. Under Cowen's leadership, Stellar is the Multiple Listing Service for real estate professionals who value clarity, stability, and support in a real estate market and industry defined by change.

https://www.stellarmls.com

Michael Miedler
President and CEO, Century 21 Real Estate

Miedler, president and CEO of Century 21 Real Estate, oversees the nation's sixth-largest franchise with nearly 50,000 U.S. agents generating over $100 billion in annual sales. Previously global chief growth officer, he led franchise sales and focused on expanding into emerging and diverse markets, driving the brand's continued success.

https://www.century21.com/about-us/about/corporate-officers/michael-miedler

Pamela Liebman
President and CEO, Corcoran Group

Pamela Liebman is President and Chief Executive Officer of The Corcoran Group, the country's premier residential real estate firm. A force throughout the industry, Pamela has been with Corcoran since she started her career and was named President and CEO in 2000. With her strategic direction, Corcoran has achieved record sales of more than $23 billion annually, and in 2024 the firm was named the #1 residential real estate brokerage in Manhattan for the fourth year in a row by The Real Deal.

https://www.corcoran.com

INDUSTRY ICONS

Paul Boomsma
CEO, Leading Real Estate Companies of the World

Boomsma leads LeadingRE, an exclusive brokerage network with over 550 firms and 138,000 agents across 70 countries. Known for fostering collaboration and referrals among top independent brokerages, he created the Luxury Property International division in 2005 before becoming CEO in 2018, driving the network's continued growth and global influence.

https://www.leadingre.com

Philip "Phil" Soper
President and CEO, Bridgemarq Real Estate Services

Phil Soper is President & CEO of Royal LePage and President of Bridgemarq Real Estate Services. With over 21,000 agents in its Royal LePage, Royal LePage Commercial, Johnston & Daniel, Via Capitale, Les Immeubles Mont-Tremblant, and Proprio Direct businesses, it is the largest real estate brokerage firm in Canada. Soper has guided the company with steady leadership, fostering growth and stability across its extensive network for more than two decades.

https://www.bridgemarq.com

Philip White, Jr.
President and CEO, Sotheby's International Realty

White Jr. oversees nearly 1,000 company-owned and franchised offices of Anywhere Real Estate's luxury brand as well as Sotheby's International Realty, the nation's fourth-largest real estate brand. Joining as COO in 2004, he became CEO of the affiliate network in 2013 and expanded his leadership to include company-owned offices in 2019.

https://www.sothebysrealty.com/eng/philip-white

RAVING REFERRALS FOR REAL ESTATE AGENTS

Rich Barton
C-Founder & CEO, Zillow Group

Rich, co-founder and co-executive chair of Zillow, has been instrumental in transforming the real estate industry. CEO from 2004 to 2010 and again until August 2024, he previously founded Expedia, leading it to a public spinoff. Rich also co-founded Glassdoor and serves on boards for Netflix, Qurate, and Zillow.

https://www.zillowgroup.com/people/rich-barton

Rick Davidson
Chairman and CEO, Cairn Real Estate Holdings

Davidson leads Cairn Real Estate Holdings, overseeing JP and Associates REALTORs (JPAR), a fee-based brokerage with over 4,000 agents in 60+ offices across 28 states. In 2023, JPAR expanded into California and introduced an agent health benefit program. Previously, Davidson served as CEO of Century 21 Real Estate from 2010 to 2017.

https://www.cairnre.com/leadership

Rick Haase
President, United Real Estate

Rick Haase, President of United Real Estate and COO of United Real Estate Group, oversees 14,300 agents generating $20.8 billion in annual sales. With over 30 years of experience, he has elevated United to the 8th largest brokerage nationally, introduced agent-focused programs, and previously served as CEO of Latter & Blum.

https://www.unitedrealestate.com

INDUSTRY ICONS

Robert Reffkin
Co-Founder and CEO, Compass

Robert Reffkin founded Compass in 2012, inspired by his mother, a longtime real estate agent. Under his leadership, Compass became the #1 real estate brokerage in the U.S., surpassing $1 trillion in sales in the last 10 years. A Columbia University graduate (B.A. & M.B.A.), Robert previously worked at McKinsey, Goldman Sachs, and as a White House Fellow. He has completed 50 marathons in 50 states, raising $1 million for charities, including America Needs You, which helps first-generation college students. His book, No One Succeeds Alone, supports nonprofits empowering young people, with all proceeds donated to their cause.

https://www.compass.com

Ryan Schneider
President and CEO, Anywhere Real Estate

Ryan Schneider, CEO and President of Anywhere Real Estate Inc., leads the nation's largest real estate enterprise with 195,000 agents generating $636 billion in annual sales. Since taking the helm, he has reorganized the company, streamlined its leadership structure, and reinforced its position as an industry leader.

https://anywhere.re/team-member/ryan-m-schneider

Shannon McGahn
Chief Advocacy Officer, National Association of REALTORs

Shannon McGahn is the chief advocacy officer for the National Association of REALTORs®, overseeing political affairs and local, state, and federal policymaking for the nation's largest trade association. The first woman in NAR's 112-year history to hold this role, she brings over 25 years of government experience on behalf of NAR's members who live and work in communities across America.

https://narnxt.REALTOR/speaker/shannon-mcgahn

Stefan Swanepoel
Founder & Executive Chairman, T3 Sixty

An experienced executive known for quickly identifying solutions and executing with focus and efficiency. Under his leadership, T3 Sixty has become the largest management consulting firm in residential real estate, driven by a team of exceptional leaders delivering strategic guidance and results for the brokerage industry's top organizations.

https://www.swanepoel.com

Stephanie Anton
President, Corcoran Group

As President of the Corcoran Affiliate Network, Anton drives the growth of Corcoran's global franchise business, expanding its presence across premium urban and second-home markets since its 2020 launch. A respected industry leader, Anton's strategic focus has positioned Corcoran as one of the fastest-growing franchise brands in real estate.

https://www.corcoran.com/about-us/display/23512

Sue Yannaccone
President and CEO, Anywhere Brands

As president and CEO of Anywhere Brands, Yannaccone leads the world's largest real estate brokerage network, including Coldwell Banker, Sotheby's International Realty, Century 21, ERA, Better Homes and Gardens Real Estate, and Corcoran Group. Overseeing 195,000 agents generating $636 billion in annual sales, she drives operational efficiency and strategic growth.

https://anywhere.re

Tami Bonnell
Co-Chair, EXIT Realty Corp. International

An international speaker and 30-year real estate veteran, Bonnell is passionate about investing in people and advancing diversity. A proud member of the National Women's Council of REALTORs®, she has built three major brands and joined EXIT Realty Corp. International in 1999, becoming Co-Chair in 2021.

https://exitrealty.com

INDUSTRY ICONS

Tamir Poleg
Co-Founder and CEO, The Real Brokerage

As co-founder and CEO of The Real Brokerage, Poleg leads one of the fastest-growing U.S. brokerages. Founded in 2014, Real became the 18th largest brokerage in 2023 with over 7,000 agents generating $12 billion in annual sales. Operating in all 50 states, it continues scaling with innovative tools and technology.

https://www.joinreal.com

Tom Rossiter
CEO, RESaaS.com

Tom is the President and CEO of RESAAS, a multi-award-winning global technology platform for the real estate industry. Under his leadership, RESAAS has become a trusted provider of business intelligence for brokerages, franchises, and associations. A thought leader in proptech and real estate trends, Tom previously managed global accounts for major brands, served on the Board of Directors for the Asian Real Estate Association of America, and mentors for the REACH accelerator program.

https://corporate.resaas.com/management

Tyler Smith
Founder and CEO, SkySlope (a Fidelity National Financial company)

Smith, founder and CEO of SkySlope, leads one of the industry's top digital transaction management platforms, serving over 650,000 real estate professionals in North America. SkySlope offers partners advanced tools, including transaction coordination services, offer management solutions, and forms software, enhancing efficiency and streamlining the real estate transaction process.

https://skyslope.com

Vinnie Tracey
President, Realty One Group

Tracey, President of Realty One Group since 2017, drives the brand's U.S. and international growth, adding five countries in 2023. The 21st largest brokerage and franchise brand in the U.S., Realty One Group has over 4,800 agents generating $10 billion in annual sales. Tracey previously led RE/MAX from 2004 to 2015.

https://www.realtyonegroup.com

York Bau
CEO, MoxiWorks

Baur, CEO of MoxiWorks, leads the real estate platform offering productivity tools like CRM, CMA, website builder, and recruiting solutions for brokers and agents. Backed by Vector Capital, Windermere Real Estate, Long & Foster, and Howard Hanna, MoxiWorks serves 800 brokerages, 600 MLS clients, and over 400,000 agents nationwide.

https://moxiworks.com

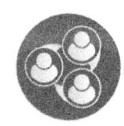

Podcasts

To help you stay apprised and educated on the latest advancements and best practices in the real estate industry, we have compiled the following list of the real estate podcasts that we find to be the most informative and beneficial for your growth. Turn your drive time into your mobile university by tuning into these insightful experts and episodes.

Agents Who Crush It In Real Estate
Hosted by: Lindsay Favazza

Want to hear the good, the bad and the ugly of Real Estate? Every two weeks Lindsay Favazza interviews some of the best REALTORs in the biz who share their stories of struggle and success. Listen in, learn and get inspired and empowered.

https://crushitinre.com/podcast

BetterLife Podcast
Hosted by: Brandon Turner

Join expert guests from business moguls to fitness gurus, from real estate tycoons to relationship experts and beyond and learn how to unlock success and build wealth without sacrificing your health and relationships.

https://abetterlife.com/podcast

BiggerPockets Real Estate Podcast
Hosted by: David Greene, Rob Abasolo

Bigger Pockets helps educate people about all aspects of real estate and real estate investing and provides tools and resources to enhance real estate knowledge, networking, marketing and dealmaking. BiggerPockets unites an online community complete with resources for anyone looking to succeed in real estate investing.

https://www.biggerpockets.com/podcasts/real-estate

Cash Flow Connections
Hosted by: Hunter Thompson

Looking to learn the intricacies of commercial real estate investing? This show features interviews with some of the leading investors, sponsors, and managers in the U.S. teaching you cash flow focused asset classes such as mobile home parks, self-storage, multi-family, and office, but virtually all types of real estate transactions will be covered.

https://cashflowconnections.com/podcast

Drive with NAR
Hosted by: Marki Lemons Ryhal, Tracey Hawkins

Get your "aha moments" on the go. This podcast provides you with insights about the sales strategies, resources, industry tools and safety tips your fellow REALTORs are using to steer their business forward and stay safe in the field.

https://d7.nar.REALTOR/magazine/drive

Elite Agent Secrets
Hosted by: Andrew Dunn, Peter Dunn

Anyone hungry for trade secrets would do well to tune in to the popular Elite Agent Secrets podcast, whose hosts share the tips and tricks they gathered while proudly "rubbing shoulders with some of the best in real estate." If you prefer a casual, conversational style, this podcast might be for you.

https://alphaempires.com

PODCASTS

Epic Real Estate Investing
Hosted by: Matt Theriault

Real estate investor and author Matt Theriault teaches you how to build wealth through conventional and creative real estate strategies. Learn how to improve your financial education, achieve realistic retirement goals in ten years or less, and enjoy the good life while you're still young enough to live it fully.

https://podcasts.apple.com/us/podcast/epic-real-estate-investing/id446611090

Financial Freedom with Real Estate Investing
Hosted by: Michael Blank, Garrett Lynch

Ready to make the jump from single family investing to apartments? Hosts Michael Blank and Garrett Lynch interview experts weekly, sharing strategies to start investing in multifamily real estate—even without prior experience or personal capital—so you can gain control over your time and wealth.

https://podcasts.apple.com/us/podcast/financial-freedom-with-real-estate-investing/id848693430

Gogopreneur
Hodted by: Gogo Bethke

Gogopreneur gets real about entrepreneurship. Gogo dives deep into the good, the bad, and everything in between, interviewing entrepreneurs from all walks of life. This podcast covers business and personal growth, raw struggles, big wins, and unfiltered truth behind building success. This is the place where you find real talk, real lessons, and real inspiration.

https://gogopreneur.com

House Party
Hosted by: Natalie Way, Rachel Stults

Discover the intersection of real estate and pop culture on the Rock The Block podcast. Hosted by Natalie Way and Rachel Stults, the show dives into the fascinating stories, trends, and connections that bring these two worlds together, offering a fresh perspective on real estate and entertainment.

https://www.REALTOR.com/authror/house-party

HousingWire Daily
Hosted by: Sarah Wheele

HousingWire Daily offers in-depth discussions on the latest real estate, mortgage, and fintech news. The podcast explores key articles and insights reported by HousingWire Media, keeping listeners informed on the trends and developments shaping the housing industry.

HousingWire.com/shows/housingwire-daily

The Iced Coffee Hour Podcast
Hosted by: Graham Stephan

The Iced Coffee Hour was created to learn from people's unique perspective in life and how they got to where they are now. Each week we interview a new entrepreneur, investor, or creator as we break down their path to success, as well as their personal finance habits. Listen in. You'll love it.

https://www.youtube.com/c/TheIcedCoffeeHour

Investing in Real Estate with Clayton Morris
Hosted by: Clayton Morris

The Investing in Real Estate podcast, hosted by Clayton Morris, focuses on creating passive income through buy-and-hold rental properties. With expert interviews, investor case studies, and proven strategies, Clayton shares insights on turnkey rentals, discounted properties, and building legacy wealth to accelerate your financial freedom and grow your real estate portfolio.

https://www.claytonmorris.com/podcast

Keeping it Real
Hosted by: D.J. Paris

Learn the success secrets from the top 1% real estate agents in the United States. This show interviews top real estate agents who share how they became successful and what advice they have for other REALTORs® wishing to increase their production.

https://keepingitrealpod.com

PODCASTS

Massive Agent Podcast
Hosted by: Dustin Brohm

The Massive Agent Podcast, hosted by Dustin, features interviews with top real estate professionals who share their secrets to building successful, profitable brands. Learn actionable strategies and insights straight from industry leaders to grow your real estate business and achieve massive success.

https://nowbam.com/massive-agent

Passive Real Estate Investing
Hosted by: Marco Santarelli

Discover how busy professionals can build substantial passive income and long-term wealth through real estate. Host Marco Santarelli of Norada Real Estate Investments shares expert strategies, insights, and advice, with a focus on passive and turnkey investments designed to simplify the process and help you achieve financial freedom.

https://www.passiverealestateinvesting.com/podcasts

Power House
Hosted by: Diego Sanchez

The Power House podcast brings the biggest names in housing to answer hard-hitting questions about industry trends, operational and growth strategy, and leadership. Join HousingWire President Diego Sanchez every Thursday morning for candid conversations with industry leaders to learn how they differentiate themselves from the competition.

https://www.housingwire.com/shows/power-house

Ready2Scale Podcast
Hosted by: Ellie Perlman

Real estate investor and syndicator Ellie Perlman hosts REady2Scale. Offering honest and insightful discussions on successful real estate investing, you'll learn proven strategies, gain inspiration, and knowledge to grow your wealth, scale your portfolio, and achieve higher goals through actionable advice and thought-provoking conversations with industry experts.

https://www.bluelake-capital.com/podcast

Real Estate & Financial Independence Podcast
Hosted by: Chad Carson

Chad Carson shares practical advice about using real estate to retire early and achieve financial independence. You'll hear in-depth episodes with tips from Chad plus interviews with other real estate investors at various levels of their financial independence journey.

https://www.coachcarson.com/coach-carson-podcast

Real Estate Disruptors
Hosted by: Steve Trang

On Real Estate Disruptors, Steve Trang interviews top real estate producers, from investors wholesaling 10 houses a month to flippers and creative strategists. Steve dives into their journeys, unique strategies, and advice for newcomers, uncovering what sets them apart and how they've built successful, thriving real estate businesses.

https://realestatedisruptors.com/interview-archives

Real Estate Espresso
Hosted by: Victor Menasce

Start your mornings with Victor J. Menasce's daily real estate investment outlook. In just 5 minutes, weekday episodes deliver high-energy insights to accelerate your success as an investor or developer. Weekend editions feature in-depth interviews with industry icons like Robert Kiyosaki, Peter Schiff, and more. A must-listen for investors!

https://podcasters.spotify.com/pod/show/victorjm

Real Estate Insiders Unfiltered
Hosted by: James Dwiggins

The real estate industry is evolving, and this podcast helps agents navigate the shifting landscape with confidence. Learn how to articulate your value, adapt to change, and implement strategies for building a profitable, sustainable business. Stay informed and ready for the future of real estate with actionable insights and expert advice.

https://realestateinsidersunfiltered.com

Real Estate Insights from Savills
Hosted by: Guy Ruddle

From the UK comes this insightful podcast. Keep yourself informed on the 'real' behind the real estate headlines, Savills brings you engaging and insightful discussion with experts across their global business on the issues that matter most in property.

https://www.buzzsprout.com/201382

Real Estate Investing Mastery Podcast
Hosted by: Alex Joungblood

On the Real Estate Investing Mastery Podcast, Joe McCall & Alex Joungblood share real world secrets on how to make a full-time income through investing in real estate - with a special emphasis on fast cash strategies like wholesaling and lease options. Listen and earn how to escape the 9-5 through stories from successful investors.

https://www.realestateinvestingmastery.com

Real Estate News Radio with Rowena Patton
Hosted By: Rowena Patton

Real estate isn't one-size-fits-all, and host Rowena Patton is here to guide you through the maze. Author of Find Your Unique Value Proposition and host of Real Estate News Radio, Rowena shares strategies for buying and selling, helping consumers navigate real estate with less stress and more fun!

https://www.buzzsprout.com/1650661

Real Estate Rockstars
Hosted by: Aaron Amuchastegui, Shelby Johnson

Make more sales and earn higher commissions by learning directly from real estate's top performers! Counting more than four-million downloads from over 100 countries, Real Estate Rockstars is the industry's most trusted, most popular podcast.Robert Kiyosaki, Barbara Corcoran, and Ryan Serhant are just a few of the many notable guests who have shared their industry expertise with the Rockstar Nation.

https://realestaterockstarsnetwork.com/shelbyjohnson

RAVING REFERRALS FOR REAL ESTATE AGENTS

Real Estate Rookie
Hosted by: Ashley Kehr, Tony Robinson

The perfect podcast for anyone starting their real estate career is the Real Estate Rookie. The hosts share their experiences and interview successful real estate professionals who offer practical advice, tips, and strategies for navigating the real estate market as a beginner.

https://www.biggerpockets.com/podcasts/real-estate-rookie

Real Estate Today
Hosted by: Stephen Gasque, Melissa Dittmann Tracey, Bill Thompson

NAR podcast Real Estate Today opens doors for buyers and sellers with critical and credible information on the real estate market. It's fast-paced and fact-packed with experts, interviews, call-ins, field reports, and timely market conditions.

https://www.nar.REALTOR/real-estate-today

RealTrending
Hosted by Tracey Velt

From HousingWire comes The RealTrending podcast featuring the brightest minds in real estate. Every week, brokerage leaders, top agents, team leaders, and industry experts share their success secrets, trends, and lessons learned navigating this ever-changing industry.

https://www.housingwire.com/shows/realtrending

RISE Real Estate Investing Podcast
Hosted by: Mayu Thava, Austin Yeh

Mayu Thava and Austin Yeh, Canadian real estate investors based in Toronto, host the RISE Real Estate Investing Podcast. Each week, they interview inspiring guests from diverse backgrounds, highlighting their challenges and triumphs as they successfully navigate the world of real estate investing.

https://mtyehrealestate.podbean.com

PODCASTS

Smart Agents
Hosted by: Charles Curry

Whether you're a new real estate agent or an experienced broker aiming to grow your business, The Smart Agents Podcast delivers value. Learn from top producers sharing lead generation strategies and marketing experts offering insights on building your brand online to take your real estate career to the next level.

https://www.smartagents.com/podcast

The 13% Podcast
Hosted by: Lance Billingsley

The 13% Podcast with Lance Billingsley uncovers why 87% of real estate agents fail — and how you can join the top 13% who succeed. Real estate offers freedom and flexibility, but without boldness, patience, integrity, and discipline, success is out of reach. Lance and his expert guests share the mindset, strategies, and habits of top agents to help you become the person you're meant to be, thrive in your business, and build a great life.

https://www.youtube.com/@the13percentpodcast

The Data Driven Real Estate Podcast (by PropertyRadar)
Hosted by: Aaron Norris, Sean O'Toole

The Data Driven Real Estate Podcast, hosted by Aaron Norris and Sean O'Toole, offers real estate professionals insights into data-driven sales, hyperlocal marketing, and industry trends. Each episode features industry leaders sharing strategies to enhance business success taking advantage of the latest real estate trends.

https://www.propertyradar.com/data-driven-real-estate-podcast

The Faithful Agent
Hosted by: Garrett Maroon

If you're a Jesus-loving, Gospel-following, believer in Christ, this podcast is for you. Garrett Maroon guides conversations with faith as the focus. Learn how to deepen relationships and build a Christ-centered business and life.

https://www.buzzsprout.com/1653892

The Millionaire Real Estate Agent Podcast
Hosted by: Jason Abram

Join Jason Abrams and his Mega Agent guests as they break down the models and systems behind their success. Discover actionable strategies that drive big profits and help agents build even bigger, more fulfilling lives through insightful discussions and expert advice.

https://millionaireagentpodcast.com

The Norris Group Real Estate Radio Show
Hosted by: Aaron Norris

The Norris Group Real Estate Radio Show is hosted by author, California real estate trainer, investor, and hard money lender, Bruce Norris. The show focuses on California real estate trends and the current market correction, how to survive, and how to profit as an investor, builder, REALTOR, and mortgage professional. Bruce Norris interviews the real estate leaders, both local and national, that change and influence the real estate and investing industries.

https://www.thenorrisgroup.com/radio-show

The Real Estate InvestHER Show
Hosted by: Liz Faircloth, Andresa Guidelli

The Real Estate InvestHER Show empowers female real estate investors to achieve balance and financial freedom. Co-hosts Liz Faircloth and Andresa Guidelli feature inspiring women who share practical tools for growing rental portfolios, flipping houses, and building successful businesses—all while prioritizing family, self-care, and the mindset for lasting success.

https://www.therealestateinvesther.com/podcast

The Real Estate Syndication Show
Hosted by: Whitney Sewell

The Real Estate Syndication Show features daily interviews with top commercial real estate entrepreneurs. Hosted by Whitney Sewell, the podcast helps active investors master syndication and improve their businesses while educating passive investors on smart strategies to diversify into real estate. A valuable resource for anyone who is serious about real estate investing.

https://lifebridgecapital.com/podcast

PODCASTS

The Real Word
Hosted by: Byron Lazine

Byron Lazine offers three different podcasts with fresh and insightful perspectives on the real estate industry. The episodes are from their professional perspective, and they discuss current industry news that should be relevant to all real estate professionals.

https://byronlazine.com/learn

The REtipster Podcast
Hosted by: Seth Williams

The REtipster Podcast reveals how to make great money investing in real estate with low risk, high impact, and plenty of freedom to enjoy life. Host Seth Williams shares insights from his land investing business and self-storage facility operation, offering inspiration and strategies for both new and experienced investors.

https://retipster.com/category/podcast

Top of Mind
Hosted by: Mike Simonsen

Ready to dive into the big trends sharing the real estate market? Join Altos founder Mike Simonsen for The Top of Mind podcast as he interviews the smartest leaders, thinkers, and doers in the industry today.

https://www.housingwire.com/shows/top-of-mind

Vancouver Real Estate Podcast
Hosted by: Adam, Matt Scalena

If you're in Vancouver, BC, this podcast is your go-to resource. Hosted by top local REALTORs Adam and Matt Scalena, it offers expert advice, market insights, and strategies to help you navigate Vancouver's competitive real estate market with confidence.

https://www.vancouverrealestatepodcast.com

RAVING REFERRALS FOR REAL ESTATE AGENTS

Women Rocking Real Estate
Hosted by: Jen Percival

The Women Rocking Real Estate podcast empowers women in the real estate industry. The episodes cover a wide range of topics to assist women in scaling their businesses with the most up-to-date tactics. These topics include demanding clients, REALTOR mistakes, and real estate terms.

https://jenpercival.com/the-podcast

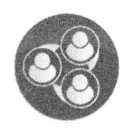

Recommended Resources

As a real estate professional, you are always looking for the most advanced and beneficial products, services, and training. That's why we have researched and compiled a list of top companies and recommended resources to help you elevate and optimize your performance, productivity, and profitability.

Agentology (powered by Verse.io)

Agentology, powered by Verse.io, is a cutting-edge lead conversion platform designed for real estate professionals. It connects agents with qualified leads through rapid response, follow-up, and personalized engagement. By leveraging AI and human touch, Agentology helps agents maximize lead potential, improve conversion rates, and grow their business efficiently.

https://agentology.verse.io

America's Preferred Home Warranty

America's Preferred Home Warranty (APHW) offers flexible, reliable protection for homeowners and real estate professionals. With the unique freedom to choose your own contractor for repairs, APHW ensures convenience and control. Their comprehensive plans cover essential systems and appliances, providing peace of mind and added value during real estate transactions.

https://www.aphw.com

Appraisal Nation

Appraisal Nation is a leading provider of nationwide appraisal management services, delivering accurate, timely, and reliable valuations for real estate professionals. Trusted by lenders, brokers, and agents, Appraisal Nation combines advanced technology with exceptional customer service to streamline the appraisal process and ensure compliance with industry standards across the United States.

https://www.appraisalnation.com

ATG (Advanced Tax Group)

Advanced Tax Group specializes in strategic tax and protection solutions designed to preserve and protect wealth for real estate professionals and investors. With expertise in business and personal taxes, asset protection/estate planning, and proactive tax planning, they help clients safeguard their assets, reduce tax exposure, and build financial resilience. Their personalized approach ensures compliance while optimizing long-term wealth preservation, making them a trusted partner in achieving long-term tax efficiency

https://advancedtaxgroup.com

RECOMMENDED RESOURCES

Attom Data Solutions

ATTOM Data Solutions is a leading provider of property data and analytics, delivering comprehensive insights for real estate, mortgage, and insurance industries. With a robust data platform covering property values, neighborhood trends, and market performance, ATTOM empowers businesses to make informed decisions, drive growth, and uncover opportunities in the housing market.

https://www.attomdata.com

Back At You

Back At You provides powerful social media, marketing, and back-office solutions tailored for real estate professionals. Its platform simplifies social media management, automated content creation, lead generation, and transaction coordination. Trusted by top brokerages and over 150,000 real estate agents, Back At You helps you save time, build your brand, and grow your business with ease.

https://www.backatyou.com

Bekins Moving Solutions

Bekins Moving Solutions is a trusted leader in residential and commercial moving services, providing seamless relocation experiences nationwide. With a commitment to exceptional customer care, Bekins offers comprehensive solutions, including packing, storage, and transportation. Their expert team ensures a stress-free move, making them a preferred choice for homeowners and businesses.

https://www.bekins.com

BombBomb

BombBomb turns emails into results with video messaging. Record a personal message with your camera, record your screen, or upload existing video. Trim, add captions, and more with easy editing tools.

https://bombbomb.com

BuildASign

BuildASign is a leading online provider of custom signage, offering high-quality, affordable solutions for businesses, real estate professionals, and individuals. With easy design tools and fast delivery, BuildASign helps agents create eye-catching yard signs, banners, and promotional materials to enhance branding, attract attention, and grow their business effectively.

https://www.buildasign.com

Canva

Canva is a user-friendly graphic design platform that empowers real estate agents to create stunning visuals effortlessly. With customizable templates, drag-and-drop tools, and a vast library of images and fonts, Canva makes designing professional-quality marketing materials, social media graphics, and presentations simple and accessible for everyone, regardless of design experience.

https://www.canva.com

Catalyze AI

Catalyze AI is an innovative platform that uses predictive analytics and artificial intelligence to help real estate professionals identify potential buyers and sellers. By leveraging data-driven insights, Catalyze AI enables agents to focus on high-probability leads, streamline prospecting efforts, and close more deals, driving greater efficiency and business growth.

https://www.catalyzeai.com

Children's Miracle Network

REALTORs can partner with Children's Miracle Network (CMN) to make a meaningful impact in their communities. By donating a portion of each transaction or hosting fundraising events, agents support local children's hospitals. This partnership enhances brand reputation, builds trust with clients, and helps provide life-saving care to children in need.

https://childrensmiraclenetworkhospitals.org

RECOMMENDED RESOURCES

CINC

CINC Pro is an all-in-one real estate platform designed to help REALTORs generate, nurture, and convert leads efficiently. With powerful tools for lead management, automated follow-ups, and customizable marketing campaigns, CINC Pro empowers agents to streamline workflows, build stronger client relationships, and close more deals, all from one intuitive system.

https://www.cincpro.com

Coach Simple

CoachSimple.net isn't just a coaching platform—it's a game-changer for visionary entrepreneurs, thought leaders, and content creators who demand results.

This next-generation AI-powered system revolutionizes the way you coach, mentor, and scale success. With seamless goal tracking, intelligent task automation, and deep performance analytics, CoachSimple.net transforms accountability into action. Whether you're building a brand, leading a movement, or scaling a high-impact business, our cutting-edge technology adapts to your unique style—helping you unlock exponential growth, boost productivity, and create lasting impact.

Elevate your influence. Simplify success. Coach smarter with

https://www.coachsimple.net

Curbio

Curbio is a turnkey home improvement solution designed to help real estate agents and sellers maximize property value. Specializing in pre-sale renovations, Curbio handles everything from project management to execution, with no upfront costs. Sellers pay at closing, ensuring a hassle-free experience and faster, higher-value home sales.

https://curbio.com

eCommission

eCommission provides real estate agents with financial flexibility by offering advances on pending commissions. With a simple, fast application process and no credit checks, eCommission allows agents to access funds when they need them most. This service helps agents manage cash flow, invest in their business, and achieve financial stability.

https://www.ecommission.com

Fello

Fello is a client relationship platform designed for real estate agents to stay top-of-mind with your clients long after the transaction. By automating personalized check-ins, value-driven updates, and milestone celebrations, Fello helps you nurture lasting relationships, build loyalty, and generate more referrals from your sphere of influence.

https://hifello.com

Fidelity National Title

Fidelity National Title is a trusted leader in title insurance and escrow services, providing comprehensive solutions to ensure seamless and secure real estate transactions. With unparalleled expertise, advanced technology, and a commitment to exceptional customer service, Fidelity empowers real estate professionals and their clients to close deals with confidence and efficiency.

https://www.fntic.com

First American Home Warranty

First American Home Warranty provides comprehensive protection for homeowners by covering the repair or replacement of essential home systems and appliances. With reliable service, 24/7 support, and a network of trusted contractors, First American helps you add value to transactions while offering buyers peace of mind and budget protection.

https://homewarranty.firstam.com

RECOMMENDED RESOURCES

First American Title

First American Title is a leading provider of title insurance and settlement services, ensuring secure and seamless real estate transactions. With a history of innovation and reliability, First American offers advanced technology, expert guidance, and exceptional customer service, helping buyers, sellers, and real estate professionals close deals with confidence.

https://www.firstam.com

FollowUpBoss

FollowUpBoss is a powerful CRM platform designed for real estate professionals to streamline lead management and client communication. With tools for automated follow-ups, team collaboration, and performance tracking, FollowUpBoss helps agents and brokers stay organized, nurture relationships, and convert more leads into closed deals, driving business growth and success.

https://www.followupboss.com

HOA.com

HOA.com offers REALTORs the opportunity to become Certified HOA Specialists, establishing you as the go-to expert for HOA communities. This certification enables you to win more listings by mastering HOA-specific rules, fees, and regulations. You can also leverage HOA.com's co-marketing campaigns to turn your vendors into proactive marketing partners. By collaborating with trusted service providers, you can amplify your reach, build lasting relationships, and attract more referrals from homeowners in the communities you serve.

https://HOA.com/CHS

HomeLight

HomeLight is a powerful platform that connects REALTORs with motivated buyers and sellers in their area. By leveraging data-driven insights and personalized recommendations, HomeLight helps agents grow their business, close deals faster, and connect with clients ready to buy or sell, making it an essential tool for real estate success.

https://www.homelight.com

Homes.com

Homes.com is a trusted real estate platform that helps you connect with motivated buyers and sellers. With high-visibility listings, lead generation tools, and customizable marketing solutions, Homes.com empowers you to showcase properties, build your brand, and grow your business while reaching an engaged audience actively searching for their next home.

https://www.homes.com

HouseAmp

HouseAmp is a real estate platform that empowers agents to help sellers prepare their homes for sale with no upfront costs. From repairs to staging, HouseAmp funds presale improvements, enabling faster sales and higher offers. Agents streamline the process, delivering a better experience for clients and maximizing property value.

https://www.houseamp.com

Immobel

Immobel provides enterprise SaaS platforms for the real estate industry in 19 languages, powering global brands with robust analytics, business intelligence, and GDPR compliance. Immobel Global Referral Networks facilitate $7–10 billion in transactions annually. Trusted by Sotheby's International Realty, Century 21, ERA, BHGRE, Coldwell Banker, and Corcoran. The MLS Match Referral Network serves professional and MLS organizations in 80 countries. Immobel property search portals include Century21Global.com, RILivingGlobal.com and SFPropertySearch.com.

https://www.immobel.com

Inside Real Estate (BoldTrail)

BoldTrail by Inside Real Estate is an innovative platform designed to help real estate professionals manage and grow your business. With advanced tools for lead generation, CRM, marketing automation, recruiting, and back office tools like transaction management and commission tracking, BoldTrail empowers agents, team leaders and brokers to streamline operations, enhance client relationships, and drive greater success in your market.

https://boldtrail.com

RECOMMENDED RESOURCES

Knock

Knock.com empowers REALTORs to offer clients a seamless buying and selling experience. With innovative solutions like the Knock Home Swap, agents help clients buy their dream home before selling their current one. Knock simplifies transactions, eliminates contingencies, and provides REALTORs with tools to close deals faster while enhancing client satisfaction.

https://www.knock.com

LegalShield

LegalShield provides REALTORs affordable access to legal support, offering you and your clients peace of mind and protection in every transaction. From contract reviews to advice on disputes, LegalShield's network of experienced attorneys ensures you're covered. REALTORs can navigate legal complexities confidently, saving time, reducing risk, and focusing on growing their business.

https://www.legalshield.com

Lone Wolf Technologies

Lone Wolf Technologies, Inc. provides real estate professionals everywhere a unified hub to manage transactions, marketing, and back-office operations effortlessly. From document management to digital signatures and client collaboration, our tools simplify workflows, boost productivity, and empower you to grow your business with confidence and deliver outstanding service to your clients.

https://www.lwolf.com

LUXE Luxury Listing Designation

Become a Luxury Listing Specialist and start winning more luxury listings with confidence! LuxuryListingSpecialist.com equips you with the tools, training, and strategies to attract high-end clients, market luxury properties effectively, and elevate your brand. Gain the expertise you need to dominate the luxury real estate market and grow your business.

https://luxurylistingspecialist.com/luxe.html

Luxury Presence

Luxury Presence is a leading marketing platform for real estate professionals, specializing in custom websites, branding, and digital marketing strategies. Designed for agents and brokers in the luxury market, Luxury Presence helps elevate your online presence, attract high-end clients, and grow your business with cutting-edge tools and exceptional service.

https://www.luxurypresence.com

Movoto

Movoto partners with top teams and agents to connect these real estate professionals with qualified buyers and sellers. Movoto helps its partners grow their businesses through its innovative platform by providing exclusive live transfer introductions, actionable insights, and smart recommendations. This enables agents to close deals faster while delivering exceptional client experiences.

https://ojo.com

MoxiWorks

MoxiWorks is a leading real estate technology platform designed to help agents and brokerages streamline their business. With tools for CRM, marketing automation, lead nurturing, and transaction management, MoxiWorks boosts productivity and client engagement. Its integrated solutions empower real estate professionals to grow their business and close more deals efficiently.

https://moxiworks.com

National Association of REALTORs

The National Association of REALTORs® (NAR) is America's largest trade association. NAR provides members with industry-leading resources, advocacy, market insights, and educational opportunities. As the voice of real estate, NAR empowers agents and brokers to succeed while promoting professionalism and ethical practices nationwide.

https://www.nar.REALTOR

RECOMMENDED RESOURCES

Payload

Payload is a secure digital payment platform designed for real estate transactions. It simplifies earnest money deposits, commission payments, and vendor disbursements with fast, transparent, and compliant processes. REALTORs and brokers benefit from streamlined workflows, reduced paperwork, and enhanced client trust, ensuring smooth financial transactions every step of the way.

https://payload.com/real-estate

Pillar To Post

Pillar To Post is North America's leading home inspection company, providing comprehensive inspections to help REALTORs and their clients make informed decisions. With detailed reports, innovative technology, and trusted expertise, Pillar To Post ensures a smooth transaction process, giving buyers and sellers confidence and peace of mind during real estate deals.

https://pillartopost.com

Place

Place.com is a leading platform that empowers real estate professionals to build scalable and profitable businesses. Offering tools for lead generation, client management, and operational efficiency, Place.com helps agents and teams streamline workflows, maximize productivity, and deliver exceptional service, ensuring long-term success in the competitive real estate market.

https://place.com/team

PODS

PODS offers flexible moving and storage solutions that help REALTORs provide added convenience to their clients. With portable moving and storage containers, clients can easily declutter, stage homes, and transition between properties. PODS helps simplify moving and storage, enhances client satisfaction, and helps REALTORs close deals faster by ensuring homes are market-ready.

https://www.pods.com

Property Management Inc

Property Management Inc. (PMI) provides comprehensive solutions for real estate professionals looking to expand into property management. With tools for residential, commercial, and vacation rental management, PMI helps REALTORs grow their business, streamline operations, and generate recurring revenue while delivering exceptional service to property owners and tenants alike.

https://www.propertymanagementinc.com

Property Radar

PropertyRadar is a powerful data platform that helps real estate professionals uncover opportunities and grow their business. With detailed property and owner data, REALTORs can identify motivated sellers, target specific markets, and streamline marketing campaigns. PropertyRadar empowers agents with actionable insights to close more deals and stay ahead in competitive markets.

https://www.propertyradar.com

Real Grader

Real Grader helps real estate professionals optimize their online presence and build stronger personal brands. By assessing digital footprints across social media, websites, and search engines, Real Grader provides actionable insights and tools to improve visibility, reputation, and engagement, empowering REALTORs to attract more clients and grow their business effectively.

https://www.realgrader.com

RealScout

RealScout is a collaborative home search platform that connects REALTORs and their clients through a seamless, personalized experience. With powerful tools for client engagement, market insights, and lead conversion, RealScout helps agents, teams and brokerages deliver exceptional service, build trust, and close more deals by turning the home search process into a competitive advantage.

https://www.realscout.com

RECOMMENDED RESOURCES

Realty.com

Realty.com connects REALTORs with motivated buyers and sellers through its innovative real estate marketplace. Featuring high-visibility agent profiles, exclusive leads, and advanced marketing tools, Realty.com helps agents grow their business, enhance their online presence, and build lasting client relationships, making it a valuable resource for real estate professionals nationwide.

http://realty.com

REDX

REDX is a lead generation platform designed for real estate professionals to grow their business. By providing accurate contact information for expired listings, FSBOs, and other lead sources, REDX helps agents prospect efficiently, connect with motivated sellers, and build a steady pipeline of opportunities to close more deals and drive success.

https://www.redx.com

RESaaS.com

RESAAS.com is a global platform designed for real estate professionals to connect, collaborate, and share referrals. With tools for networking, lead generation, and market insights, RESAAS empowers agents and brokers to expand their business, access exclusive opportunities, and grow their referral network within a trusted community of industry professionals.

https://www.resaas.com

Ring Central

RingCentral is a leading cloud-based communications platform designed to help real estate professionals stay connected. With features like voice, video, messaging, and team collaboration tools, RingCentral streamlines communication, enhances productivity, and supports seamless client interactions, enabling REALTORs to manage their business effectively and deliver exceptional service anytime, anywhere.

https://www.ringcentral.com

ShowingTime+

ShowingTime+ is a comprehensive real estate software platform that streamlines showings, marketing, and client collaboration. With tools for scheduling, feedback, market insights, and listing management, ShowingTime+ empowers REALTORs to save time, enhance efficiency, and deliver exceptional service. It's designed to simplify transactions and help agents grow their business effortlessly.

https://www.showingtime.com

SkySlope

SkySlope is a trusted transaction management platform for real estate professionals, streamlining document management, compliance, and client communication. With features like digital signatures, audit tracking, and automated workflows, SkySlope simplifies the closing process, saves time, and ensures accuracy, enabling agents and brokers to focus on growing their business.

https://skyslope.com

The CE Shop

The CE Shop is a leading provider of online real estate education, offering pre-licensing, post-licensing, and continuing education courses. Designed for convenience and success, The CE Shop's industry-approved curriculum helps REALTORs stay informed, meet licensing requirements, and advance their careers with flexible, engaging, and accessible learning solutions.

https://www.theceshop.com

The International MLS (IMLS)

The International MLS (IMLS) is a global property listing platform connecting real estate professionals with international buyers and sellers. With worldwide exposure, referral opportunities, and a network of trusted agents, IMLS empowers REALTORs to expand their reach, grow their business, and access a broader audience in the global real estate market.

https://www.theimls.com

RECOMMENDED RESOURCES

Transactly

Transactly simplifies real estate transactions with a platform that streamlines communication, task management, and document sharing. Designed for agents, brokers, and transaction coordinators, Transactly offers tools to improve efficiency, reduce stress, and close deals faster. Its automation and support services allow real estate professionals to focus on growing their business.

https://transactly.com

VIU by HUB

VIU by HUB is an innovative digital insurance platform designed to simplify the insurance process for real estate professionals and their clients. Offering tailored insurance solutions, VIU enhances the home buying and selling experience by providing quick, reliable coverage options, creating added value and peace of mind for homeowners and agents.

https://www.viubyhub.com

Weekly Real Estate News

Weekly Real Estate News (WREnews.com) delivers timely market insights, industry trends, and expert analysis to help real estate professionals stay informed and succeed. Founded by John G. Stevens, a respected industry leader, WREnews.com provides essential updates on housing, mortgages, and market shifts, ensuring agents, lenders, and investors have the knowledge they need to thrive in today's dynamic real estate landscape.

http://wrenews.com

Wise Agent

Wise Agent is more than a CRM platform - it's a trusted tech partner for real estate professionals. This powerful, all-in-one platform combines contact management, lead automation, transaction management, and marketing tools to help brokers and agents streamline their business and maximize success. By offering cutting-edge technology, intuitive automation, and personalized support, Wise Agent empowers members to stay organized, build relationships, and close more deals. With Wise Agent, you're not just adding software; you're adding a team dedicated to your growth—all at an affordable price.

https://wiseagent.com

Wizehire

Wizehire is an all-in-one hiring platform designed for real estate professionals to find top talent quickly and easily. With optimized job ads, applicant tracking, and expert hiring support, Wizehire helps brokers and agents attract qualified candidates, streamline the hiring process, and build high-performing teams to grow their business.

https://wizehire.com

Workman Success Systems

Workman Success Systems is a business coaching company that's the only one of its kind. They specialize in real estate teams and companies, helping them achieve Predictable Greatness™ as they adopt the proven Workman Success systems, processes, and tools.

https://workmansuccess.com

Ylopo

Ylopo is a cutting-edge digital marketing platform designed for real estate professionals to generate, nurture, and convert leads. With advanced tools like AI-driven lead follow-up, dynamic property ads, and personalized client engagement, Ylopo empowers agents and teams to grow their business, enhance their online presence, and close more deals.

https://demo.ylopo.com

RECOMMENDED RESOURCES

Zillow

Zillow is a leading real estate platform that helps REALTORs connect with millions of buyers and sellers. With tools for lead generation, listing promotion, and market insights, Zillow empowers agents to grow their business, enhance their visibility, and build strong client relationships in today's competitive real estate market.

https://www.zillow.com

National Networking Organizations

Success in real estate is built on relationships, and national networking organizations provide the perfect platform to expand your connections, exchange referrals, and grow your business. In this chapter, we explore top national networking groups that help real estate professionals build trust, collaborate with industry leaders, and generate consistent referral opportunities nationwide.

Alignable

Alignable is a free online business network for small business owners across North America. Members use Alignable to connect within their local business community or in other markets across the country. Members can access industry insights and share updates about their business. While this is a great platform to connect with people online, you will need to take your conversations into the real world if you hope to build solid referral partnerships through this platform.

Alignable.com

Achieve Systems

Achieve Systems is dedicated to providing the systems needed to help entrepreneurs, business owners, and professionals acquire high level success. This includes strategic relationships, leads, collaboration, business coaching systems, conferences, daily mastermind calls, industry influencers, events, revenue streams, and more. Improve your learning, create a support system, and connect with professionals who are mission-driven.

AchieveSystemsPro.com

BNI - Business Network International

BNI is the world's leading business referral organization with over 335,000 Members in over 11,000 BNI Chapters worldwide. In 2024 alone, BNI Members shared over 16 million valuable new client referrals and generated over $25 billion (USD) in revenue for their fellow members. Many BNI Chapters are currently meeting using BNI Online™, a powerful and convenient platform that enables Members to continue sharing new client referrals. BNI Members are actively supported by regional, national, and global BNI staff that provide the training, structure, and the technology needed for the continued success of BNI Members. Each chapter allows just one person to represent each professional category. This gives participants exclusivity in their area of service helping them connect and collaborate with complementary business owners and professionals.

BNI.com

C-Suite Network

C-Suite Network™ prides itself as the world's most trusted network of C-Suite Leaders, with a focus on providing growth, development, and networking opportunities for business executives with titles of Vice President and above with annual revenues of $5 million or greater. If you're looking to connect to executives, he C-Suite Network helps create lasting business relationships, connections, and insights among senior leaders.

C-SuiteNetwork.com

NATIONAL NETWORKING ORGANIZATIONS

Christian Business Alliance

The CBA helps Christian businesspeople connect, collaborate and form strategic partnerships with other believers in business. After realizing a lack of fellowship opportunities for business-minded Christians, the CBA was formed and now has chapters across the US and around the world.

TheCBA.org

EngagePro

EngagePro helps turn the people you meet into trusted relationships who want to do business with you. Their easy-to-use EngagePro software tool has been described as being the "know-like-trust" online platform to implement the "Go-Giver" principles. Subscribers see results in just a few days. Imagine escaping the noise of online and digital marketing and building trusted relationships, referral partners and real results.

EngagePro.com

Eventbrite

Although not a networking organization, Eventbrite is an online platform listing live events and experiences in your local market. Their mission is to bring the world together through live experiences. Here you can search for and find local business and networking opportunities led by local chambers of entrepreneurs.

Eventbrite.com

eWomen Network

For women looking to connect with other entrepreneurial women, check out the eWomenNetwork. They offer their Accelerated Networking™ at over 2,000 online and in-person events each year. You'll find customers, innovative ideas, and breakthrough resources to help you succeed. They connect more than 500,000 women through 118 local chapters across North America providing members with resources, networking, and more.

eWomenNetwork.com

G7 Networking

G7 Networking is dedicated to helping business professionals build meaningful relationships rooted in biblical principles. Their locally-based chapters feature a diverse group of members representing all sorts of businesses, so that members can stay connected while growing their referral business and faith. They strive to create a special space where spiritual growth is encouraged alongside professional development.

G7Networking.com

HOA.com

HOA.com is the #1 referral network for professionals who serve homeowners. The vision began as "The Home Owner Alliance" and quickly expanded once the domain HOA.com was secured in 2020. Now this national network unites tens of thousands of top trusted contractors, REALTORs, and other home services businesses and professionals who provide services specific to homeowners. A unique feature of this network is that they have Referral Partner Managers who actively assist their Certified Pros in creating strong referral partnerships to generate referrals for years to come.

HOA.com/grow

LeTip

LeTip International is the oldest and one of the most trusted business networking groups in the country. They truly are the business referral network that started it all. LeTip prides itself on building more than just strong business relationships. Their business networking group cultivates a lifetime business networking group model based on building, sustaining, and supporting strong relationships between businesspeople. LeTip members form a close-knit family of non-competing businesses. LeTip members spend time learning about each other's business, powering their ability to make better referrals. By becoming well-versed in each other's industries, they can make higher-quality referrals. These high-level tips turn their local business referral network chapters into powerful and result driven sales forces.

LeTip.com

NATIONAL NETWORKING ORGANIZATIONS

Master Networks

This business networking company has chapters starting up around the country. They believe in the power of growing your business through relationships and connecting with others. Professional and personal development are a key part of their organization as they help professionals gain access to top training.

MasterNetworks.com

MeetUp

Meetup is a platform for finding and building local events and communities. You can use Meetup to find networking groups, real estate investor associations, and other events that bring people together. Check out local events, join a group to meet people, make friends, grow a business, and explore your interests. Thousands of events are happening every day, both online and in person so it's a great place to get connected in your local community.

MeetUp.com

National Association of REALTORs

The National Association of REALTORs® (NAR) is America's largest trade association, representing more than 1.5 million members involved in all aspects of the residential and commercial real estate industries. NAR and its employees have demonstrated a commitment to creating and fostering a culture that puts its members first, advances diversity and inclusion, leads change and emphasizes respect, communication, and collaboration.

NAR.REALTOR

Network In Action

Network In Action International believes that the perfect mix of technology and face to face networking will help your business grow. All Network In Action groups have only one mandatory monthly meeting as opposed to a weekly obligation. Their mobile app helps keep you connected throughout the month, potentially freeing up over 80 hours a year so that you can focus on what's important: Growing your business. Check their website to explore their various chapters across the United States.

NetworkInAction.com

One Business Connection

Since 1997, One Business Connection (1BC) has been connecting and empowering business owners and professionals. From their headquarters in Denver, CO, 1BC prides itself on being a success organization that puts you in contact with the connections, the ideas, and the people you need to grow your business. 1BC is committed to helping their members grow both personally and professionally providing its own success library on success, motivation, and inspiration.

OneBusiness.com

TEAM Referral Network

TEAM Referral Network has since grown to over 100 chapters across several states. TEAM Referral Network includes weekly meetings with your chapter, training programs, business development, and most importantly, quality business relationships. Members are encouraged to meet one-on-one with other members to get to know each other on a deeper level.

TeamReferralNetwork.com

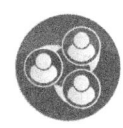

Top 20 Real Estate Referral Groups

In today's digital world, Facebook groups have become powerful hubs for real estate agents looking to exchange referrals, grow their network, and close more deals. This chapter highlights the Top 20 Real Estate Referral Groups on Facebook, where agents can connect with trusted professionals across markets, share leads, and build profitable referral partnerships. Whether you're looking for out-of-state referrals or niche-specific connections, these groups offer endless opportunities to expand your business and boost your commission pipeline.

1. Real Estate Agent Referral Network & Marketing Tips

Led by Debbie Mauro and Raymond Sjolseth, the Real Estate Agent Referral Network & Marketing Tips Group is a global platform for networking, mentoring, and sharing best practices. It's a space where real estate professionals exchange wins, industry insights, and leads, fostering growth and inspiration for agents worldwide. Join their weekly real estate virtual coffee mastermind sessions Thursday mornings on zoom by going to

MPREALTORMastermind.com.

RAVING REFERRALS FOR REAL ESTATE AGENTS

2. Real Estate Community

The Real Estate Community group is a fun and supportive space for real estate professionals to connect. Members can ask questions, share market insights, discuss trends and opportunities, post funny real estate memes and photos, and seek advice or support. It's all about learning, laughing, and growing together.

3. REALTOR Networking & Social Media Tips

Created by Natalie Ridderbos, a social media expert, this group is designed to help REALTORs network and exchange social media marketing tips. It's a dynamic community focused on using social media to build brands, share best practices, and support each other in leveraging online platforms for real estate success.

4. Let's Talk Real Estate

The Let's Talk Real Estate group is a supportive space for real estate professionals to ask questions, share market trends, and discuss opportunities. It's a fun community where members can also post memes, seek advice, vent, and stay informed about the latest happenings in the real estate world.

5. Inside Real Estate Discussion Group

A community that's designed for real estate professionals focused on business growth and scaling. Members share strategies, discuss industry challenges, and connect to expand their referral networks. It's all about collaboration—exchanging ideas, tools, tips, and best practices to help everyone stretch, grow, and achieve greater success in real estate.

6. Real Estate Conversations

This group is an online space for discussing real estate, sharing market insights, and connecting with buyers, sellers, and professionals. It's perfect for networking, learning, and exchanging advice on investments, home buying, and industry trends.

FACEBOOK GROUPS

7. Real Estate Lead Gen Scripts & Objections

Real Estate Lead Gen Scripts & Objections provides a supportive community where agents get candid advice on lead generation and overcoming objections. Its mission is to help real estate professionals build the life they deserve, fostering business transparency and long-lasting impact within the industry.

8. All Things Real Estate

This group is a fun, lighthearted space for sharing real estate memes, funny stories, and even bad real estate photos. It's designed to connect like-minded individuals, offer advice, and create a sense of community where everyone can laugh, share experiences, and feel heard in the world of real estate.

9. Real Estate Connections

An online community where members engage in discussions about real estate, share market insights, and connect with industry professionals, buyers, and sellers. It provides a platform for networking, learning, and exchanging advice on property investments, home buying, and market trends.

10. Real Closers

A collection of Real Estate professionals committed to sharing, networking, and growing together! The group members build relationships, ask questions, share wins and seek advice about working in the real estate business. They are all about collaboration, networking, sharing best practices, stories and insights.

11. Real Estate 101

The Real Estate 101 group is a welcoming community for real estate professionals at all experience levels. Members can share advice, ask questions, and discuss strategies, trends, and industry basics. It's a great place to build your knowledge and network while staying informed on key developments in the real estate world.

12. Real Estate Agent & Loan Officer - Referrals, Leads & Networking

Designed for all Real Estate Agents and Loan Officers to connect, share marketing tips, and increase referrals and leads. Whether you're just starting or scaling your business, you'll find valuable resources and ideas to help grow your network and business success, no matter your experience level.

13. Real Estate Agents Group

A friendly online space that brings together real estate enthusiasts to chat about buying, selling, investing, and market trends. It's a great spot to ask questions, exchange tips, and connect with others who share a passion for real estate, whether you're just starting out or an experienced professional.

14. Lab Coat Agent Referrals

A dedicated space for real estate agents to exchange client referrals nationwide. It's a trusted community where agents connect, share referrals, and help clients find top professionals in different markets. The group ensures referrals stay within a network of vetted, experienced agents, making it a valuable resource for growing business and expanding connections in the real estate industry.

15. Pop-Bys For REALTORs®

For busy real estate agents, this service offers quick, Amazon-delivered closing gifts, pop-bys, and staging items. Skip the hassle of shopping, driving, and waiting in line while getting supplies and thoughtful gifts that help strengthen client relationships. Save time and focus on growing your business with ease.

16. California Agents and REALTORs

Looking for an agent to refer clients to in California? Connect with top real estate professionals to exchange referrals, share insights, and stay ahead of trends. Network, collaborate, and expand your reach while ensuring expert service for your clients and lucrative referral fees and commissions for you.

FACEBOOK GROUPS

17. All REALTORs and related Professionals

This group consists of all real estate professionals in real estate related industry such as REALTORs, Brokers, Property Managers, Investors, Developers, Lenders, Accountants, Attorneys, Lawyers, Notaries, Home Inspectors, Appraisers, Bankers, Mortgage Brokers, Pre-sale Developers, Staging company and anyone related to the Real Estate Industry from all over the world.

18. Real Estate Agent Referrals Group

A digital community where agents from across the nation connect to exchange client referrals. Members engage in discussions, share opportunities, and offer insights. This platform fosters trust and collaboration, helping agents grow their businesses by building valuable relationships and leveraging referrals to expand their reach and resources.

19. The Preferred Real Estate Referral Network

For real estate professionals to connect, collaborate, and exchange client referrals. It provides a valuable space for agents, brokers, and industry experts to share knowledge, insights, and opportunities, fostering growth and expanding business networks across regions. Trust and collaboration drive success within this community.

20. Real Estate Agent Referral Network

Dedicated to real estate professionals, including agents, lenders, companies, and brokerages globally. It facilitates collaboration and business expansion by connecting diverse industry experts. The community thrives on shared opportunities and mutual growth, offering a brokerage-neutral platform where professionals can build valuable relationships and drive success.

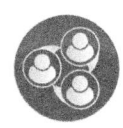

Become a Raving Referrals Co-Author

If you love what you've read and are interested in elevating your credibility and visibility by being a featured co-author in one of our upcoming industry related Raving Referrals books, we want to hear from you. We're looking for quality experts and influencers with subject matter expertise in the following areas:

- Raving Referrals for Accountants
- Raving Referrals for Attorneys
- Raving Referrals for B2B Sales
- Raving Referrals for Business Coaches
- Raving Referrals for Car Sales Pros
- Raving Referrals for Charities
- Raving Referrals for Chiropractors
- Raving Referrals for Doctors
- Raving Referrals for Electricians
- Raving Referrals for Financial Advisors
- Raving Referrals for General Contractors
- Raving Referrals for Home Service Pros
- Raving Referrals for HVAC Pros

- Raving Referrals for Insurance Pros
- Raving Referrals for Life Coaches
- Raving Referrals for Marketing Pros
- Raving Referrals for Network Marketing Pros
- Raving Referrals for Orthodontists
- Raving Referrals for Painting Pros
- Raving Referrals for Personal Trainers
- Raving Referrals for Plumbing Pros
- Raving Referrals for Property Managers
- Raving Referrals for Solar Pros
- Raving Referrals for Veterinarians

To begin a conversation and explore the possibilities of partnership on an upcoming Raving Referrals book, call (480) 400-0996 or go to *RavingReferrals.com/coauthor*

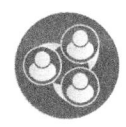

Become a Raving Referrals Certified Trainer

Are you ready to take the stage and empower people to have more income, more influence, and more Impact?

Then consider getting trained and approved as a Raving Referrals Certified Trainer. This program helps solidify your knowledge and mastery of attracting Raving Referrals. It also propels your credibility and visibility and opens new income streams to unlock the financial freedom you desire and deserve.

Imagine speaking to dozens or even hundreds of REALTORs and home service Pros who are all listening and learning from you as you teach and train the content you've just learned. As your expert status grows, so will the opportunities and referrals that come your way.

As a Raving Referrals Certified Trainer, you can:

- Create powerful and profitable referral partnerships
- Win more clients as a trusted expert in your local market
- Be an influential local leader in the world's fastest growing referral network
- Earn lucrative recurring commissions for years to come

Sharing our program with local professionals and businesses can help you attract more clients for your business, while adding a lucrative long-term income stream.

Ideal candidates exude the following qualities:

- Charismatic
- Inspiring Leader
- Passionate Promoter
- Natural Networker
- Well Connected & Respected
- Involved in Your Community
- Actively Serves in Your Charity or Church
- Confident Public Speaker/Trainer
- Active User of Social Media
- Has Existing Fans & Followers

To learn more about this powerful program, call (480) 400-0996 or go to *RavingReferrals.com/certification*

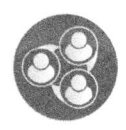

About the Authors

BRANDON BARNUM

Often referred to as the "King of Referrals," Brandon is an award-winning serial entrepreneur, coach, consultant, speaker, trainer, and workshop leader. He serves as CEO of HOA.com – the #1 Referral Network for Home Service Professionals, and as the Chairman of the Board for The Christian Business Alliance. He is a highly sought-after expert in referrals, marketing, sales, joint ventures, business development, and business growth strategies.

While a single Dad, in 1997, Brandon was an early technology innovator featuring real estate property listings from REALTORs that he partnered with and promoted. After learning the art and science of referrals, he increased his annual income 10X from 20K to $200K in just 18 months. Brandon has since closed over $500 million in transactions by referrals and has founded multiple local and online referral platforms and networks connecting 5 million members in 195 countries including over 250,000 real estate agents.

RAVING REFERRALS FOR REAL ESTATE AGENTS

Brandon has been featured internationally on TV, radio, and several books, including Cracking the Millionaire Code and Zero to Hero, and in magazines including The Wall Street Journal, Business Journal, and Newsweek, to name a few.

Brandon is passionate about empowering real estate sales professionals with a step-by-step system for attracting profitable prospects and expanding their income, influence, and impact.

To contact Brandon for executive coaching, workshops or keynote speaking:

Phone: 480-400-0996

Email: Brandon@RavingReferrals.com

Web: *www.RavingReferrals.com*

LinkedIn: *LinkedIn.com/in/brandonbarnum*

To book Brandon as a speaker for your event or podcast: *www.BrandonBarnum.com*

ABOUT THE AUTHORS

VERL WORKMAN

Verl Workman is the CEO and Cofounder of Workman Success Systems, a Master Coach, Business Consultant, and Keynote Speaker.

Verl makes it his personal mission to develop amazing coaches. It takes thorough vetting and intense training, but it all starts with being a master coach himself, who leads by example.

Verl brings deep real-estate, leadership, and coaching experience to every business relationship. His coaching clients represent the elite agents, teams, and brokers in the world; but they didn't necessarily start out that way. By identifying the "why" behind each goal, he is able to help his clients achieve greatness.

Verl is also an accomplished speaker and presenter—one of just a handful of presenters to earn the Certified Speaking Professional (CSP) designation from the National Speakers Association. His experience and expertise in all aspects of sales, marketing, promotion, management, and technology have enlightened and empowered thousands of professionals to expand their knowledge and achieve their goals.

Verl's contagious style and sales and management mastery make him not just an ideal coach, but the consummate coach's coach.

Verl Workman's Credentials & Accomplishments

- Founder & CEO, Workman Success Systems – Leading a premier coaching and consulting firm dedicated to helping real estate professionals scale their businesses with proven systems and strategies.
- Certified Speaking Professional (CSP), National Speakers Association – A prestigious designation held by the world's top speakers, recognizing excellence in professional speaking.
- President, RISMedia's Top 5 in Real Estate Network – Leading an exclusive network of top-producing real estate professionals committed to industry excellence.
- Co-Founder, Pinnacle Quest Consulting & Verl Workman Seminars – Developing high-impact training programs that empower agents, teams, and brokers to achieve peak performance.

- Co-Founder, Automation Quest (Acquired by Homes.com, 1999) – Innovating early real estate technology solutions that streamlined operations and enhanced productivity for agents nationwide.

- Successful Real Estate Agent & Business Owner – Decades of hands-on experience in buying, selling, and building businesses, ensuring real-world expertise in every keynote, coaching session, and consulting engagement.

- MBA from the School of Hard Knocks – A lifelong entrepreneur who has built, sold, and scaled businesses, Verl delivers battle-tested strategies that actually work in today's market.

For coaching, workshops, or keynote speaking inquiries:
Email: *speaking@WorkmanSuccess.com*

Real Estate Coaching & Business Growth:
Website: *www.WorkmanSuccess.com*

Book Verl as a Speaker:
Website: *www.VerlWorkman.com*

Follow Verl on Social Media:
- Instagram: @VerlWorkman
- LinkedIn: Verl Workman
- Facebook: @Workmansuccess
- YouTube: Workman Success Systems
- Twitter/X: @VerlWorkman

We invite you to leave a review of this book on Amazon and Goodreads

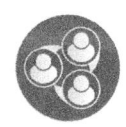

Expertise Publishing

Your knowledge, experience, and unique perspective have the power to elevate your authority, grow your business, and inspire others—and publishing a book is one of the most impactful ways to do it.

In today's digital world, being seen, heard, and READ is more achievable than ever, with social media and innovative publishing tools giving authors unprecedented visibility.

At Expertise Publishing, we help entrepreneurs, professionals, and thought leaders turn their expertise into powerful books that build credibility, attract clients, and expand influence. Whether you're looking to establish yourself as an industry leader, share your insights, or create a lasting impact, our publishing platform provides the tools and guidance to bring your vision to life. Start your journey today at *ExpertisePublishing.com* and turn your knowledge into a powerful asset for success!

Visit *ExpertisePublishing.com* today and start your journey to greater success, opportunities, and impact.

Made in United States
Orlando, FL
22 August 2025